I0827813

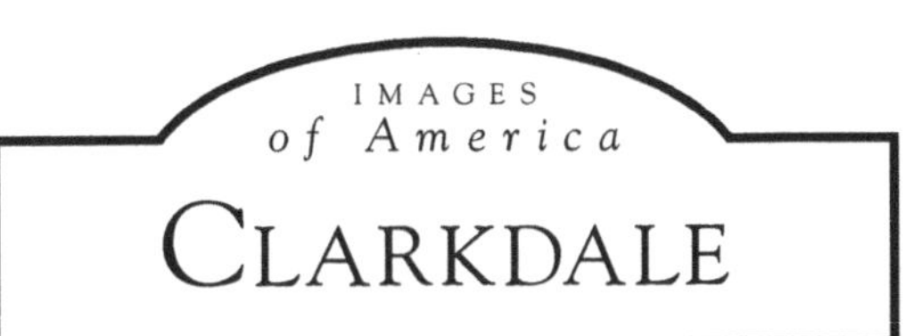
IMAGES
of America
CLARKDALE

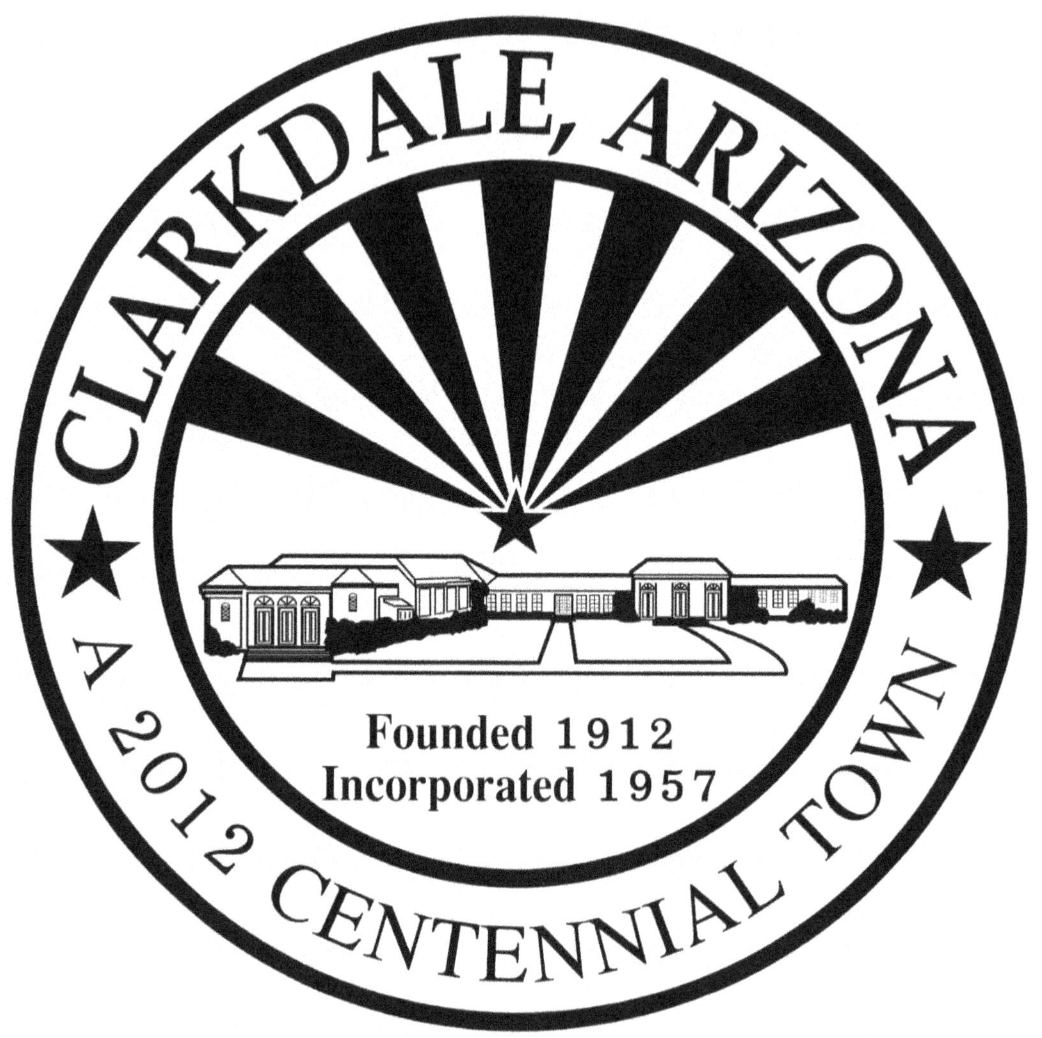

Pictured here is the seal of the historic town of Clarkdale. (Courtesy Town of Clarkdale.)

On the Cover: Clarkdale's commercial center on Main Street is located between Upper Town and Lower Town. The building exteriors have changed little since their original construction in 1915. Note the attractive architectural variations of the roof parapets. The 1939 movie *Hotel for Women* dates the photograph. Cars line the street, indicating business was good in Clarkdale in this pre–World War II era with the smelter producing copper full time. (Courtesy John Bell.)

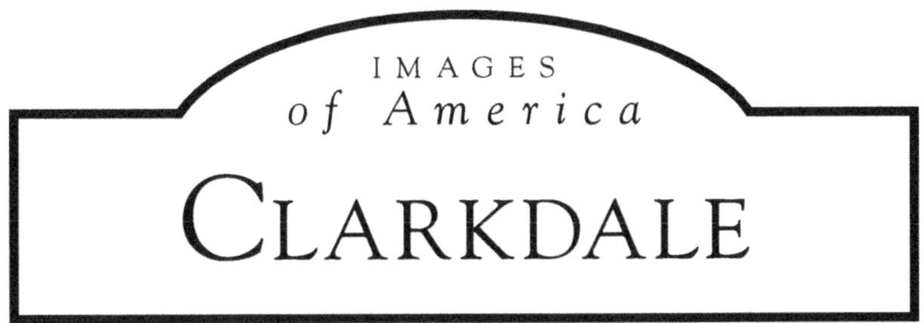

Paul A. Handverger and the Clarkdale Historical Society

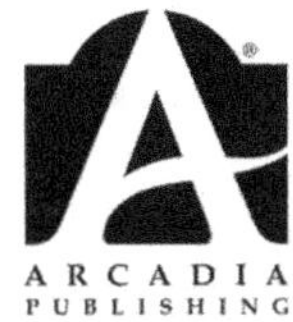

ISBN 978-1-4671-3139-1

Published by Arcadia Publishing
Charleston, South Carolina

Library of Congress Control Number: 2013948139

For all general information, please contact Arcadia Publishing:
Telephone 843-853-2070
Fax 843-853-0044
E-mail sales@arcadiapublishing.com
For customer service and orders:
Toll-Free 1-888-313-2665

Visit us on the Internet at www.arcadiapublishing.com

Dedicated to the individuals, historical societies, and museums that have contributed to preserving the history of Clarkdale, making this book possible.

Contents

ACKNOWLEDGMENTS

The author expresses thanks to the Clarkdale Historical Society and Museum for their support in this project. Special thanks go to members Drake Meinke, Mary Lu Estlick, James and Dinah Gemmill, Jerry Wiley, and Cindy Lowry. Three lifetime Clarkdale residents, Bob Beltz, Jerry Wombacher, and Armida Zepeda, were most helpful in providing first-hand knowledge and material and as tour guides in the preparation of this book. My most grateful appreciation goes to Cindy Emmett and Linda Greene Smith for their hours of support and work on this project.

Thanks also go to the following people for providing background discussions, local history, photographs, and documentation: Betty Dickenson Kent, Charles Kent, John Tavasci, Tim Coons, Vicky and Steve Anderson, Ellie Bauer, Curtis Lindner, Pat Fairfield, Janice Benatz, Christine Keller, Gayle Mabery, Wayne Debrosky, and Mickey Ryan. Special thanks go to outstanding local historian Glenda Farley, and to exemplary author and historian William Cowan for his much appreciated support.

Thanks go to James McMeekin, Helen Killebrew, and Helga Freund of the Verde Historical Society for supplying photographs from the archives of the Clemenceau Heritage Museum. Thanks also go to Janeen Trevillyan of the Sedona Heritage Museum for making available photos from their collection, and to Colleen Holt for assistance in obtaining archive photos from the Jerome Historical Society. Appreciation goes to Matthew Guebart, United States Park Service archeologist, for providing photographs and a unique opportunity to photograph artifacts at Tuzigoot National Monument. Thanks go to Sheila Stubler of the Fort Verde State Park for support. Thanks to Nancy McConlogue for her encouraging support.

Special thanks to Alyssa Jones of Arcadia Publishing, who, in a most positive way, helped me through the publishing process.

A most grateful thank-you to my wife, Roberta Handverger, for her patience, aide, support, and encouragement throughout this writing process and during our lifetime together.

Thanks again to all above. To those I may have missed, my sincere apologies. All errors of commission or omission are mine alone.

Introduction

Clarkdale could be the representative all-Arizonan town. It lies under blue skies near the center of the state in one of America's most spectacular natural settings beside the Verde River green belt, bordered by the White Hills, the red and yellow Mogollon Rim, and the massive, looming, once copper-rich Black Hills. Today, Clarkdale is a community of 4,000 encompassing a Yavapai-Apache reservation, three museums, the Verde Canyon tourist railroad, Yavapai College, Tuzigoot National Monument, lodges, churches, and several businesses, all amidst diverse outdoor recreational activities. This original company-planned town, listed in the National Register of Historic Places, is a community whose land and many cultures have a long and fascinating history.

The town of Clarkdale celebrated its centennial in 2012, the same year that Arizona observed its statehood centennial. Arizona promotes its heritage by the five Cs—copper, citrus, cattle, cotton, and climate. Copper led to the building of the early 20th century smelter town. Clarkdale's orchards once grew many varieties of fruit. Cowboys drove thousands of cattle from surrounding ranches to the Clarkdale stockyard for shipping by railroad. Indians grew cotton and wove cloth at the Tuzigoot Pueblo long before Europeans entered this land. Clarkdale's climate averages a comfortable 63 degrees Fahrenheit annually. Clarkdale, bestowed with the five C Arizona legacies, has a sixth C from the name of the town's builder—William A. Clark.

The town lies at the northern end of the 500-square-mile Verde Valley. The elevation of the community is between 3,350 and 4,600 feet at the base of the rugged 7,800-foot Black Hills that dominate the western view. The Verde River flows along Clarkdale's eastern edge.

Clarkdale sits amidst varied, colorful rocks that record eons of Arizona's natural history. Rock formations within 20 miles of the town are the same formations as those exposed in the Grand Canyon 80 miles away.

To understand Clarkdale's history, one has to begin at the dawn of time. The community's deeply buried basement rocks consist of 1.73-billion-year-old volcanic strata that erupted under an ocean. This ancient volcanism deposited seafloor sulfide-rich copper, zinc, gold, and silver found in the nearby Black Hills. These metals led to the building of the smelter town of Clarkdale. Subsequent uplift above the seas was followed by millennia of erosion. Ancient oceans again advanced over the metal-rich units, covering them with sandstone, mudstone, and limestone. Visible in the surrounding mountains are formations that reveal a long geologic history of beaches, seas, coral reefs, tidal flats, sand dunes, rivers, volcanic eruptions, tectonic fracturing, deposition, erosion, and fossils of extinct life. Today, the ancient submarine metal deposits are a mile above sea level due to uplift followed by erosion that exposed the ore outcrops.

Clarkdale sits upon the two- to eight-million-year-old Verde Formation evident as flat-lying white and tan strata in the nearby hills. This formation provided shelter, home sites, and construction materials for Indians for millennia; in modern times, town builders used the clay from this formation to make the distinctive multihued bricks of Clarkdale's historic buildings.

The first inhabitants of this region were the Paleo-Indians, who had immigrated here by 11,600 years ago at the end of the ice ages. They were hunter-gatherers of game and wild plants. Paleo-Indian fluted spear points, called Clovis points, have been found in the Clarkdale region.

From 10,500 B.C. to about 200 A.D., Archaic Indians roamed in the Verde Valley. These hunter-gatherers, beginning 4,000 to 5,000 years ago, developed domesticated crops of corn, beans, and squash. Archaic Indians living in caves in Sycamore Canyon nine miles north of Clarkdale left behind split-twig figurines. The development of agriculture introduced permanent living conditions with pit houses replacing temporary brush structures. Using local vegetation, they made baskets for storage, trays, bowls, and water haulage. Bows and arrows and the first crude ceramic pottery were introduced. Well-made clay pottery appeared at the end of the Archaic Indian era.

About 400–500 A.D., Sinagua Indians immigrated into the Verde Valley. Over the next millennium, the Sinagua developed an irrigation-based agriculture that supported an increasing population. Along the Verde River near Clarkdale are many cave dwellings on cliff faces and several multistory pueblos on ridges and hilltops. Irrigation ditches more than 1,500 years old have been identified. Excavation of these sites revealed highly decorated pottery, woven-dyed cotton cloth, and ball courts indicating a permanently based society far above hunter-gatherer subsistence living.

Tuzigoot National Monument is a Sinagua pueblo located near Peck's Lake and the Verde River. The pueblo consists of 87 first-floor rooms and 23 second-story rooms estimated to have housed 225 people living in a complex agricultural and trading society. Irrigated fields produced corn, cotton, squash, beans, agave, and prickly pear. Pottery was made of volcanic rock and clay. Jewelry was made from local azurite, malachite, and hematite. Other artifacts—made from seashells, turquoise, and pipestones—indicate trading was conducted far outside the Verde Valley.

Several natural disasters affected the Sinagua. Volcanic eruptions near Flagstaff occurred between the years 1064 to 1250, followed by a drought from 1276 to 1299, and floods in 1358 and the 1380s. These events affected food supplies and living conditions in the region. The Sinagua suddenly abandoned Tuzigoot in 1425, disappearing from history. The reasons for their departure are unknown, but it may have been crop failures due to drought, salt build up in the irrigated fields, disease, or war.

In the first half of the 16th century, Spanish explorers claimed today's American Southwest for Spain. In 1583, 1598, and 1604, Moqui (today's Hopi) guides led gold-seeking Spanish expeditions on their Palatkwapi Trail into the Verde Valley. The Moqui used this trail to obtain minerals for pigments and jewelry. On their way to the reported metal outcrops, the Spanish expeditions stopped at the then oasis at Haskell Spring in today's Clarkdale. They examined the future Jerome ores, but left quickly, discouraged by the apparent lack of gold. In 1769, the region became the Alta California province of New Spain.

Following the Sinagua departure, the only inhabitants living in the region until the mid-1800s were small Indian clans of roving hunter-gatherers. By the mid-1500s, Yavapais from western Arizona had immigrated into the Verde Valley. The Spanish in 1583 describe meeting these Indians in today's Clarkdale; they called them "Cruzados" because they wore crosses on their heads. The Apaches, coming from New Mexico, entered the Verde Valley sometime after the Yavapais. Linguistic studies identify a fundamental difference between these two nations. The Yavapai language is Yuman with its origins from the lower Colorado River region. The Apache language is Athabascan with its origins in the northern Arctic regions.

The Yavapais and Apaches lived in seasonal encampments using brush wikiups for shelter. Small patches of corn, beans, and squash were cultivated. Acorns, agave, cactus fruit, mesquite beans, berries, seeds, and game were their basic foods. Their only domestic animals were dogs and turkeys until the introduction of horses by the Spanish into the Americas. Handcrafted baskets of all sizes and shapes, depending upon their purpose, were skillfully made out of local plants.

Following the Mexican War of Independence from Spain in 1821, the region became the New Mexico Territory under Mexican governance. During this time, American mountain men on beaver-trapping expeditions went up the Verde River in the 1820s and 1830s through the future site of Clarkdale.

The United States, under the Manifest Destiny concept, conquered Mexico in the War of 1848, seizing most of today's American Southwest. In 1863, Pres. Abraham Lincoln established the Arizona Territory by splitting the New Mexico Territory in half.

The mid-1860s to the mid-1870s are the transition years between the past and the present for Arizona. This brief period brought a major influx of gold miners into the Prescott region, farmers and ranchers to provide food for the increasing Yavapai County population, government officials to administer the Arizona Territory, and the US Army to subjugate the Indians.

The first Anglo-Americans into the Verde Valley arrived in 1865 when farmers moved into Lower Verde. Indian attacks prompted a plea from these farmers for military support. Soldiers arrived in August 1865 establishing Camp Lincoln, and eventually Camp Verde, to conduct operations against the Indian nations. After the defeat of most of the Indian clans of central Arizona, Pres. Ulysses S. Grant implemented the Rio Verde Reservation in 1873. This 800-square-mile reserve encompassed most of the Verde Valley including the future towns of Clarkdale, Cottonwood, and Jerome.

In April 1873, more than 1,500 Yavapais and Apaches were moved next to the Verde River south of Peck's Lake near today's Cottonwood. The river was a breeding place of malarial mosquitoes, and by September, more than 1,000 Indians were ill and death became almost a daily occurrence. A five-mile irrigation ditch, today's Cottonwood Ditch, was hand dug by the Indians, and in 1874, a bounty of food grew on 56 irrigated acres.

Because of the malaria, the reservation headquarters and tribes moved on June 2, 1874, to the "Hot Water Spring" as named by the Indians. This is today's Haskell Spring that became Clarkdale's main water source in the early 20th century. In February 1875, a total of 1,476 Indians were forced out of the Rio Verde Reservation. President Grant annulled the reservation two months later, opening the land to settlement under the Homestead and Mining Acts. The potential irrigable lands, abundant water, long growing season, and mineral resources in the mountains were common knowledge. Soon farmers tilled the rich soil watered by irrigation ditches while prospectors explored for ores in the Black Hills and ranchers ran large herds of cattle on the open grasslands.

In 1875, George Kell lived in an adobe house at Haskell Spring where he farmed irrigated gardens. Here on August 17, 1875, Riley and Rebecca Casner had a son, George Washington Casner—Clarkdale's earliest known Anglo birth.

There is a common perception that Clarkdale is the "son" of Jerome. In reality, they are "sibling" communities conceived a few months apart. On April 17, 1876, George Kell was elected recorder of the Verde Mining District with the duty of documenting mining claims under the federal mining law. He conducted this responsibility at his Haskell Spring home using the address "Old Indian Reservation, Camp Verde, Arizona Territory." One of the first mineral claimants was Morris Ruffner, a farmer-prospector living at Peck's Lake in 1875. Ruffner and others staked the first Jerome mineral claims in 1876. In 1904, *The Jerome Mining News* reported that these original claimers "set up our assaying outfit at Kell's ranch, now known as the Haskell-Kirwagen ranch, where we tested the ores, one of our party Doctor O'Dougherty being a practical assayer. Being satisfied with the results of the tests made from the ores, we proceeded to form the Verde Mining District, John Boyd being elected President, Doctor O'Dougherty as Secretary, and G.V. Kell, Recorder."

Before the town of Clarkdale was built, the area was called the Upper Verde. Several families lived on irrigated homesteads beside the Verde River, Peck's Lake, and at spring locations. In 1911, a headline boasted of "The Verde Valley, the garden spot of the new state." A productive farming economy grew a variety of crops from 1875 into the first two decades of the 20th century. During the 1880s, ranchers ran up to 40,000 head of cattle over the grass-covered Verde Valley region; however, by 1900 the cattle had overgrazed the vegetation and their hooves had created hard-packed bare ground.

In 1912, Clark began to construct the United Verde Copper Company (UVCC) smelter and a model company town near the Verde River. That same year, the Atchison, Topeka & Santa Fe Railway tracks, financed by Clark, reached Clarkdale.

Over the next 38 years, the UVCC smelter became one of the world's major copper producers, dominating Clarkdale's land and the lives of its multicultural residents. This period, the focus of this book, is covered in detail in chapters five, six, seven, and eight.

Between 1915 and 1920, smoke pollution from the Clarkdale smelter, the United Verde Extension smelter in nearby Clemenceau, and the Tapco generating plant extinguished the area's farming economy. The industrial age replaced the agricultural age in Clarkdale.

The 1953 notification by Phelps Dodge that the Jerome mine and Clarkdale smelter were shutting down was like a death notice for the sibling communities. Their future appeared to be ghost towns as most families left for employment elsewhere, abandoning their houses. Many of the lively ethnic neighborhoods around Clarkdale disappeared, leaving no traces today.

In 1953, Phelps Dodge sold Clarkdale and the smelter to Allison Steel Company, which wanted the millions of tons of iron-rich slag. In 1957, the town's citizens incorporated Clarkdale. Residents were buying the former company-owned homes. Over the years, the town obtained ownership of the roads, parks, swimming pools, dispensary, hospital, community church, administrative buildings, and the Clark Memorial Clubhouse. The Peck's Lake recreational area and the golf course were initially leased to the townspeople.

A new life for Clarkdale began in 1959. A mile west of the abandoned smelter, the Phoenix Cement mine and plant (now the Salt River Materials Group) and trucking company began operations to furnish cement for the Glen Canyon Dam project. Employment opportunities expanded, and Clarkdale's population grew.

In 1960, the town, after passing through several corporate owners, was purchased by Clarkdale Realty, a division of Gulf States Land and Development, which began actively selling off the company homes and lands. In 1969, Clarkdale Realty granted 60 acres within Clarkdale to the Yavapai-Apache Nation as a reservation. A federal program helped the Native Americans replace their old houses that lined dirt roads with modern utility-equipped homes on paved roads.

Within a decade, Clarkdale's population grew as most of the remaining abandoned company houses were sold and remodeled. The sale of the former UVCC lands led to new homes and subdivisions in the community. In 1975, Clarkdale annexed land that included the Yavapai College site and the Haskell Spring locale.

Significant town events for the remainder of the 20th century into the 21st century are presented in chapter nine.

One

Prologue
The Land

Clarkdale's oldest basement strata are the same 1.73-billion-year-old ocean floor volcanic rocks that host the copper ore deposits of Jerome. Younger formations have since buried these basement rocks more than a half mile below today's surface in Clarkdale. These upper units reveal the history of life through geologic time. The 400-million-year-old Devonian Martin dolomite contains coral reefs and traces of petroleum. The 350-million-year-old seashell-rich Mississippian Redwall is the source of the lime used in the manufacture of cement at the Clarkdale plant. Early land plants are preserved in carbon-rich layers in the region's 300-million-year-old red bed strata.

Beginning over 10 million years ago, today's Verde Valley began forming by deep fracturing of the crust that slowly lowered the valley floor. From eight to two million years ago, a large, shallow, freshwater lake formed throughout the slowly sinking Verde Valley. This lake deposited layers of brown clays, tan sands, and white limestone that surround and underlie Clarkdale. These bedded rocks, named the Verde Formation, host fossilized reed plants, freshwater mollusk shells, and evidence of prehistoric elephants, lions, and camels. The Verde Formation and the Mississippian Redwall limestone are Clarkdale's groundwater aquifers.

At the end of the ice age 10,000 years ago, Clarkdale was a verdant grassland area cut by the wide, shallow, slow moving Verde River. Peck's Lake formed out of a cutoff portion of the meandering Verde River. This Eden-like setting began changing in the late 19th century with overgrazing, dropping of the water table, drying up of water sources, diminishing rainfall, and the erosive effects of incised drainages.

Geology has shaped Clarkdale's history. The copper ores, cement resources, construction materials, flat topography, soil, and water have made its land the setting for multiple cultures over millennia. Eons of volcanic activity, sedimentary deposition, and tectonic fracturing interspersed by periods of erosion have created Clarkdale's picturesque setting amidst sculptured shapes, rainbow colors, and encompassing mountains. The Mogollon Rim outcrops a few miles north of Clarkdale present the spectacular Colorado Plateau strata known worldwide for its awe-inspiring national parks.

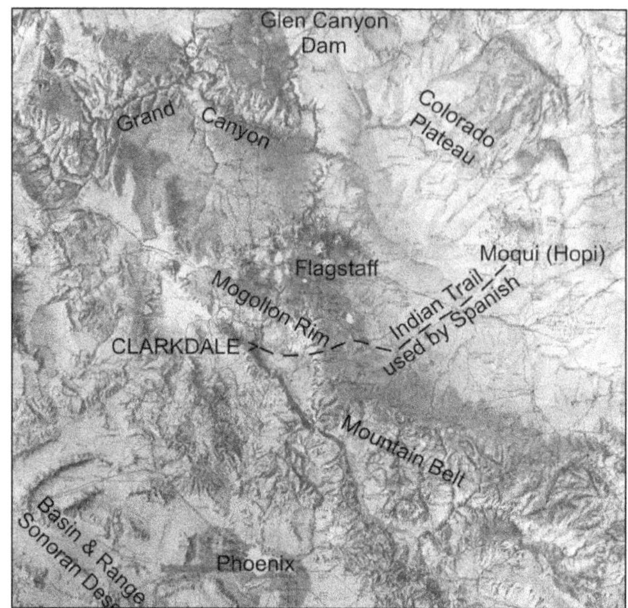

Clarkdale is located where the mountain belt of uplifted ancient basement rocks of central Arizona meets the flat-lying colorful younger sedimentary strata of northern Arizona's Colorado Plateau. The Mogollon Rim separates these distinct topographic provinces. The Mogollon Rim and the Verde Valley were formed by crustal fracturing. A long geological history made Clarkdale's region one of the continent's unique geological environments. (Author's collection.)

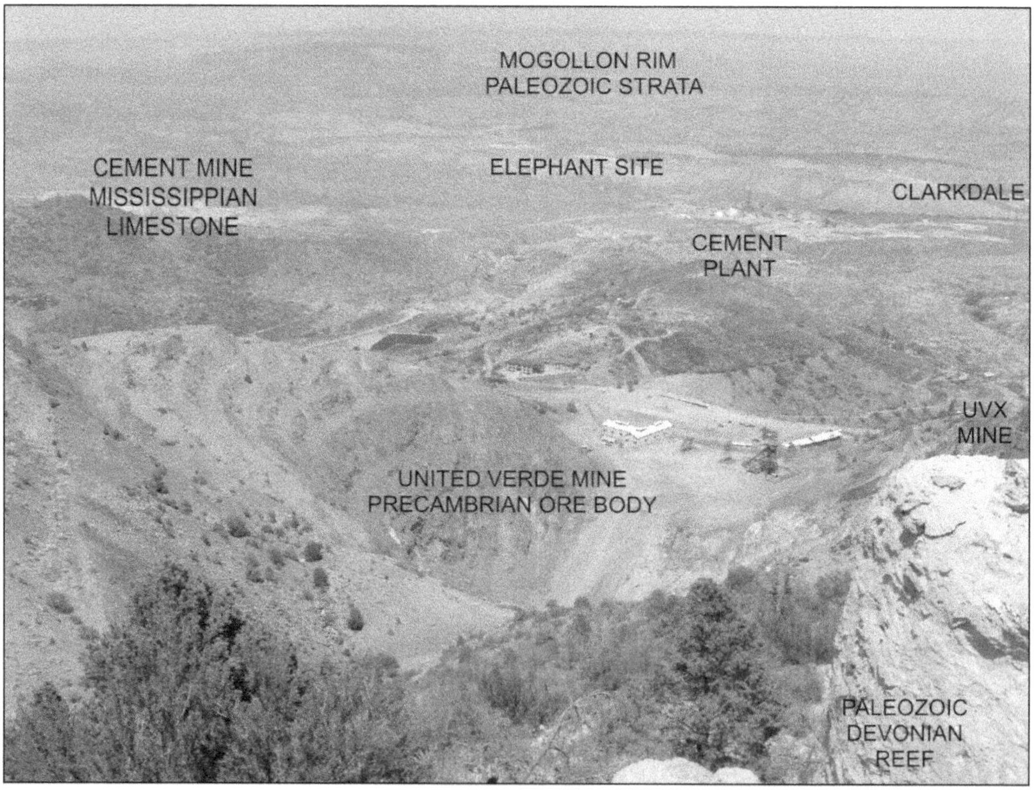

This Jerome-Clarkdale scene shows 1.73 billion years of geologic history ranging from some of Arizona's oldest rocks at Jerome's mine to some of its youngest in Clarkdale's lakebeds below. The coral reef outcrop (lower right) indicates a history of coral formation in a subtropical ocean about 400 million years ago, continental plate movements, and uplift and erosion exposing fossil corals a mile high and 250 miles from the nearest sea. (Author's collection.)

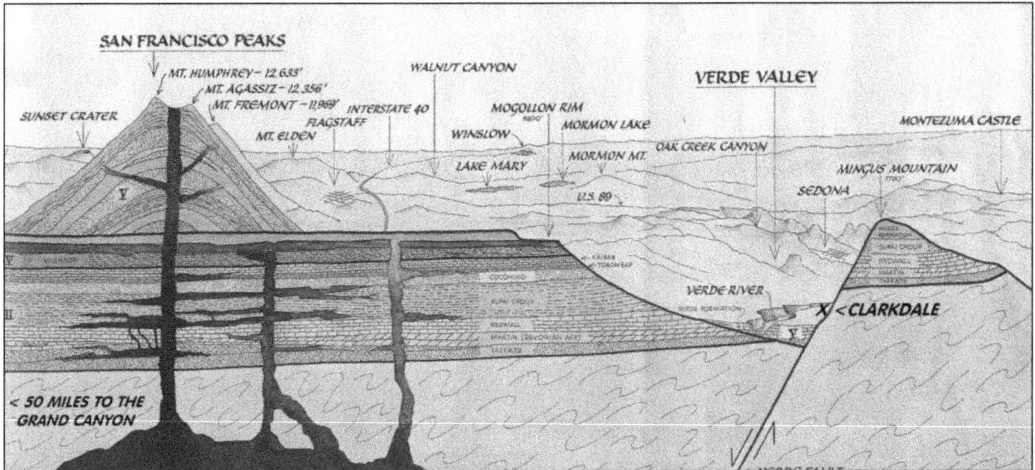

This cross section presents the subsurface units from Clarkdale to Flagstaff. It shows the Verde Fault as one of the many fractures that down-dropped the Verde Valley, and exposed the Mogollon Rim flat-lying sedimentary strata that project under Flagstaff and on to the Grand Canyon, where the same strata are again exposed. Clarkdale lies at the base of Mingus Mountain. (Courtesy Zion Natural History Association.)

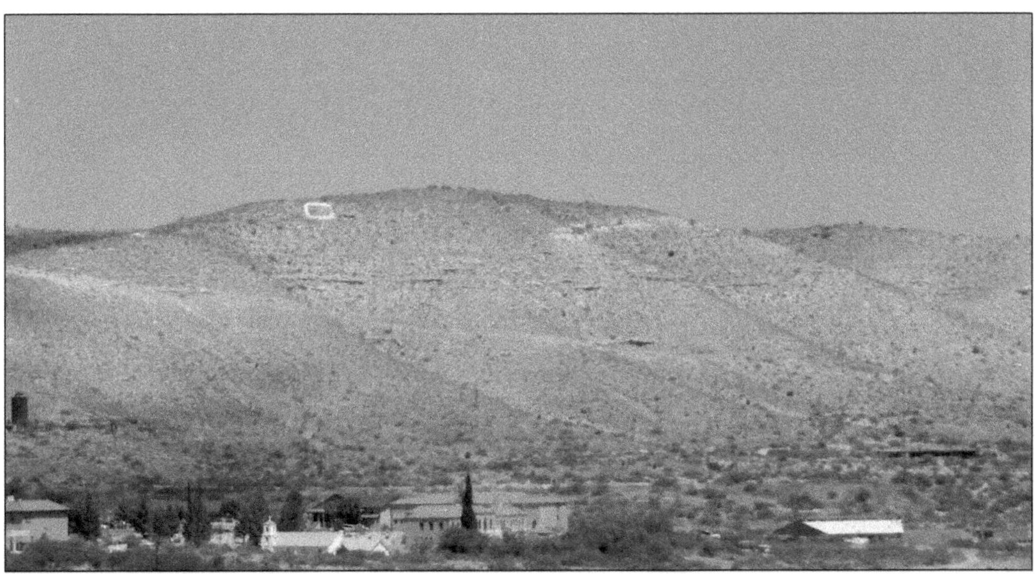

Flat-lying white- and tan-bedded formations surround and underlie Clarkdale. These beds, named the Verde Formation, were deposited eight to two million years ago in a valley-wide, shallow water lake. The formation locally consists of more than 3,000 feet of water-laid mud, sand, and limestone deposited while the Verde Valley was sinking. (Author's collection.)

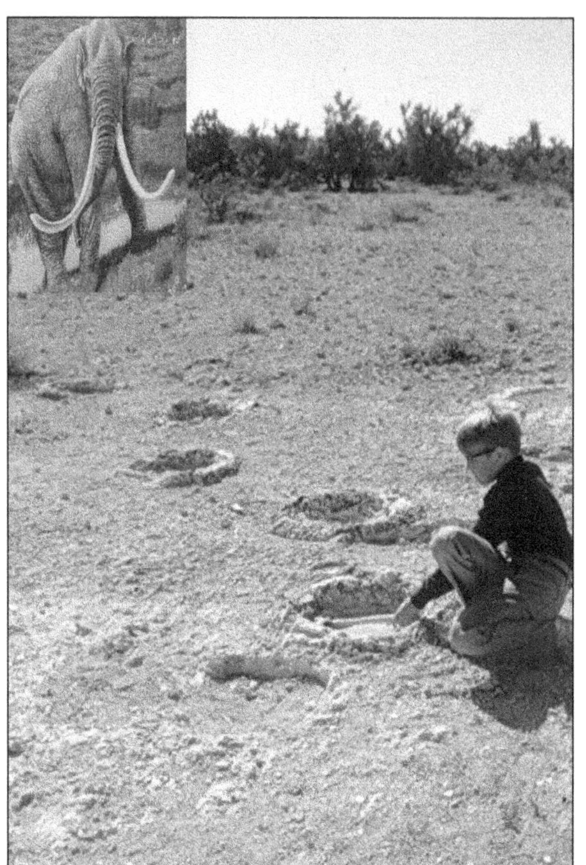

The Verde Formation lake beds contain fossilized reed plants, fresh water mollusks, and animal bones. This photograph shows the footprints of an elephant that walked across a mud flat of the shallow Verde Lake a few million years ago. The salt and gypsum beds near Camp Verde developed during the final evaporative stages of the lake two million years ago. (Author's collection.)

In 1979, a Northern Arizona University geologist excavated a three-million-year-old fossil elephant (Stegomastodon) head in a Verde Formation mudstone. The skull was discovered on cement plant land in the hills on the edge of Clarkdale's border. The tusks have been flattened by the weight of overlying rocks over time. A Stegomastodon palate cast with teeth and tusk roots is exhibited in the Clarkdale Historical Museum. (Courtesy Dr. Dale Nations.)

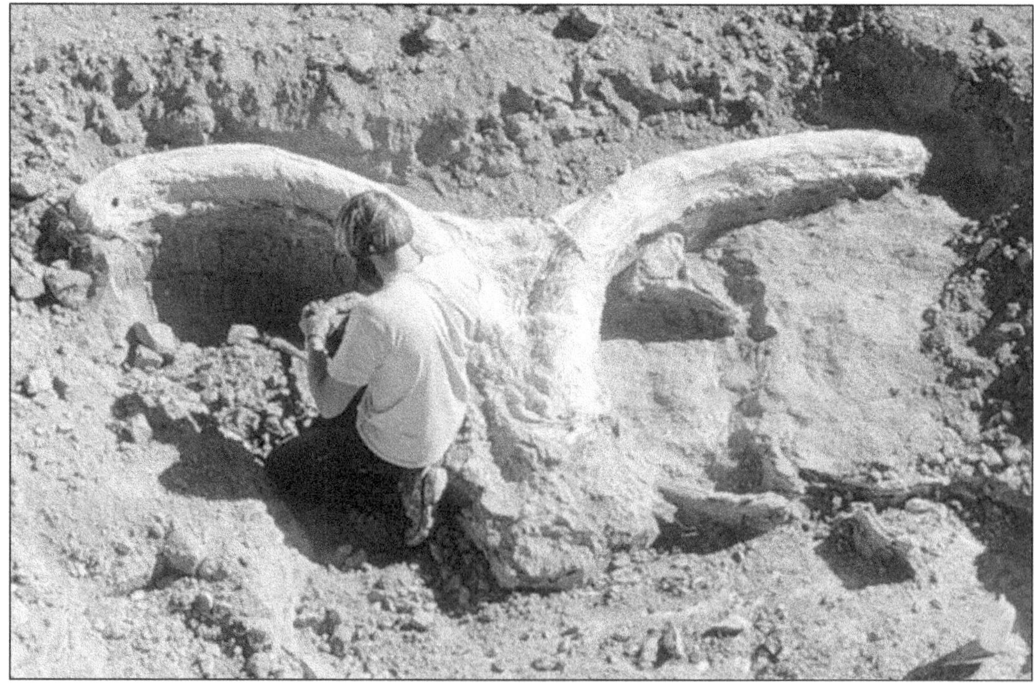

Two

The First Peoples

The earliest inhabitants of the Clarkdale area were the hunter-gatherer Paleo-Indians. They arrived in the Verde Valley more than 11,000 years ago, carrying spears bearing the distinctive Clovis points.

About 4,000 years ago, the Archaic Indians were in the Verde Valley. They left behind split-twig animal figurines, crude pottery, baskets, and evidence of domesticated beans, corn, and squash.

About 2,000 years ago, Hohokam Indians immigrated from the south into the Clarkdale region. They lived in pit shelters, fabricated basket-ware, and eventually developed clay pottery. By 500 A.D., permanent irrigated farming communities existed.

By 800 A.D., Sinagua Indians became the dominant culture for the next six centuries. Clarkdale's stretch of the Verde River has remains of several Sinagua pueblos and cliff-face cave dwellings. The excavated and restored 110-room, two-story pueblo at Tuzigoot National Monument documents this period. Farming produced a variety of ditch-irrigated crops. The culmination of the Sinagua culture occurred between 1100 and 1425 A.D.

The Sinagua Indians—for unknown reasons—hastily abandoned the region in about 1425. For the previous two centuries, Sinagua communities had been built in strong defensive positions, suggesting war may have caused the hasty exodus.

About the beginning of the 16th century, Yavapai Indians came from the west into the Verde Valley, followed in the early 17th century by Apache Indians from the east. These nomadic hunter-gatherer tribes moved according to the seasons, game movement, and plant ripening times. The total population of the central Arizona hunter-gatherer clans was at most a very few thousand. Over the next three centuries, they left little evidence of their temporary encampments. Some small corn-growing dry farming plots have been identified. Today, descendants of both Indian nations live within Clarkdale on a 60-acre portion of the Camp Verde Reservation of the Yavapai-Apache Nation.

All the Native American cultures mined, utilized, and traded the local natural resources, including copper minerals for tools, jewelry, and coloring; pipestone and gypsum for jewelry; rock tools; salt; clay utensils; chert, quartzite, obsidian, and rhyolite for arrowheads and knives; gabbro or diorite for axes; and basalt and sandstone for manos and metates.

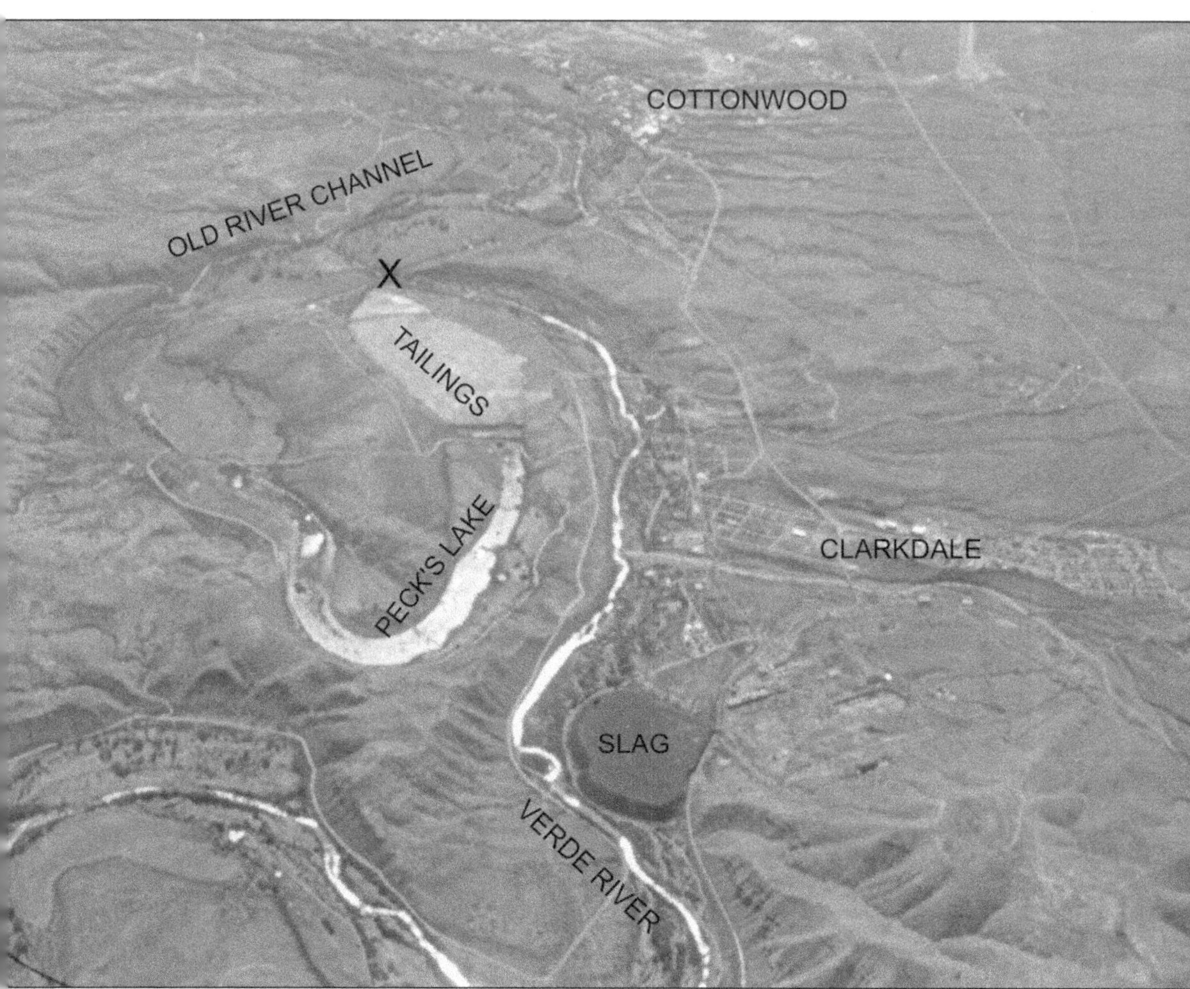

The name Tuzigoot is an anglicized Apache term for "Crooked Water" referring to Peck's Lake's shape. The lake was once part of the Verde River; however, a few thousand years ago, river erosion changed the channel near Tuzigoot National Monument (the X on the photograph) cutting off the meander from the old river channel and leaving behind the lake. The Clarkdale smelter tailings buried the former channel. Peck's Lake is one of Arizona's largest natural wetlands. (Author's collection.)

Paleo-Indians had immigrated into the Clarkdale area by 11,600 years ago, near the end of the ice ages. The lush vegetation supported a diversified, now mostly extinct, large animal population. Paleo-Indians hunted these creatures using lances tipped with distinctive fluted stone spear points archeologists call Clovis points (shown here). It is hypothesized that these early hunters exterminated many of the ice age animal species. (Author's collection.)

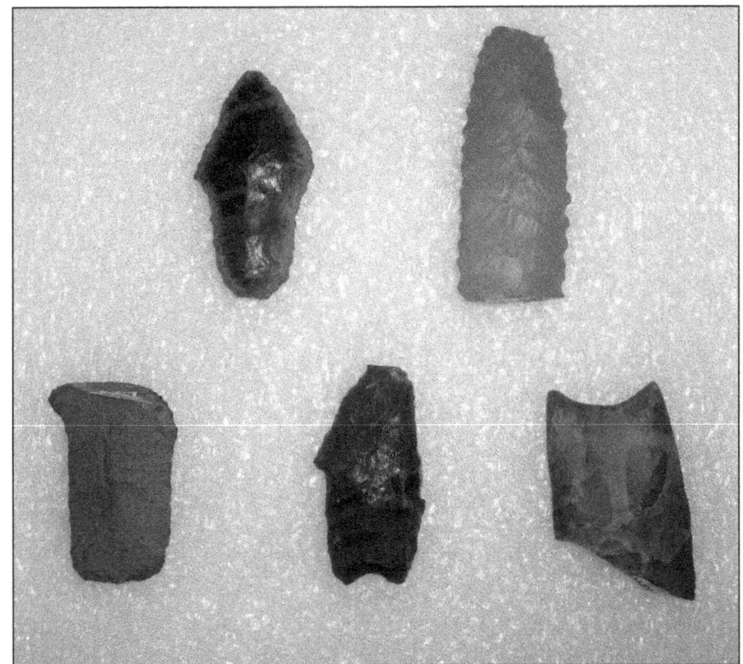

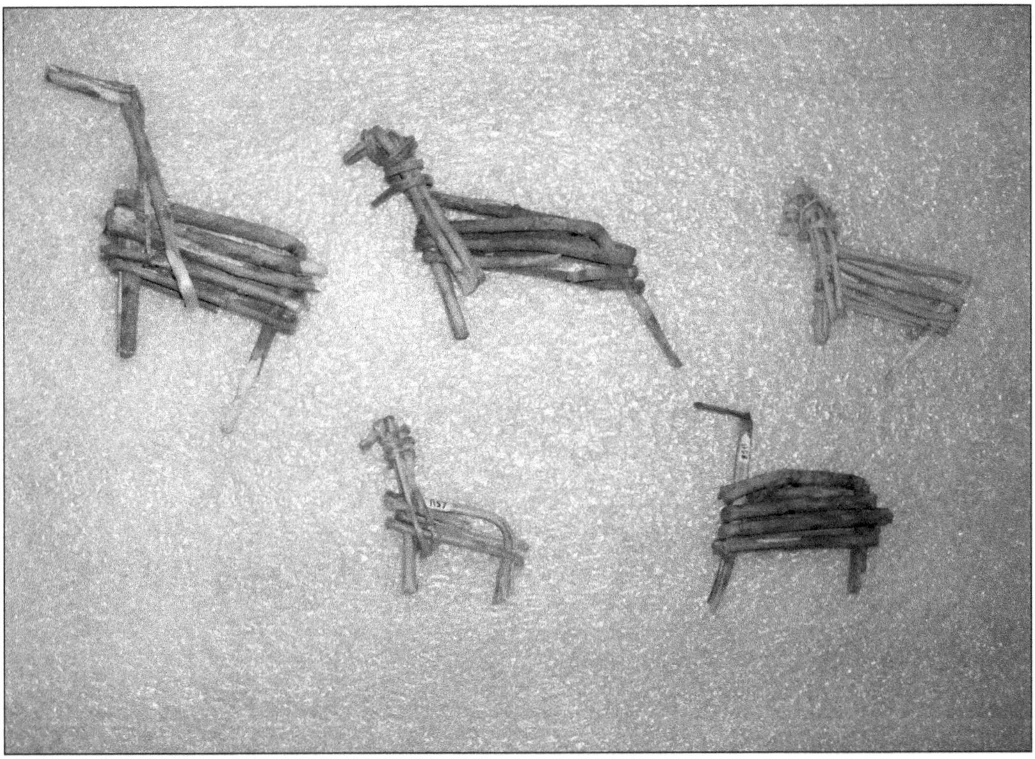

Split twig figurines were discovered in Sycamore Canyon caves eight miles north of Clarkdale. These figures were made out of one willow twig split lengthwise. The halves were then twisted, wrapped, and formed into a one-piece animal idol. Similar figurines from the Grand Canyon and Flagstaff area date between 4,400 and 2,990 years ago. (Author's collection.)

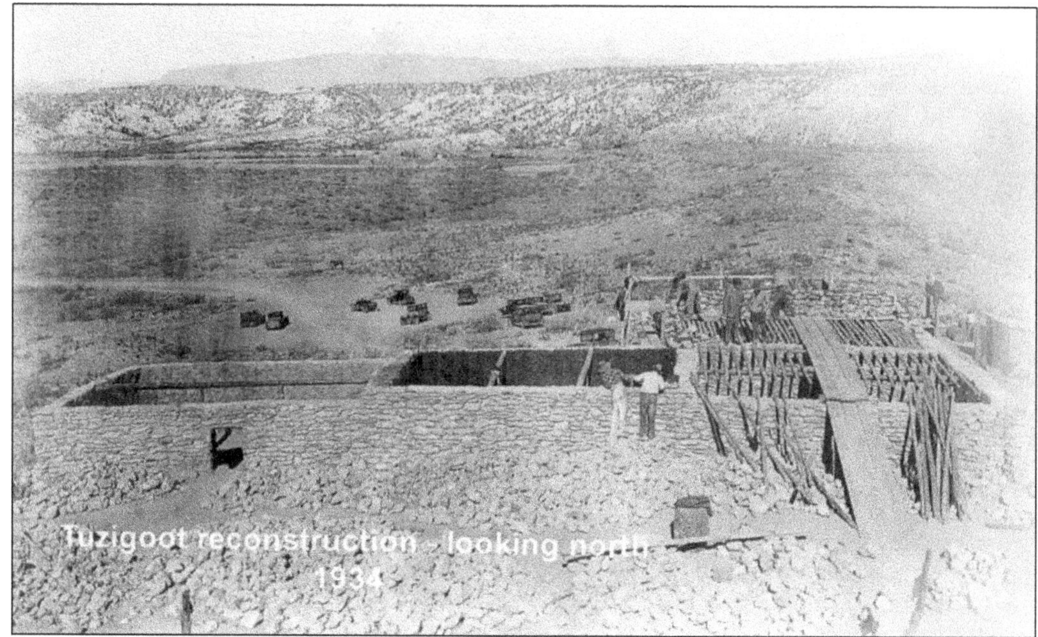

The Hohokam Indians immigrated from the south into the Verde Valley between 500 and 600 A.D. About 500 years later, the Sinagua Indians immigrated from the north into the Clarkdale area. They adopted a preexisting irrigation system and created a sophisticated society living in apartment complexes constructed of stone, adobe, and wood. The Sinagua culture culminated in the 13th and 14th centuries. (Courtesy Jerome State Historic Park.)

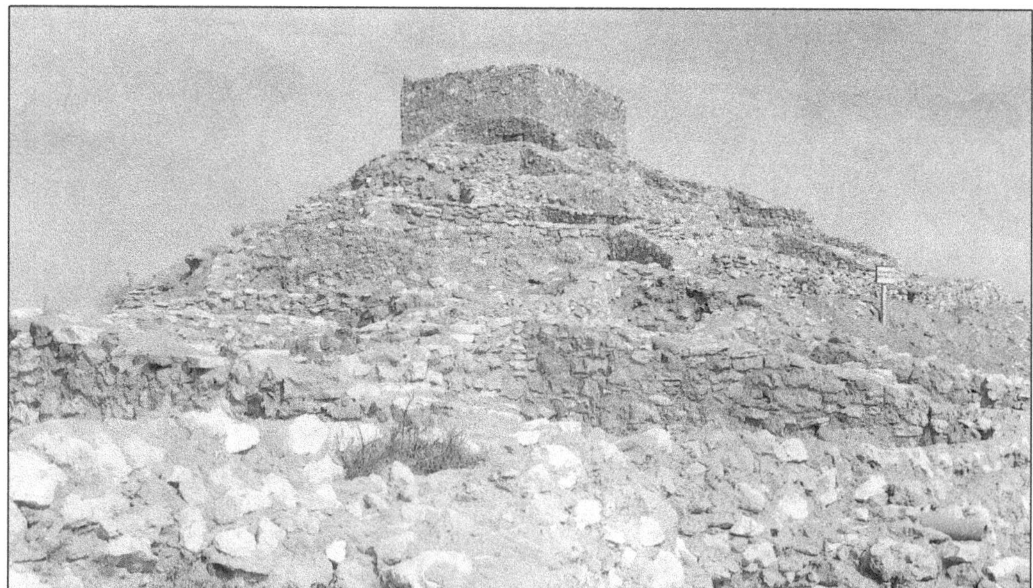

The 110-room, two-story Tuzigoot pueblo is located on a 120-foot-high hilltop. Individual families lived in one room that had cooking and heating fireplaces with adjoining storage rooms. Roof openings provided entry by means of ladders. The wood used in constructing the pueblos provides the material archeologists use in establishing absolute dates by tree ring studies and carbon-dating techniques. (Courtesy Tuzigoot National Monument.)

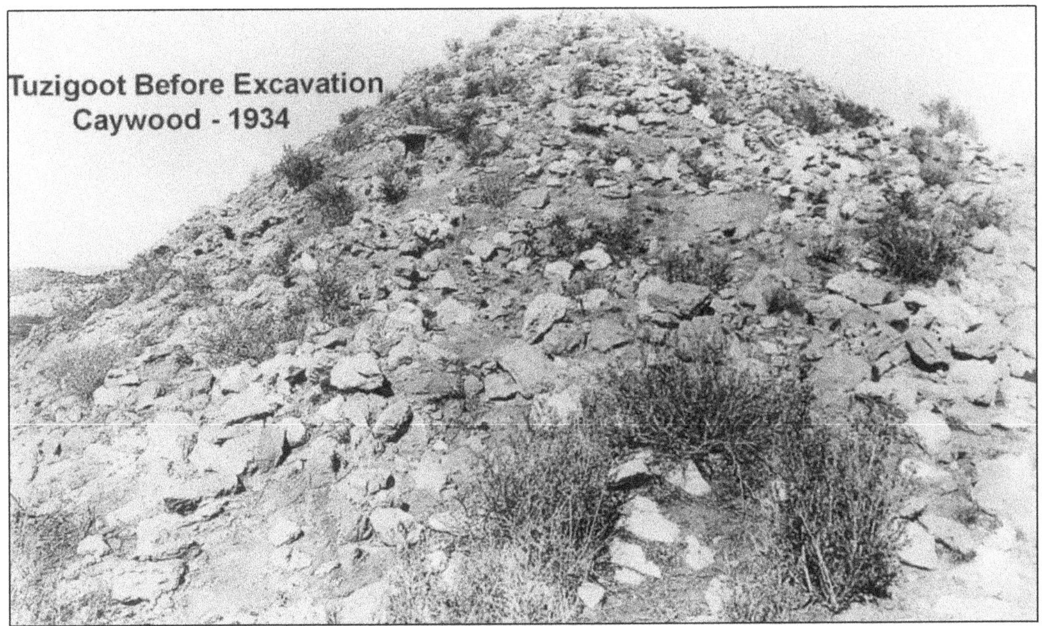

About the year 1425, the Sinagua suddenly and hastily deserted Tuzigoot and the entire Verde Valley. The speculated cause for the hasty abandonment was something external out of their control. Warfare is inferred by Tuzigoot's hilltop position in sight of other pueblos similarly located on high points along the Verde River and by the easily protected cliff housing locations found near Clarkdale and Camp Verde. (Courtesy Tuzigoot National Monument.)

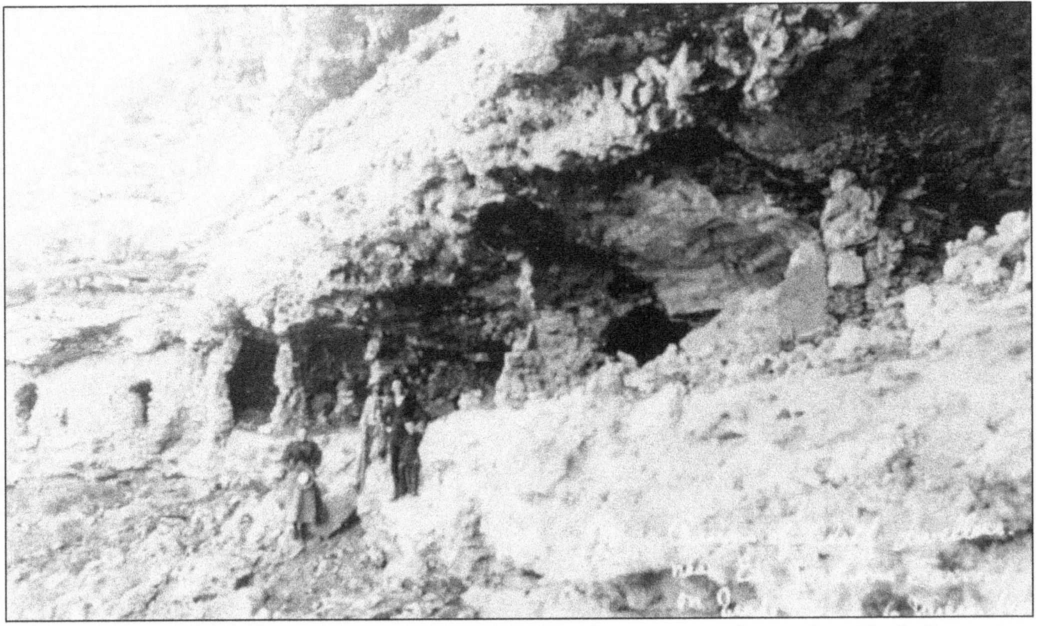

Local citizens in the early 20th century visited shallow Sinagua ruins located on Verde Formation cliff faces above the railroad tracks just north of Clarkdale. These cave dwellings, called "cavetes," are hollowed out soft clay beds situated between hard limestone strata that form the floors and the ceilings. Hand-built rock adobe walls divide and protect living and storage areas. (Courtesy Tuzigoot National Monument.)

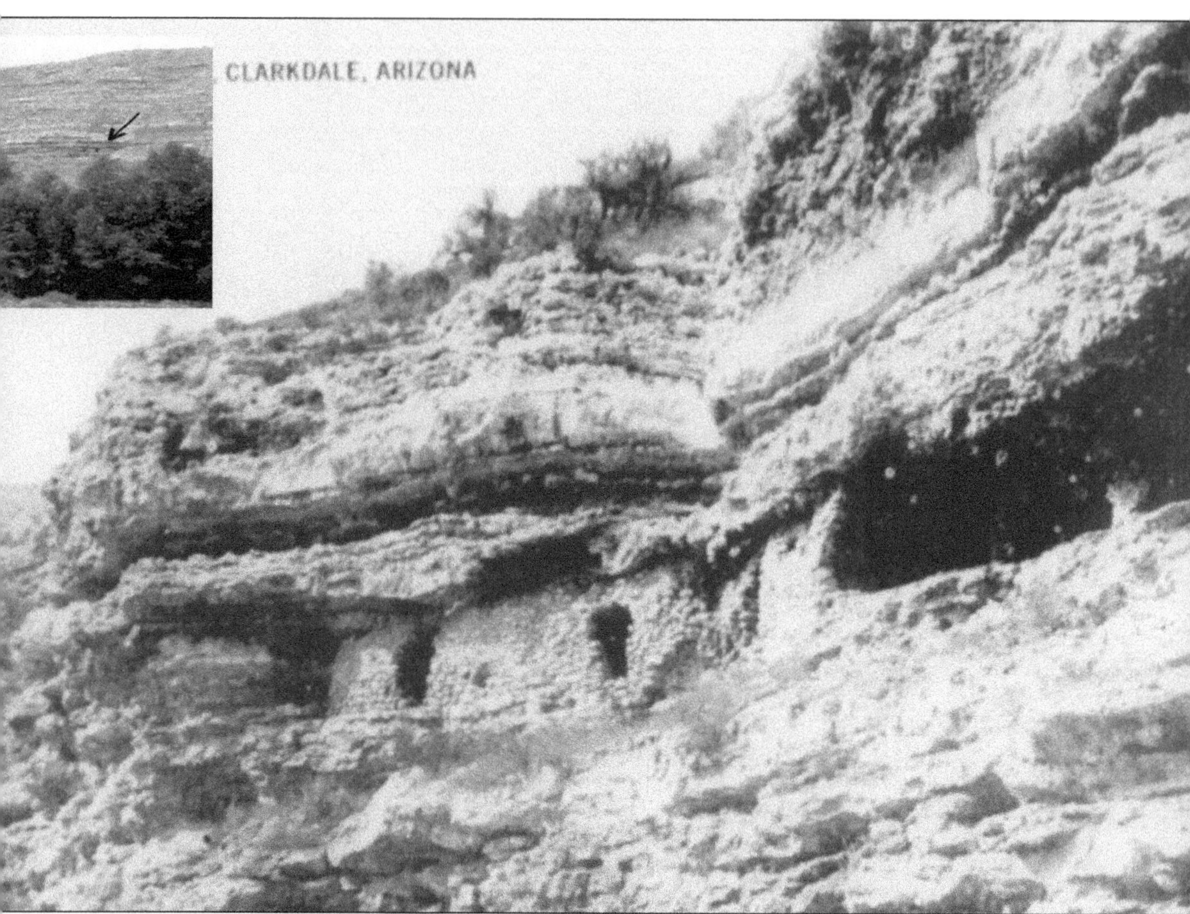

Fifty years ago, there were at least 17 Sinagua cave structures of varying sizes containing pottery shards, hair cuttings, twine, and tiny corn ears along a quarter-mile section of these cliffs. In the last half of the 20th century, pothunters removed the artifacts, and an increasing rate of natural erosion of the cliff faces has destroyed most of the cave dwellings. (Courtesy Jerome State Historic Park.)

Three

1583–1865

Yavapai, Apaches, Spanish, Mexicans, and Anglos

Sometime during the 15th and 16th centuries, Yavapai clans from the west and Apache clans from the east moved into the Verde Valley. Little is known about these hunter-gatherers, as their shelters were temporary, their numbers few, and artifacts rare.

In 1519, Spain claimed lands that included Arizona. No Spaniards came to Clarkdale for 64 years until 1583, when Antonio de Espejo with four other Spaniards seeking gold were guided by Moqui Indians on their Palatkwapi Trail (see map on page 12) to examine Indian-reported metals at the future site of Jerome. After crossing El Rio de los Reyes (the Verde River), their journal reported, "Close to it was a swamp into which flowed a stream of water. Rustic people with crosses on their heads waited for us." This was Haskell Spring, an important site in Clarkdale's history.

On November 23, 1598, Marcos Farfan de los Gados—with nine soldiers and two wives—arrived in the Verde Valley seeking gold. Progressing one league (2.6 miles) beyond the Verde River, they wrote, "As it was late, we camped that night on the slope of these hills, at a spring of water . . . very large and carrying much water almost hot." The Spanish left the oasis going up a well-used Indian trail to the mines where they described Indian mining activities including a 16-foot-deep shaft. In 1604, Gov. Juan de Onate led a third expedition to the future Jerome mines via today's Clarkdale. Onate reported abundant game, water, waterpower, forests, pastures, rich soils, and abandoned pueblos, but not the coveted gold and silver.

In 1821, Clarkdale's lands became part of newly independent Mexico. No Mexican officials entered the Verde Valley during their 27 years of governing this land. During this time, American mountain men, usually without Mexican permits, trapped beaver along the Verde River. These trappers reported Indian attacks, rampaging grizzlies, rabid wolves and coyotes, attacks by white men, and fur seizures by Mexican officials.

In May 1854, mountain man and government guide Antoine Leroux established the Leroux Trail between today's Phoenix and Winslow. He is credited with being the first United States explorer to officially describe the Tuzigoot ruins.

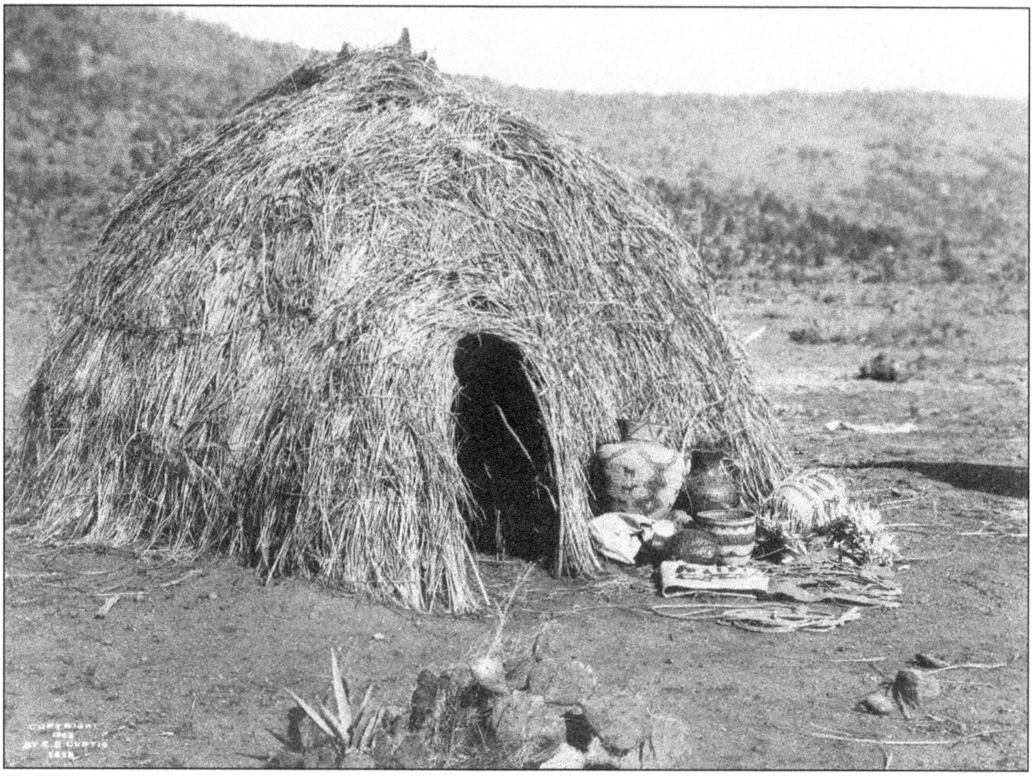

Sometime between the early 15th century Sinagua exodus and the late 16th century Spanish expeditions, two Native American nations immigrated into the unoccupied and open spaces of central Arizona. The Yavapais came from the west and the Apaches from the east. Their total population was probably only a few thousand, and by the mid-19th century, their numbers had been considerably reduced due to both Indian and white warfare and European diseases. (Author's collection.)

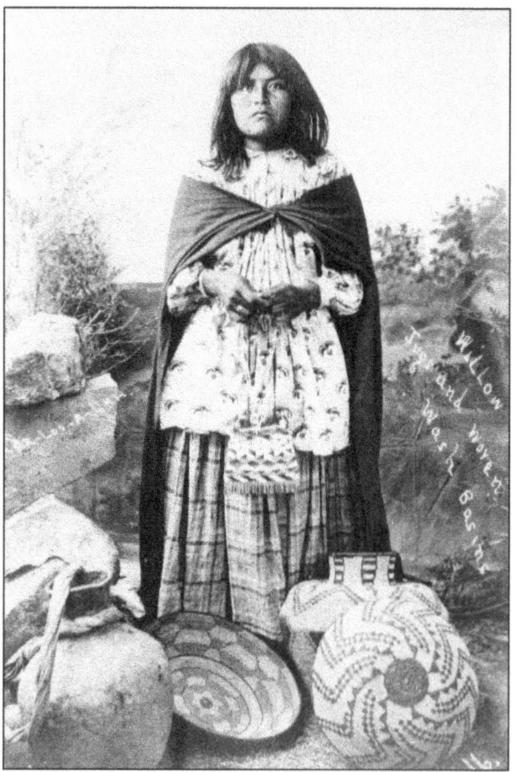

The Yavapai and Apache cultures consist of matrilineal clans of a few dozen members each. The size of hunter-gatherer clans depended upon finding adequate food. Clan members are interrelated by generation, with everybody of the same generation a brother or sister, everybody of one's parents' generation an uncle or aunt, and so on. Women were clan counselors. This Apache is in reservation dress. (Author's collection.)

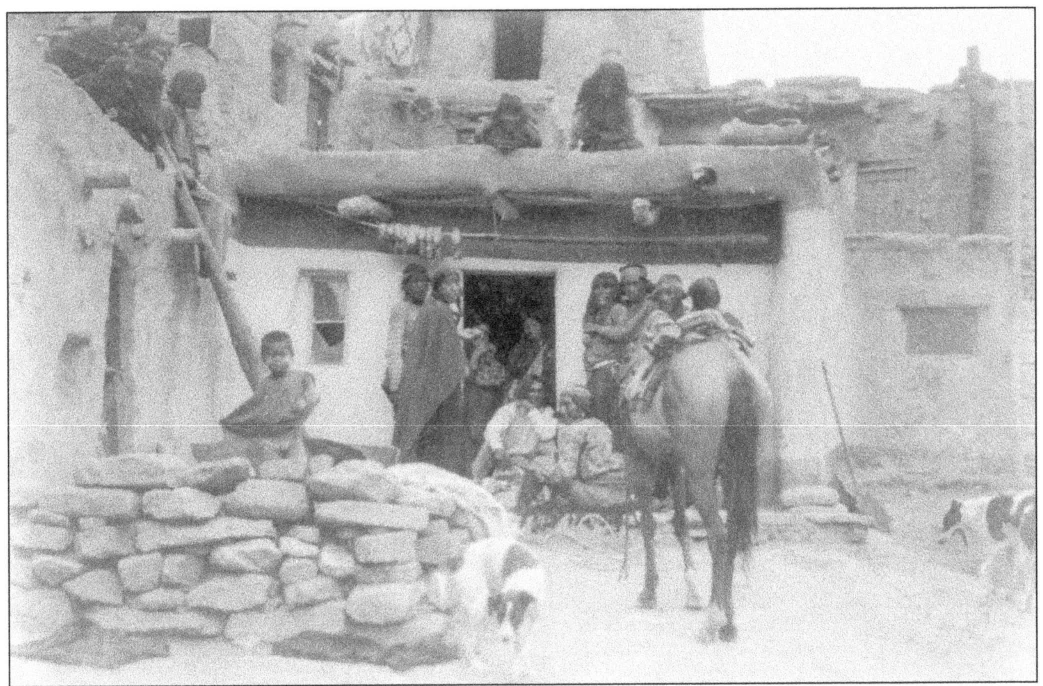

The Moquis, known today as the Hopis, are considered by some to be related to the Sinagua Indians who abandoned the Clarkdale region in 1425. Over the centuries, the Hopis walked the 150-mile-long Palatkwapi Trail (see map on page 12) from their northern Arizona mesas into the Verde Valley to obtain mineral resources. (Courtesy Clarkdale Historical Society and Museum.)

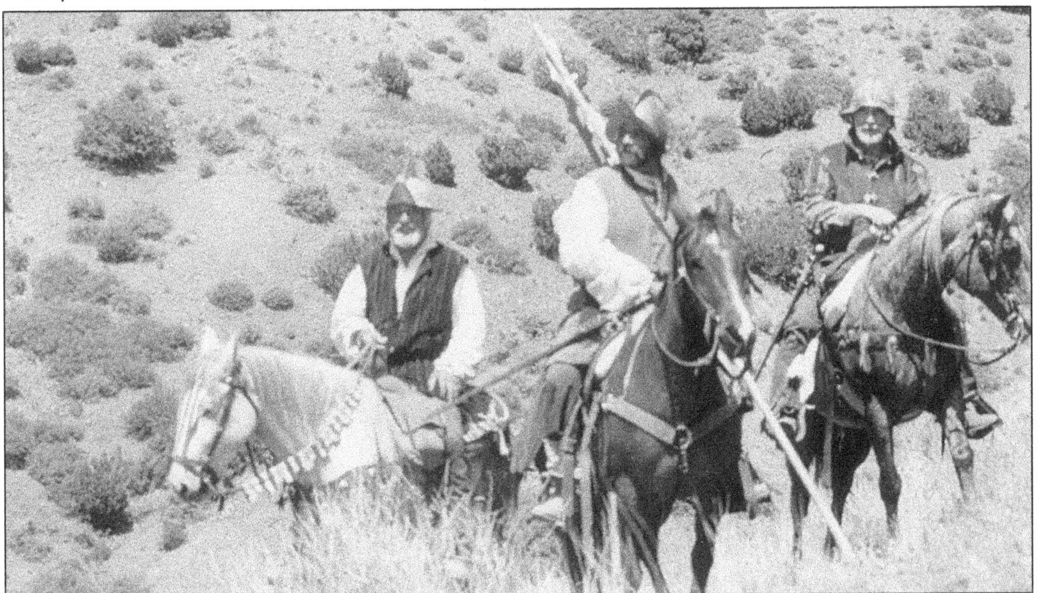

Clarkdale's Haskell Spring is a place with centuries of history. Artifacts around the once prolific spring indicate that Indians camped here for millennia. Between 1583 and 1604, three expeditions led by Spanish conquistadores seeking gold and silver stopped at the spring before going up to examine the metal outcrops at today's Jerome. In 1983, Robert Reeves, William Ensign, and Robert Munson retraced Antonio de Espejo's journey. (Courtesy Alan Reeves.)

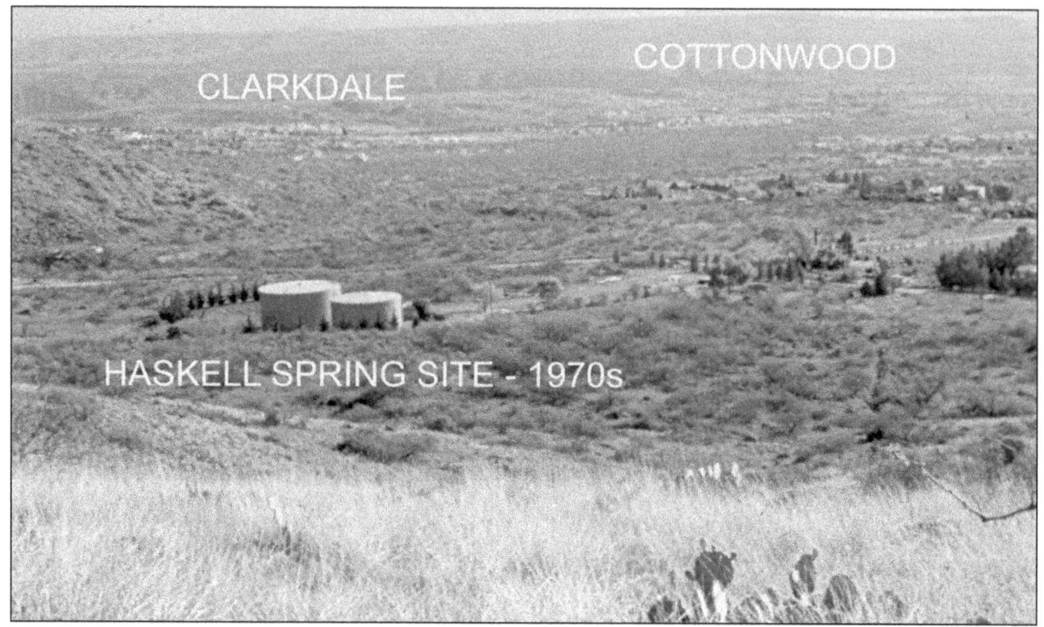

Moquis guided Marcos Farfan's Spanish expedition from their villages to the ore outcrops at today's Jerome. They forded the Verde River on November 23, 1598, and after crossing 2.6 miles of snow-covered ground, came to a spring that issued "much water almost hot" at the base of the mountain. This spring, today's Haskell Spring, is 65 degrees Fahrenheit year round, very warm relative to the cold November air. Local tribes also described the water as hot. (Author's collection.)

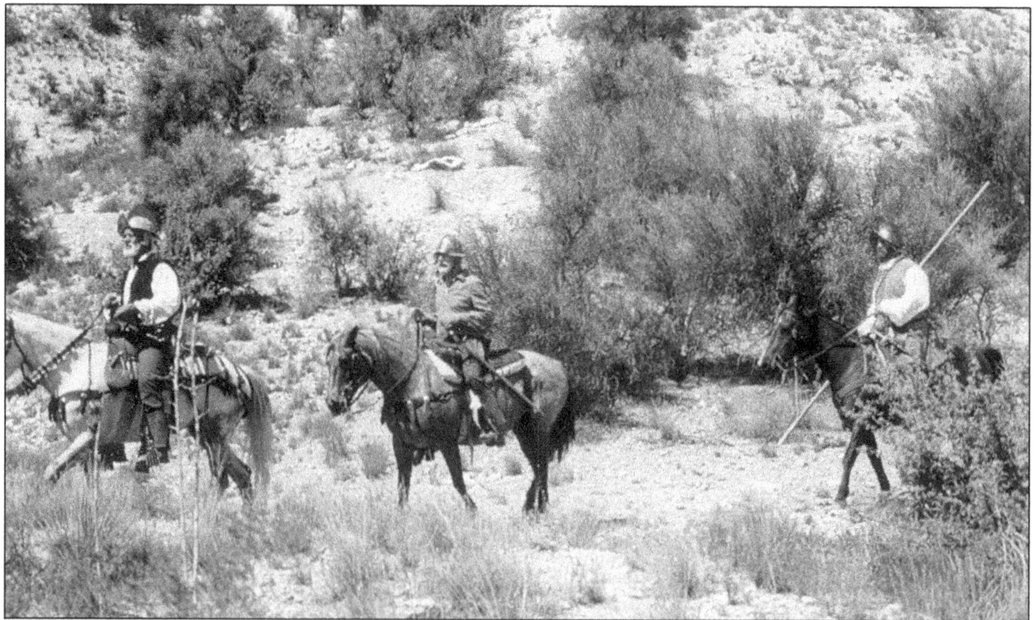

The conquistadors described evidence of centuries-old Indian mining. From the spring, "one could go up to the mine on horseback for these Indians had opened up a road." At the site, they found workings and a large dump. Espejo reported the veins as "copper mines and poor," lacking silver. Later, Farfan described the veins as wide and rich and staked land claims; however, no Spanish mining attempt was ever made. (Courtesy Alan Reeves.)

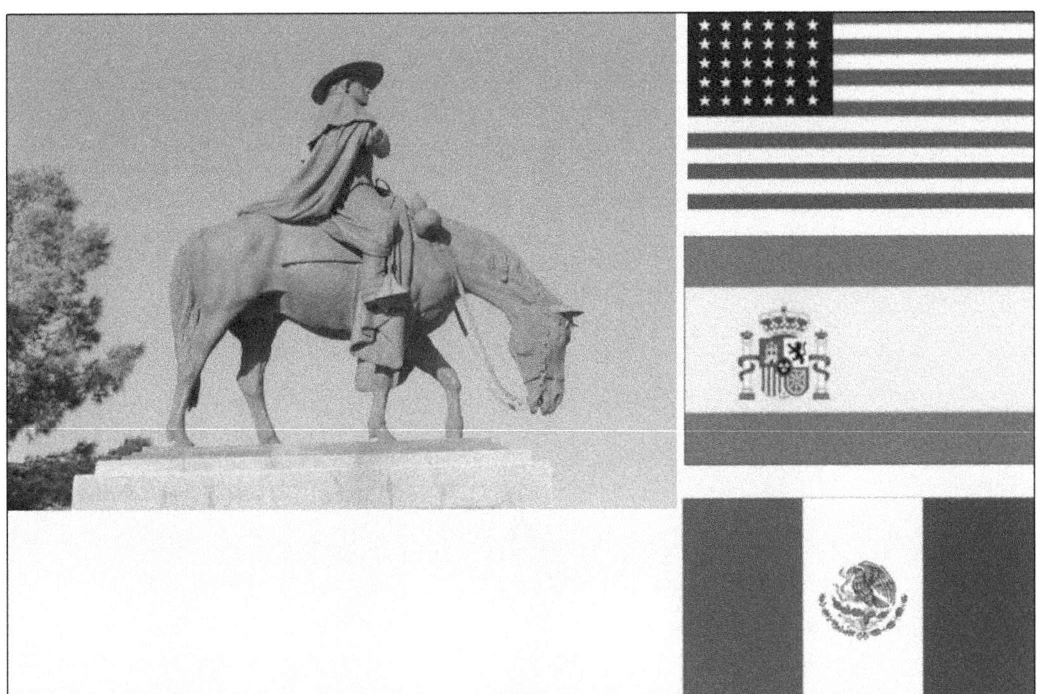

In 1699, Father Kino (statue)—mission builder and mapmaker—saw the lowermost Verde River and named it the Rio Azul. Indians controlled central Arizona, stopping Spanish expeditions coming up the Verde River in the mid-18th century and fur trappers in the early 19th century. The three flags are those of Spain, Mexico, and the United States that have flown over northern Arizona since 1519. (Author's collection.)

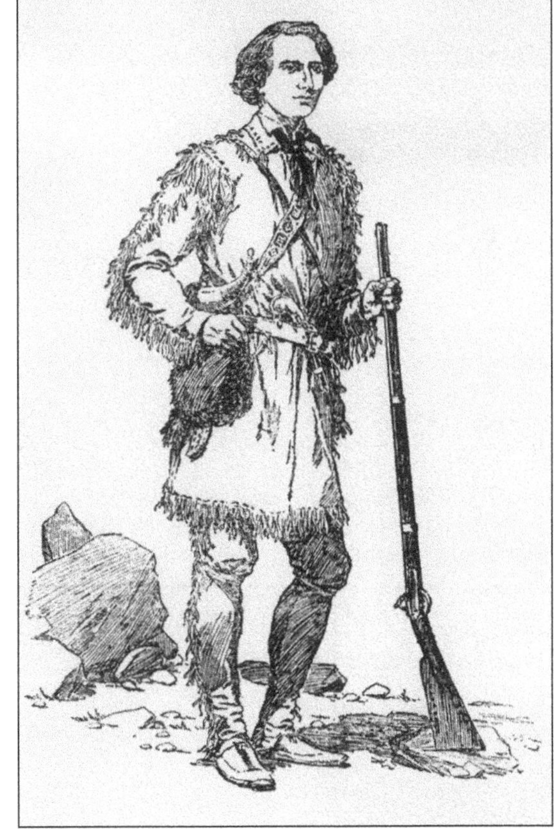

In the 1820s, several mountain men trapped beaver in Arizona. Most trespassed into the Mexican territory without authorization; hence, few records exist. Antoine Leroux, James Pattie, and Ewing Young may have trapped in the Verde Valley in 1826. Ewing Young led 43 trappers, including young Kit Carson on his first western expedition, up the San Francisco (present Verde) River past Clarkdale in 1829. (Author's collection.)

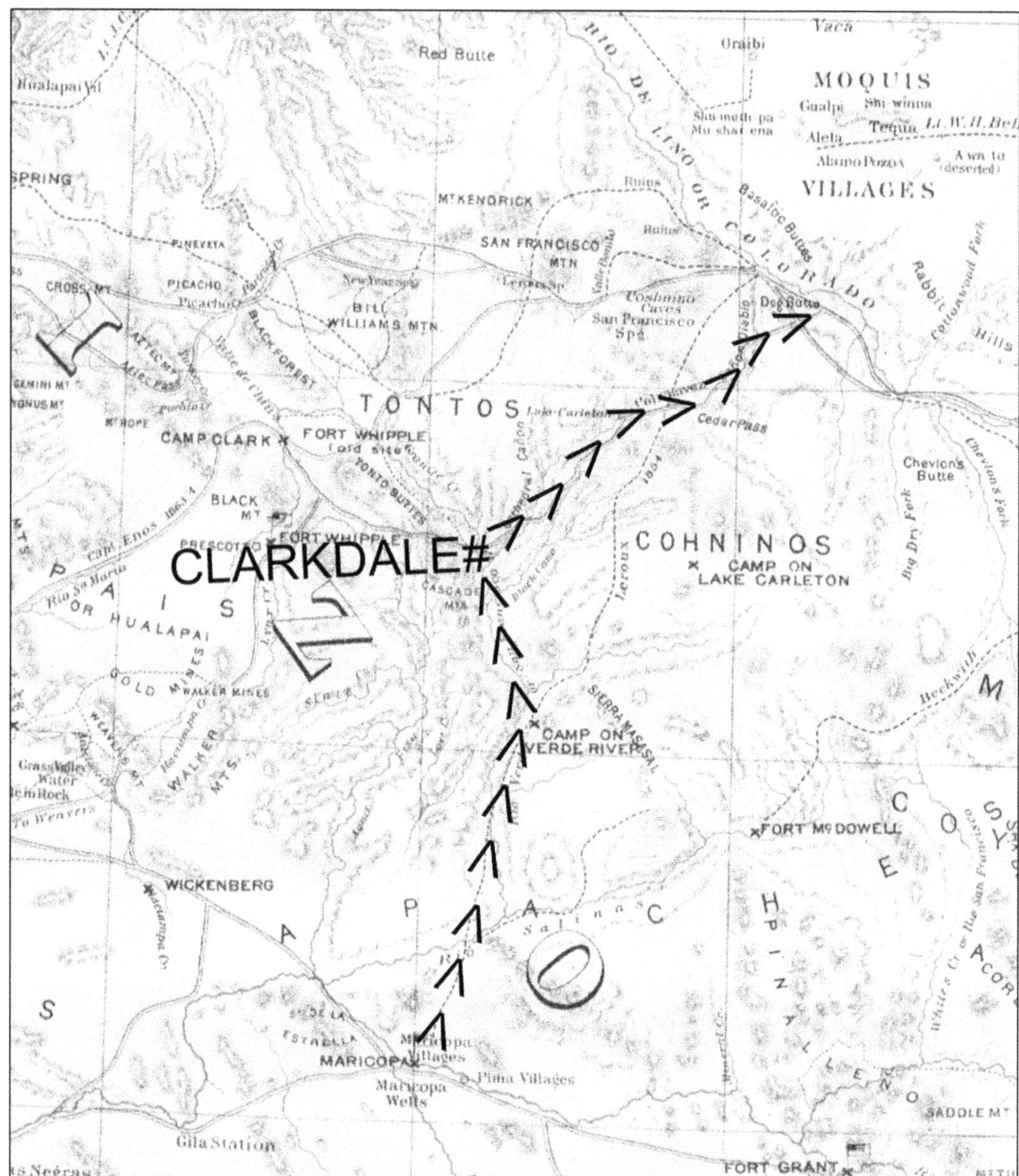

In 1853–1854, mountain man Antoine Leroux guided Lt. Amiel Whipple's 35th Parallel Pacific Railroad Survey party through northern Arizona to California. Returning to Arizona, he developed the Leroux Trail from the Salt River up the San Francisco River to the Little Colorado River. He described the Tuzigoot ruins amidst abundant water and lush vegetation. The middle section of the Leroux Trail on this 1864 Army map is misplaced; the probable route is indicated on the map. (Courtesy Western National Parks Association.)

Four

1865–1911
Pre-Clarkdale Settlement and Agriculture

The Arizona Territory, along with the nation, changed during the post–Civil War period. The Clarkdale lands transitioned from Native American, Spanish, and Mexican heritages to Anglo American agricultural and industrial societies.

Beginning in 1865, farming families—under the protection of the Army—homesteaded at today's Camp Verde. By 1872, most of the central Arizona Yavapai and Apache clans were conquered. In 1873, the Army placed 1,500 to 2,000 Indians on the Rio Verde Reservation beside the Verde River near today's Cottonwood. In June 1874, the Indians, dying in great numbers from malaria, moved to Clarkdale's Haskell Spring to get away from the mosquito-infested Verde River. A productive summer crop on river-irrigated land was harvested in 1874. However, in February 1875, the Indians were exiled in a forced winter march to the San Carlos Reservation and the Rio Verde Reservation was annulled.

Farmers, ranchers, and miners moved into the Clarkdale area immediately following the Indians' departure. An 1877 government map indicates Ruffner, Jordan, and Hawkins homesteading around Peck's Lake and Kell's adobe home and gardens at Haskell Spring.

The pre-Clarkdale area became an agricultural center of irrigated farms; Jerome and Prescott were their principal markets. In 1879 and 1898, Arizona's territorial reports to the federal government glowingly described these Upper Verde farms. Reported agricultural products included 26 different vegetables, 16 fruits, and 4 grains—plus nuts, honey, dairy products, and animals. Haskell Spring became the site of the Haskell-Kirwagen agricultural enterprise, which marketed its award-winning fruits nationally. Ranchers filled the surrounding Verde Valley with tens of thousands of cattle into the early 1890s.

Meanwhile, W.A. Clark's UVCC mine in Jerome was becoming a major copper producer. Copper was smelted at the mine site and shipped out by a narrow gauge railroad. In spite of the ore body's great size and richness, an increase in the mine's output was limited due to topographic limitations. Clark set out to build a bigger smelter, a standard gauge railroad line, and a company town in the flatlands below. With Clarkdale's construction, the Upper Verde's economy changed from agricultural to industrial.

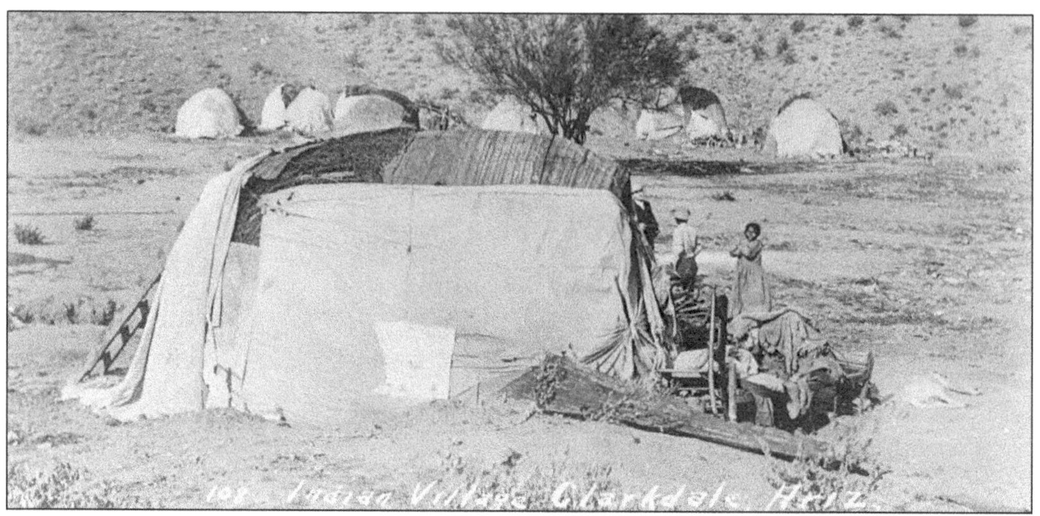

In November 1871, President Grant ordered the formation of the 800-square-mile Rio Verde Indian Reservation. In April 1873, a total of 2,300 Indians surrendered to the Army at Camp Verde, effectively ending the central Arizona Indian wars. The Rio Verde Reservation headquarters and community was established near Dead Horse State Park in Cottonwood. The Army supervised 2,000 Indians next to the slowly flowing, mosquito-infested, marshy Verde River. A malaria outbreak resulted in numerous fatalities. (Courtesy William Cowan.)

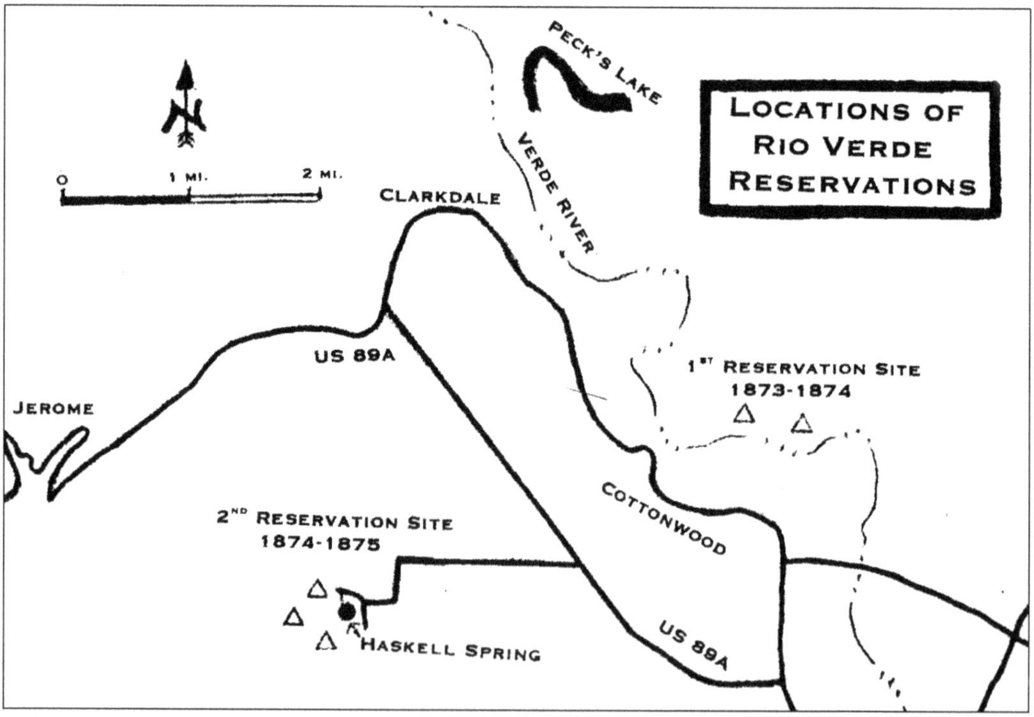

LOCATIONS OF RIO VERDE RESERVATIONS

PECK'S LAKE
VERDE RIVER
0 1 MI. 2 MI.
CLARKDALE
US 89A
JEROME
1ST RESERVATION SITE 1873-1874
COTTONWOOD
2ND RESERVATION SITE 1874-1875
HASKELL SPRING
US 89A

In June 1874, the reservation Indians and officials moved three miles west to higher ground at the base of the mountains where Haskell Spring supplied more than 250 gallons of water per minute. A tent town was built consisting of a military headquarters, hospital, kitchen and dining facility, underground jail, and a wood-frame trader's store surrounded by hundreds of wickiups in a mosquito-free environment around the healthy spring site. (Author's collection.)

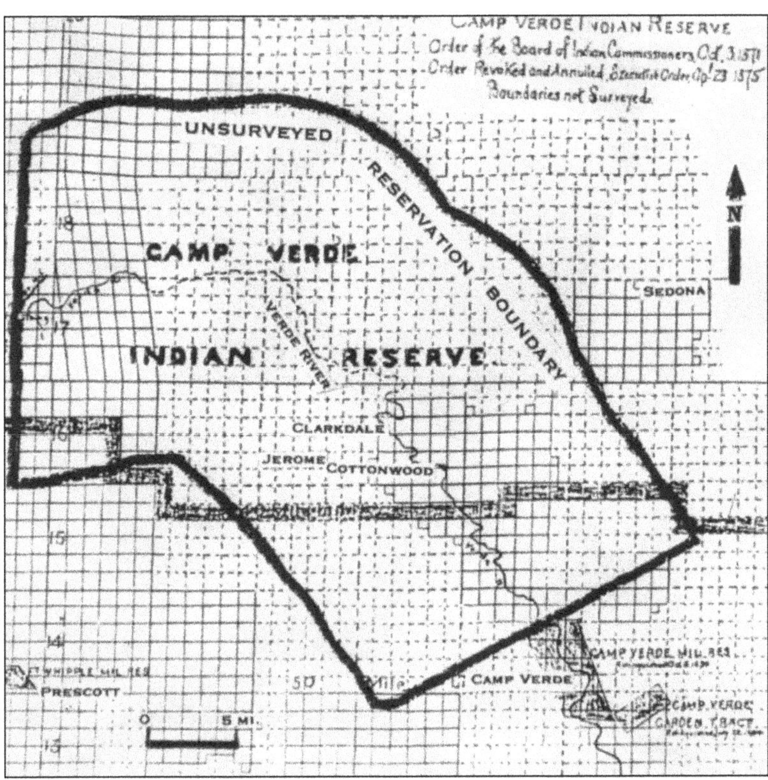

The "Indian Ring" of Tucson officials and businessmen, not wanting the Indians to become self-sufficient in food production, lobbied Washington politicians to close the Rio Verde Reservation. In February 1875, the Indians were marched out through snowy mountains, with much loss of life, to the San Carlos Reservation. It would be more than a quarter century before the remaining exiles returned to Clarkdale. (Author's collection.)

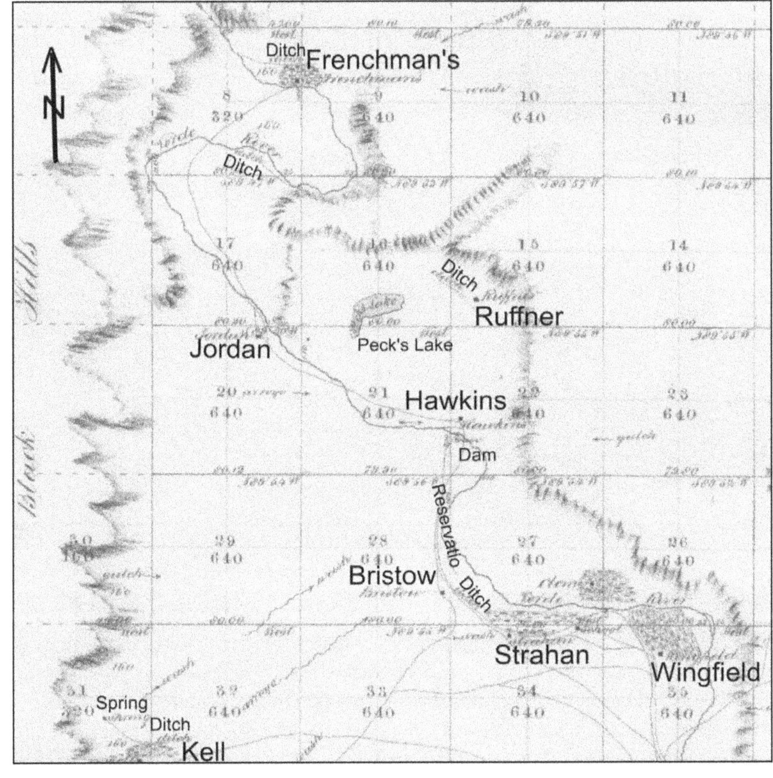

Peck's Lake is named for Ed Peck, who never resided there. In 1865, he reportedly cut hay there for the Army at Prescott. George Kell, probably Clarkdale's first Anglo resident, lived near the former Verde Reservation headquarters site at Haskell Spring. This 1877 map identifies Ruffner, Jordan, and Hawkins homesteading around Peck's Lake. The 1880 census lists Angus McKinnon and George McKinnon as living at Peck's Lake. (Author's collection.)

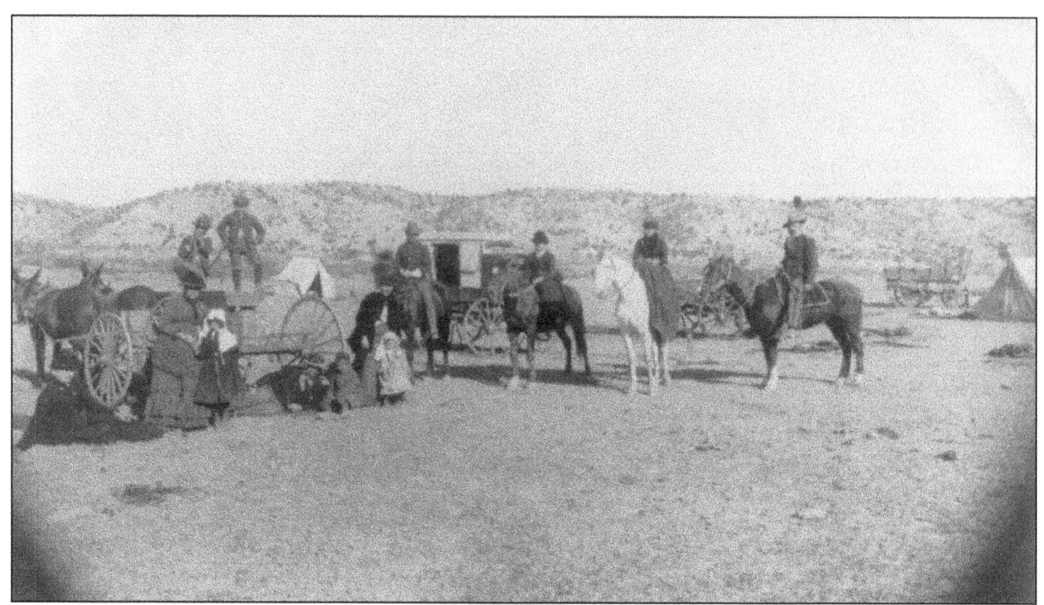

Peck's Lake has been a food resource and family recreational area since 1865. This photograph shows a campout by Fort Verde soldiers, scientists, and families in the mid-1880s. Early farmers hunted the waterfowl to supply the troops at Fort Whipple. In 1909, the Jerome Boat and Gun Club built a clubhouse at Peck's Lake. Baptism ceremonies were conducted in the lake waters. This became Clarkdale's major recreational area for decades. (Courtesy William Cowan.)

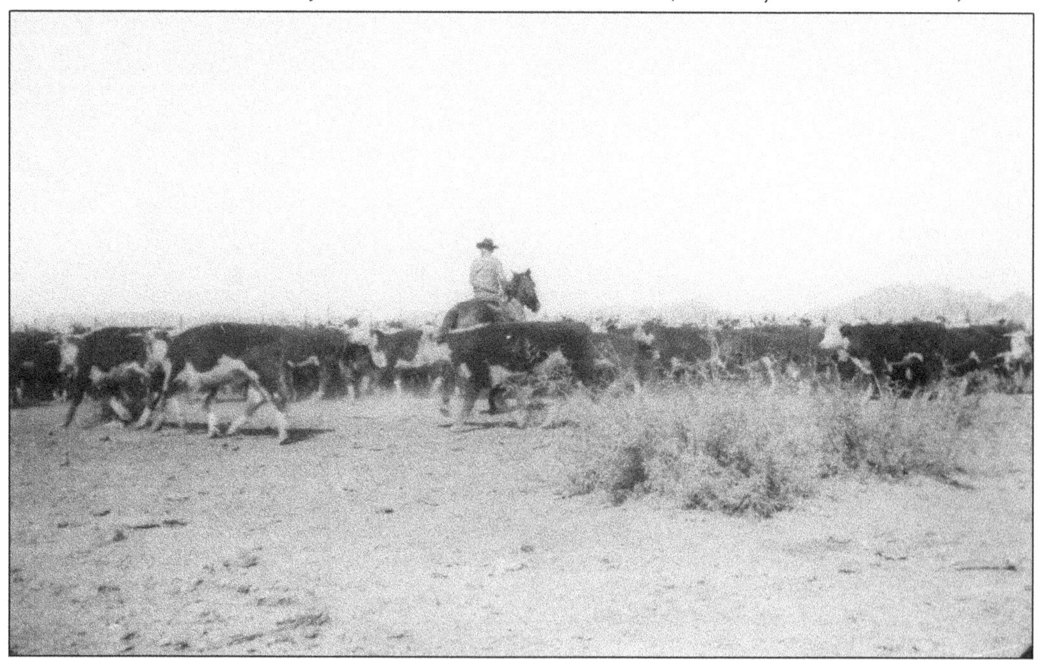

In the 1880s, Verde Valley ranchers built up large herds of cattle that grazed on the open range. In 1892–1893, drought and overgrazing killed up to 75 percent of these cattle. The remaining animals' hooves hard packed the grassless land, allowing flood runoffs to erode the topsoil and channelized washes to change the valley vegetation forever. Federal grazing regulations eventually reduced cattle numbers; few working ranches exist today around Clarkdale. (Courtesy Jane Goddard.)

Morris Ruffner lived near Peck's Lake in 1875. Ruffner, George Kell, Angus McKinnon, and seven other partners staked 10 mining claims in the Black Hills in 1876, which became the site of the future United Verde Mine. The partners recorded these claims at mining recorder George Kell's home at Clarkdale's Haskell Spring. This was the beginning of the long Jerome-Clarkdale relationship. (Courtesy William Cowan.)

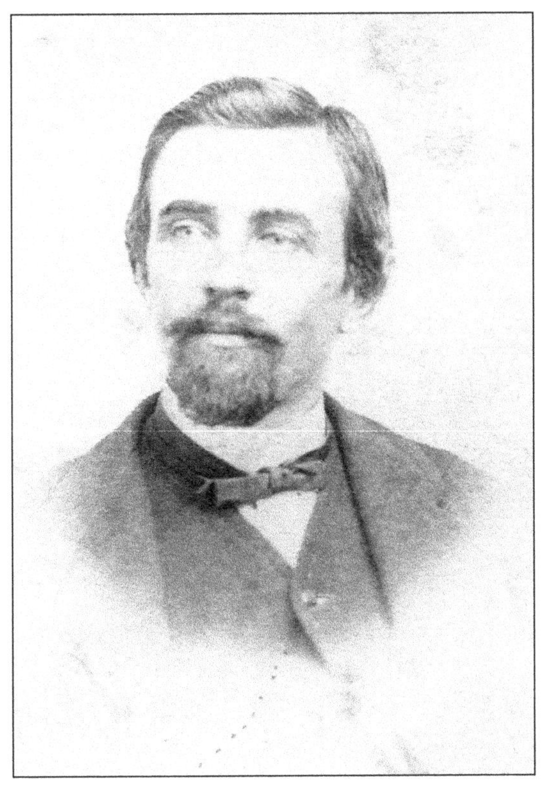

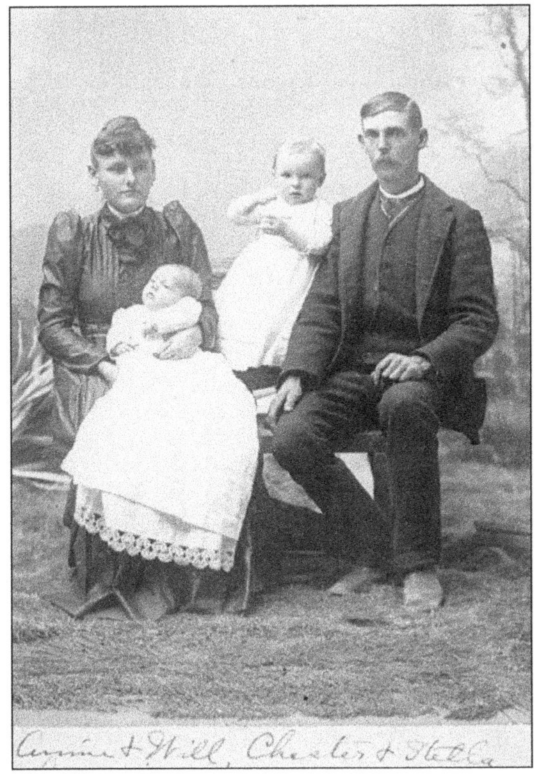

In 1895, the farmers along the Verde River north of Peck's Lake were Jack Duff, Antonio Bird, J. Muse, William Ward, William Hawkins, James Boyer, Leonard Carroll, Will Jordan, T. Hawkins, Hugh Brewer, Dan Shea, George Rich, and Con O'Keefe. The Windes, Goodwin, Wilbur, Dunn, Cannon, and Ames families reportedly lived in the area. Pictured are Will and Annie Jordan with children Stella and Chester. (Courtesy Sally Jackson.)

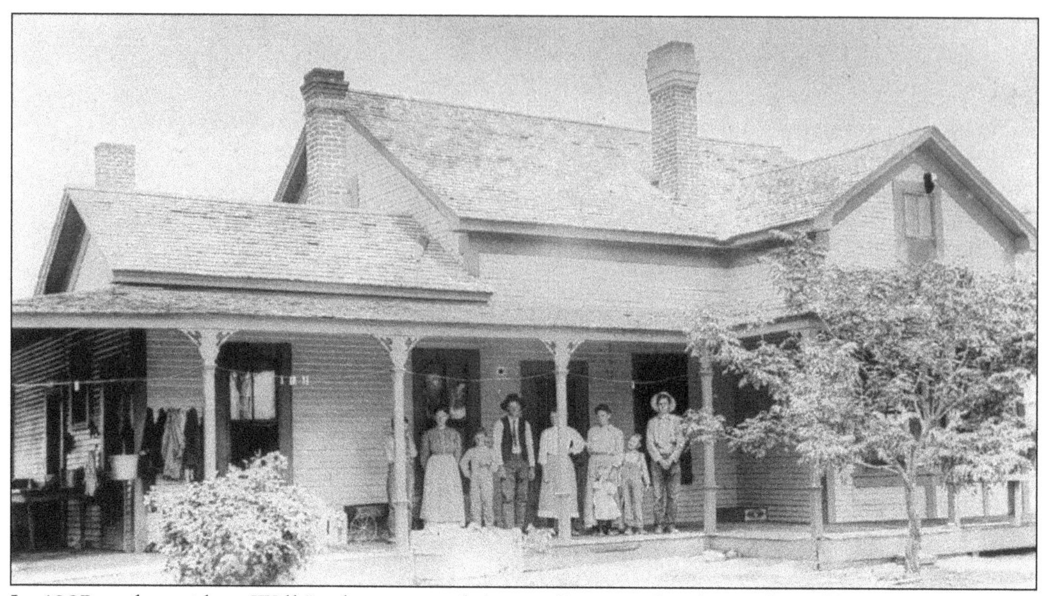

In 1887, early resident Will Jordan married Annie Bristow, daughter of neighbor James Bristow. They became the parents of nine children born in the Jordan home on Rattlesnake Hill just north of the current slag pile. Jordan developed a productive orchard and farm using Indian labor. He sold out in 1911 to UVCC. (Courtesy Sally Jackson.)

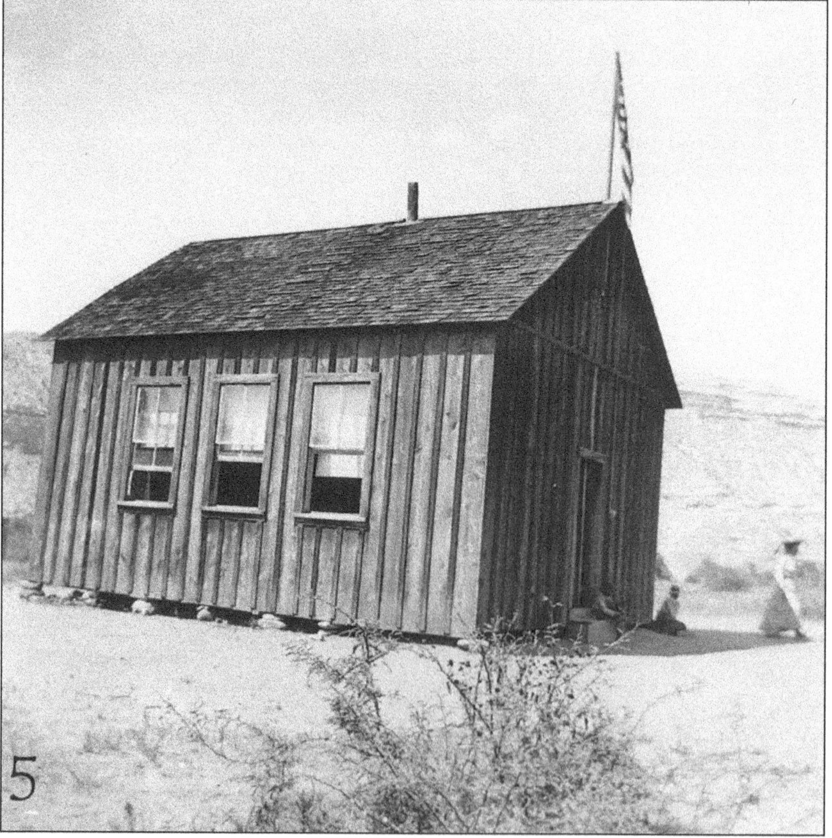

This 1904 photograph shows the first pre-Clarkdale school called the Peck's Lake School. It was just upriver from today's Clarkdale on Will Jordan's donated land. The one-room school opened November 1897 with 11 pupils. It served an average of 22 children per year until its closure in 1913. (Courtesy Sally Jackson.)

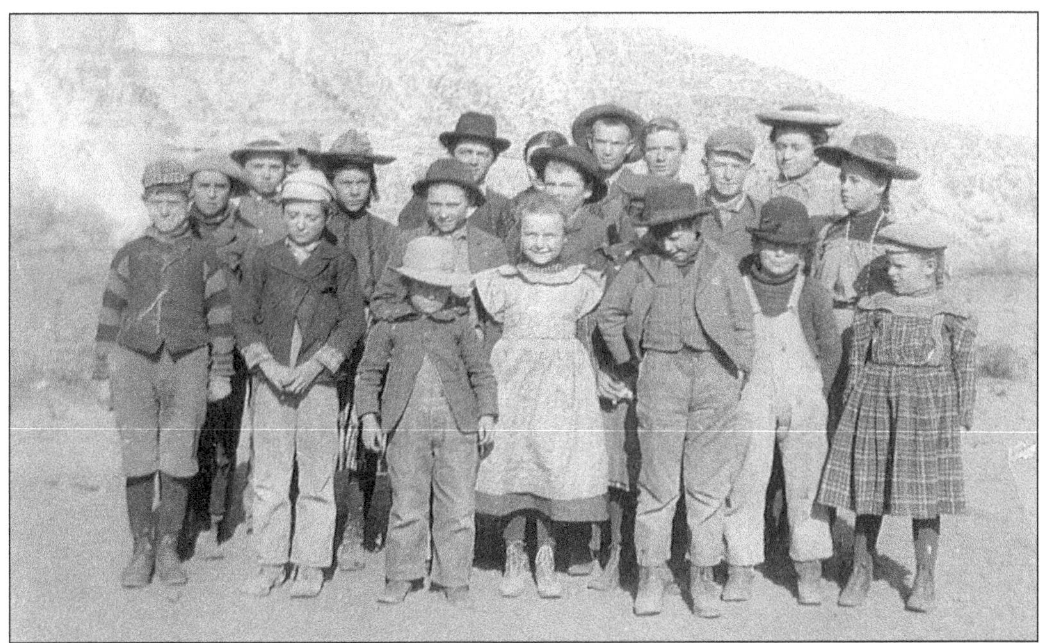

This 1904 photograph shows Mary and Henry Farley, the Jordan children, and other children of Upper Verde families. Former students tell of picking fruit from the orchards on their way to the school, which was on the east side of the Verde River a mile above today's Clarkdale. (Courtesy Glenda Farley.)

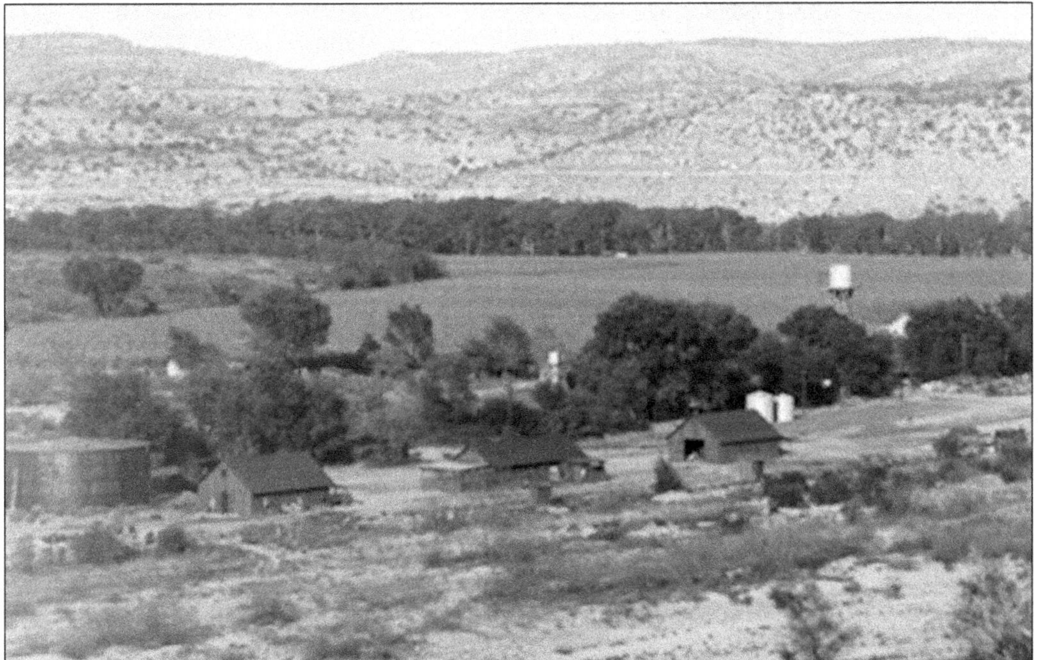

This is an early 20th-century farm near Tapco that was irrigated by the Verde River. It is one of many farms along the river all the way down to Camp Verde that made the Verde Valley one of Arizona's significant agricultural centers at the time. These farms validated the 16th-century Spanish observations that this was a land of rich soil and abundant water. (Courtesy Tim Coons.)

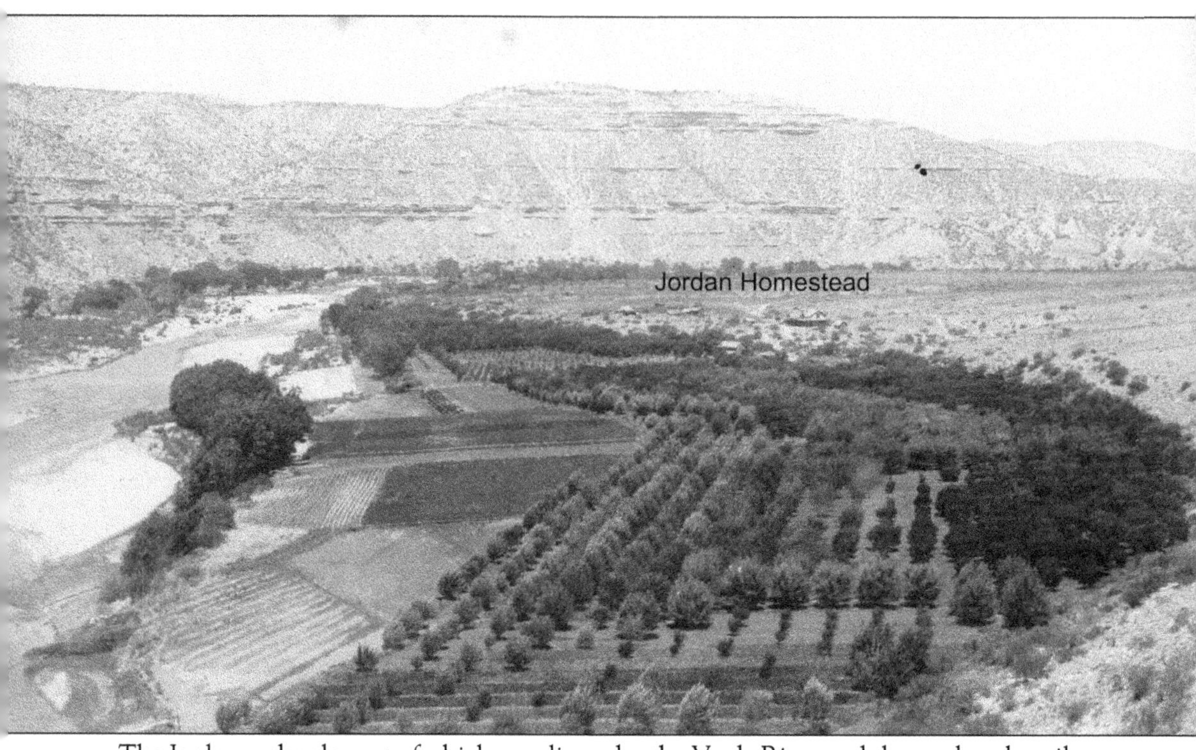

The Jordan orchards, part of which now lie under the Verde River and the smelter slag pile, were a major farming enterprise from the 1880s into the early 20th century. The Jordan home on Rattlesnake Hill is visible here. The Jordans' prolific orchards and gardens proved right Charles Willard's description of the Upper Verde in 1879 as "moist fertile ground . . . thick grass . . . a picture of greenery not often seen." (Courtesy Sedona Heritage Museum.)

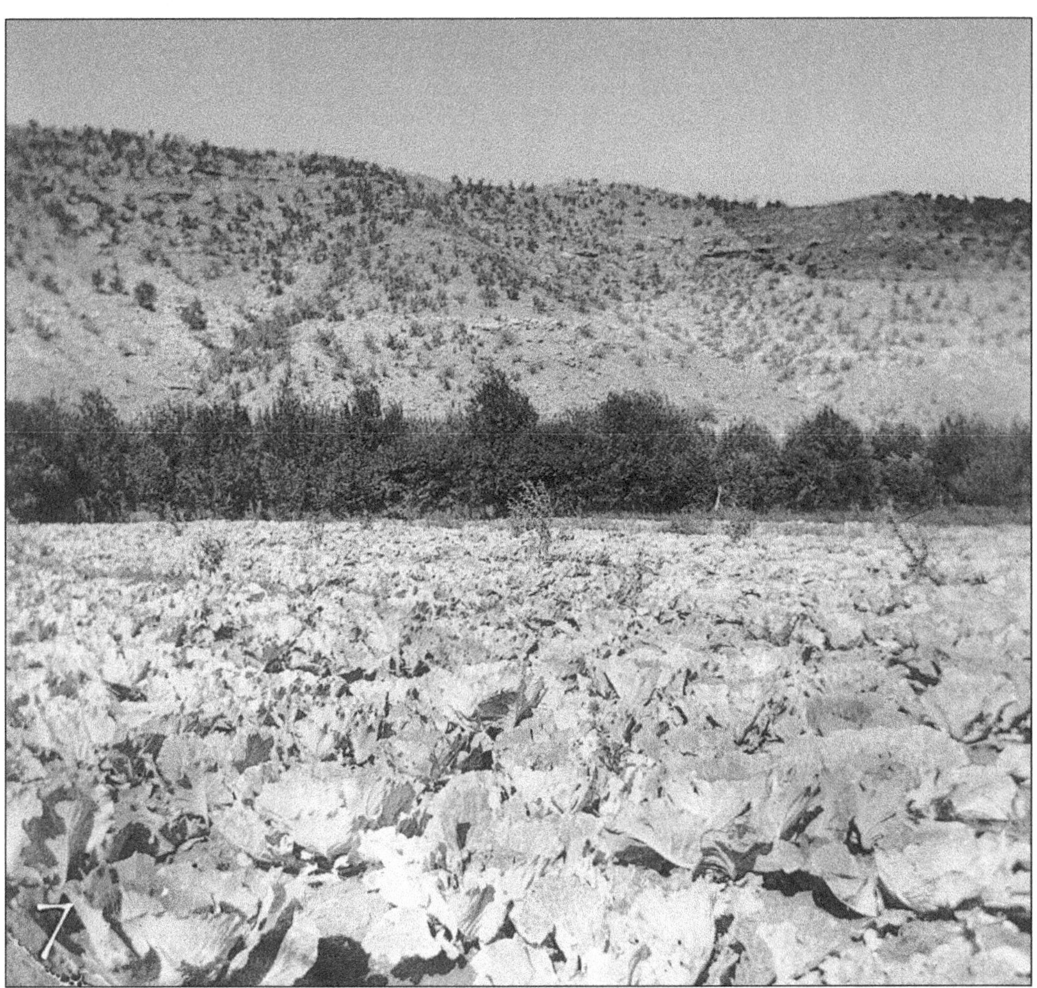

Upper Verde farms produced apples, peaches, prunes, plums, pears, apricots, cherries, persimmons, figs, dates, quinces, pomegranates, cantaloupes, grapes, melons, strawberries, watermelons, asparagus, pumpkins, peas, sweet potatoes, celery, spinach, broccoli, parsnips, okra, carrots, cabbages (pictured, with orchard in background), lettuce, tomatoes, cucumbers, turnips, pinto beans, eggplants, onions, peppers, cauliflower, chili peppers, beans, squash, milos, corn, potatoes, beets, barley, oats, wheat, alfalfa, English and black walnuts, almonds, roses, milk, and honey. (Courtesy Sally Jackson.)

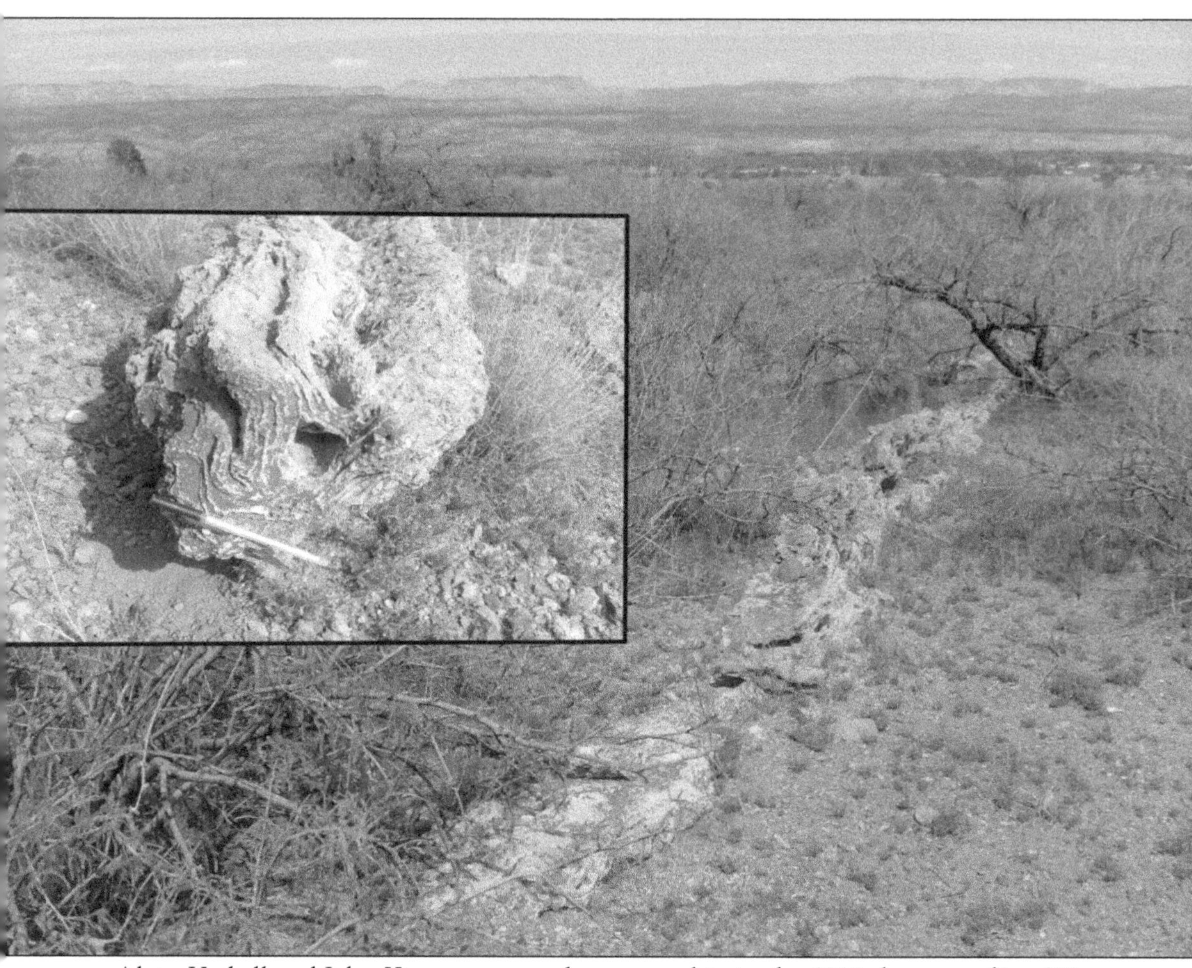

Alvin Haskell and John Kirwagen started a partnership in the 1880s homesteading 320 acres at Haskell Spring. They irrigated 100 acres producing fruits and crops. This photograph shows the remains of their main irrigation ditch, which is preserved by periodic layers of lime deposits made over a century ago. The World's Columbian Exposition, held in Chicago in 1893, awarded Haskell and Kirwagen the first-place blue ribbon for apples grown in their 1,500-tree orchard. (Author's collection.)

Five

1839–1925
Sen. William Andrews Clark

William Andrews Clark, entrepreneur and Clarkdale's creator, was born on a Pennsylvania farm on January 8, 1839. Following an education, he became a schoolmaster, law student, and perhaps a Confederate soldier in 1862. In 1863, Clark went to Montana where he made a gold strike that provided seed capital of $1,500. This cash soon made him a millionaire through investments in Montana mercantile ventures, mining, transportation, ranching, manufacturing, banking, and water.

In 1872, Clark studied mining at New York's Columbia School of Mines. Returning to Butte, he expanded into milling, smelting, newspapers, power, lumbering, sugar refining, farming, amusement parks, and streetcars. In 1905, he capitalized a railroad from Los Angeles to Salt Lake City, founding Las Vegas as a railroad town. Nevada's southernmost county carries his name.

At the 1885 New Orleans World's Fair, Clark saw ore specimens from Jerome. Following a field examination, he acquired 99.7 percent of the UVCC stock for a $360,000 outlay. In 1895, he built a narrow gauge railroad from Jerome to the mainline at Jerome Junction. This transportation upgrade from mule haulage to railroad made the UVCC a prolific cash generator.

In 1898, Clark wanted to be Montana's senator. The Constitution specified that senators were appointed to office by state legislatures, not elected by citizen voters. Clark reportedly paid $431,000 to buy 47 of the 54 legislators' votes to obtain the position. Because of Clark's overt corruption of Montana's legislators, the Senate pressured him to resign before being seated. Clark said, "I never bought a man who wasn't for sale." In 1901, Montana reappointed Clark to the Senate. This time he was accepted, but Senator Clark proved to be a poor legislator with one ironic exception. Clark's campaign shenanigans led directly to the 17th Amendment in 1913 that required senatorial elections by popular vote, not appointment.

Shortly after 1900, Clark started planning for a smelter and mainline railroad for his mine. Clarkdale resulted. He spent his last two decades living in New York and Europe while periodically visiting his western enterprises. Though he made millions in Butte, the UVCC created more than half of his more than $250 million estate.

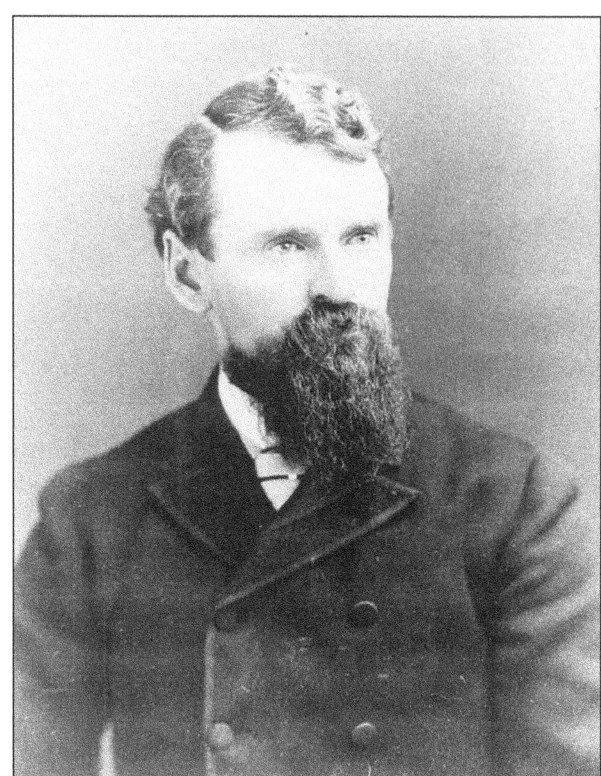

William A. Clark was driven to escape his childhood poverty. After studying law, he went west to make his fortune. He became a shrewd capitalist, finding opportunities in any field that had profit potential. Clark became one of America's richest tycoons in the gilded age of Rockefeller, Carnegie, and Morgan. Clark's estate when he died in 1925 was more than $250 million. (Courtesy Jerome State Historic Park.)

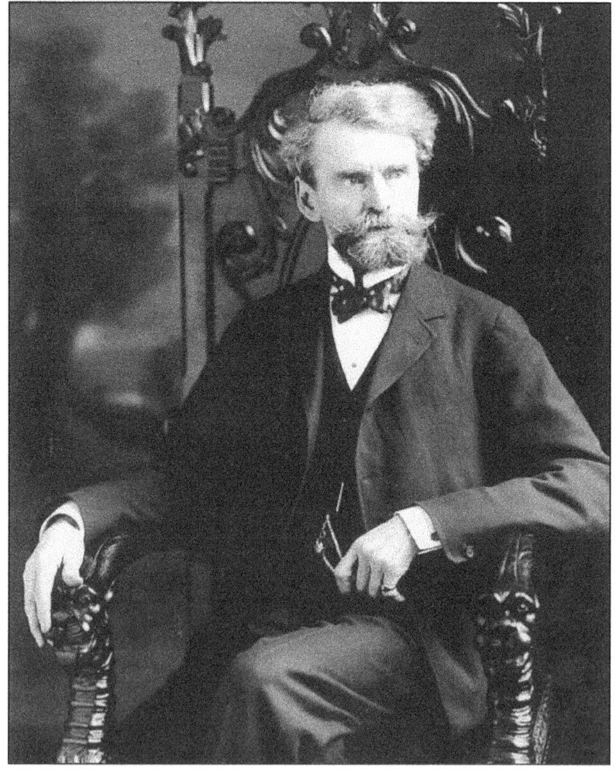

Clark was a small, red-haired man with piercing eyes, upswept mustache, and parted beard. He wore meticulous swallowtail coats. Clark's intelligence, verbal skills, and rapid gestures dominated meetings. He was a vigorous walker. Clark was generous to employees, but hard and sometimes ruthless in business affairs. He became fluent in French and German to conduct his passion of European art acquisition. Clark was a family man, taking interest in and care of his direct family and his extended family. (Courtesy Drake Meinke.)

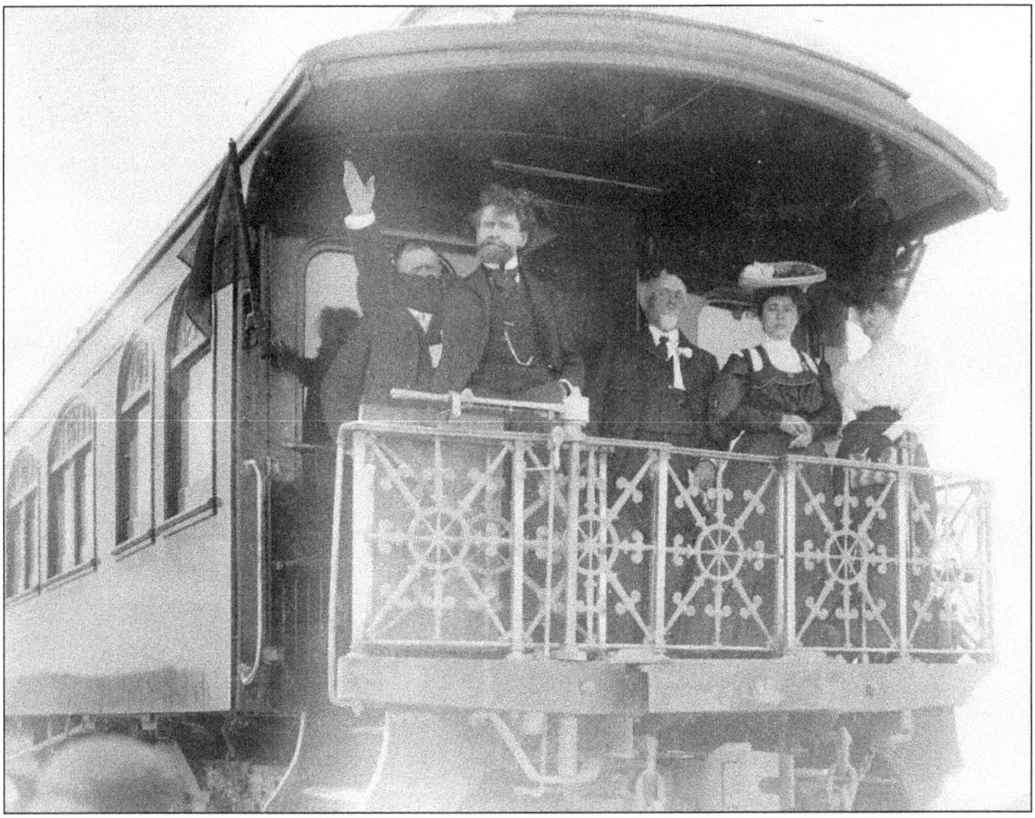

Clark traveled extensively by private railroad car from his New York City residence to examine his numerous western enterprises. In 1916, Clark's UVCC shares paid him a $222,750 dividend per month. He suffered the tragic loss of his spouse and three children during his lifetime. He last visited Clarkdale in 1924, dying a year later in New York. (Courtesy Verde Historical Society.)

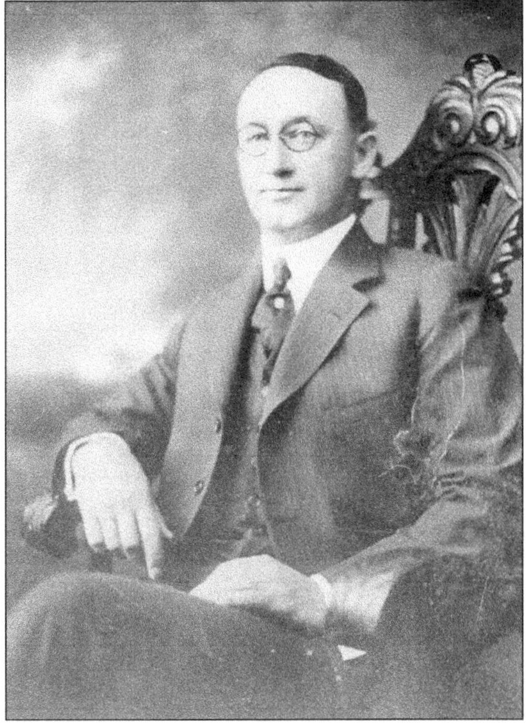

Clark kept absolute control of his enterprises, but delegated to his sons, appointing Charles W. Clark (pictured) the UVCC general manager in 1904. Owning water supplies was part of Clark's business strategy of absolute control. He established vertical property sidelines in the Verde District avoiding Butte's costly claim battles. This complex man provided his employees excellent housing, schools, and medical and recreational facilities, but always under his autocratic rule. (Courtesy Jerome State Historic Park.)

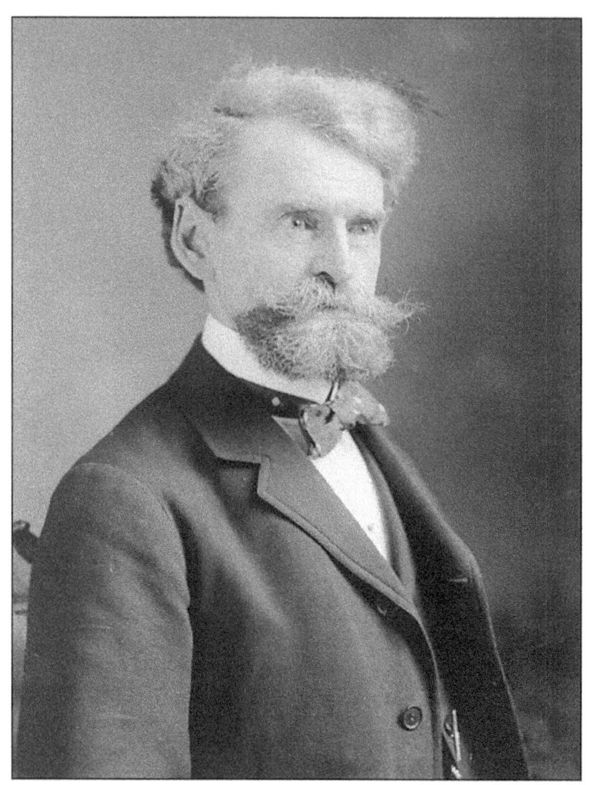

Clark's rise to becoming a US senator is a story of uncounted votes, rampant perjury, stolen ballot boxes, and flagrant bribery with the buying of Montana's legislators and judges. Following Clark's 1899 aborted appointment as Montana's senator, he was reappointed in 1901, becoming Senator Clark. He served a lackluster term, forgetting his campaign promises and accomplishing little. Senator Clark was a capitalist and a politician, but not a statesman or legislator. (Courtesy Jerome State Historic Park.)

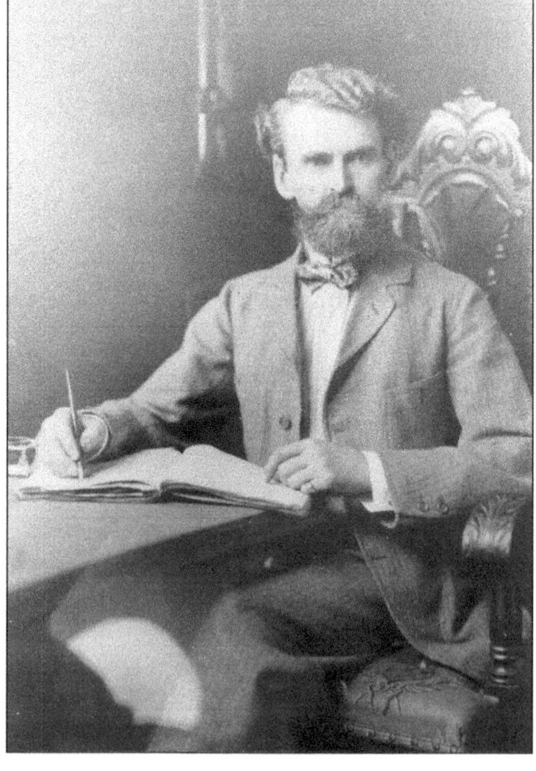

As a direct result of Clark's campaigns, Montana enacted the Corrupt Practices Act in 1912, prohibiting unlimited buying of political offices. In 2010, Clark's campaigns resurfaced in Citizens United briefs before the Supreme Court as an argument against unlimited corporate political funding. The argument failed, as the Supreme Court approved limitless corporate political donations. This voided Clark's legacy of Montana's century-old Corrupt Practices Act. (Courtesy Verde Historical Society.)

Clark reportedly spent $15 million over six years building a 121-room, 31-bathroom mansion on Fifth Avenue in New York City. The furnishings included gold-plated railings, carved panels, and imported marble and exotic woods. Sculptures and paintings occupied all rooms including a large art gallery. His art collection was donated to the Corcoran Art Gallery in Washington, DC. The family, despising the house, demolished it two years after Clark's death. (Courtesy Clarkdale Historical Society and Museum.)

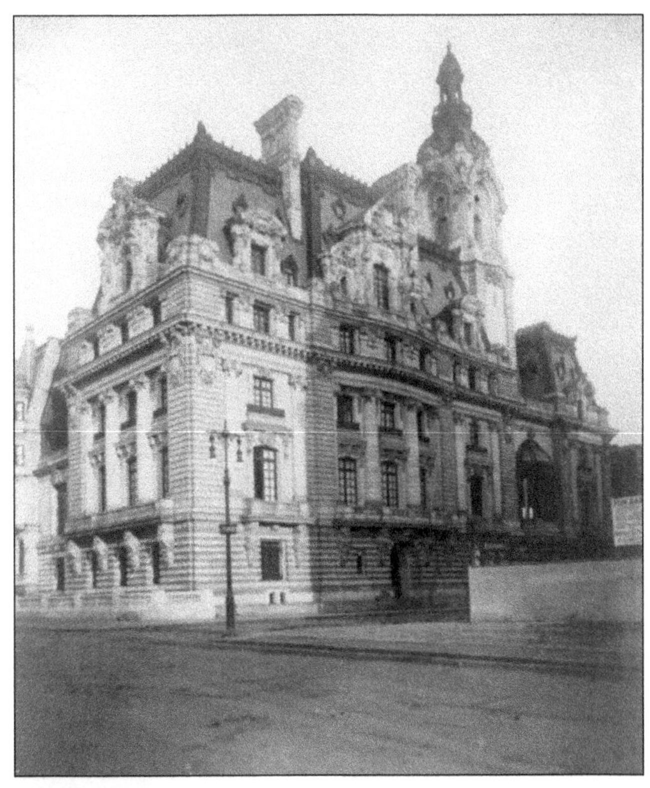

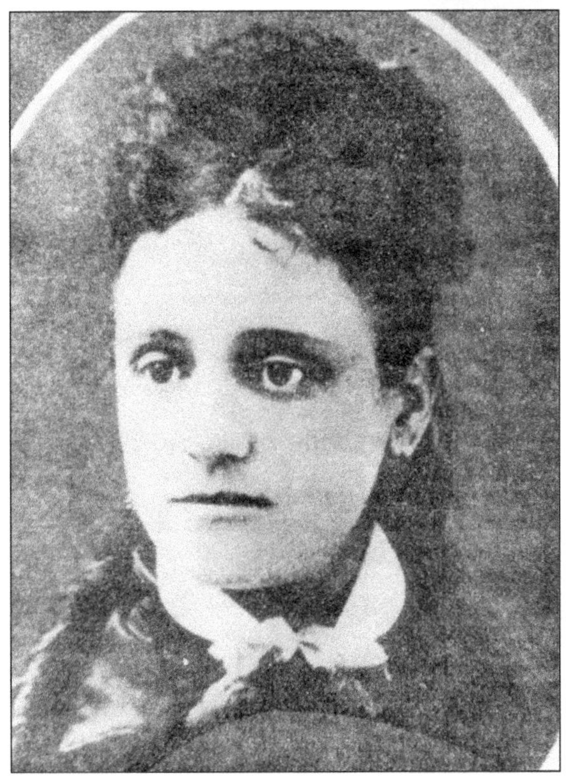

In 1869, Clark married his childhood sweetheart, Katherine Stauffer (1840–1893). They had six children. Tragedy came with the loss of an infant son followed by Katherine's death and then also that of teenage son Paul (1880–1896). The two remaining sons, Charles (1871–1933) and William (1877–1934), died within nine years of Clark's death. Katherine's daughters, Mary (1870–1939) and Katherine (1875–1974), and the daughter of Clark's second marriage, Huguette, became Clark's heirs. (Courtesy Jerome State Historic Park.)

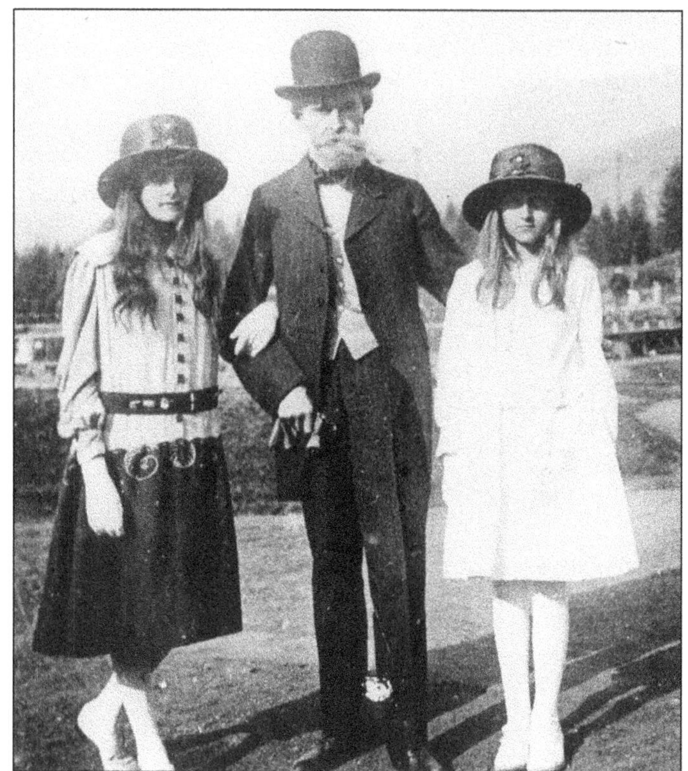

Eight years after Katherine's death, 62-year-old William Clark secretly married 23-year-old Anna Eugenia La Chapelle (1878–1963) in France. She had been his teenaged ward. They had two daughters, Louise Amelia Andrée (born in Spain in 1902) and Hugette Marcelle (born in Paris in 1906). Louise died of meningitis a week before her 17th birthday. Three of Clark's first children were older than Anna. (Courtesy Verde Historical Society.)

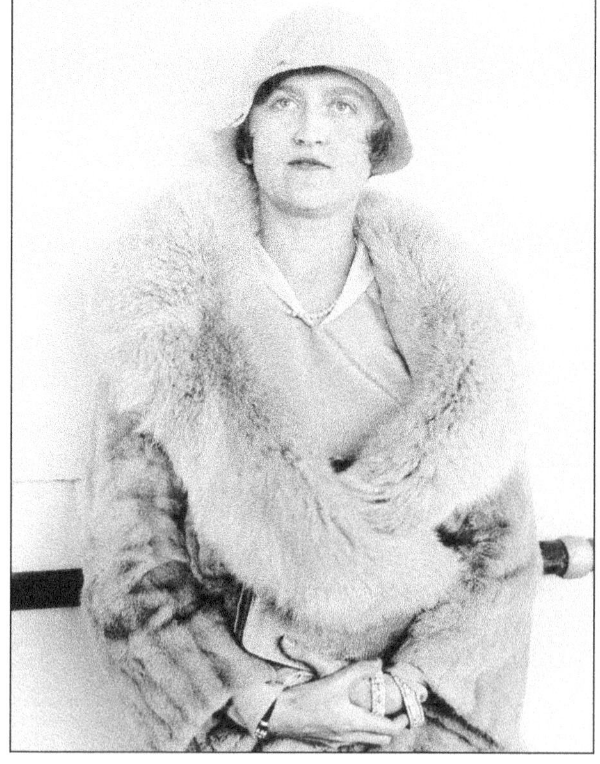

Clark's daughter Huguette, one of society's most eligible women of the 1920s, died at 104 as a recluse, isolating herself in New York City hospitals through her final decades. Her vast estate, exceeding $200 million, led to complex inheritance battles. The 172 years from her father's birth in 1839 to her death in 2012 spanned 37 of the 44 US presidents from the agricultural age through the industrial age into today's digital age. (Courtesy Verde Historical Society.)

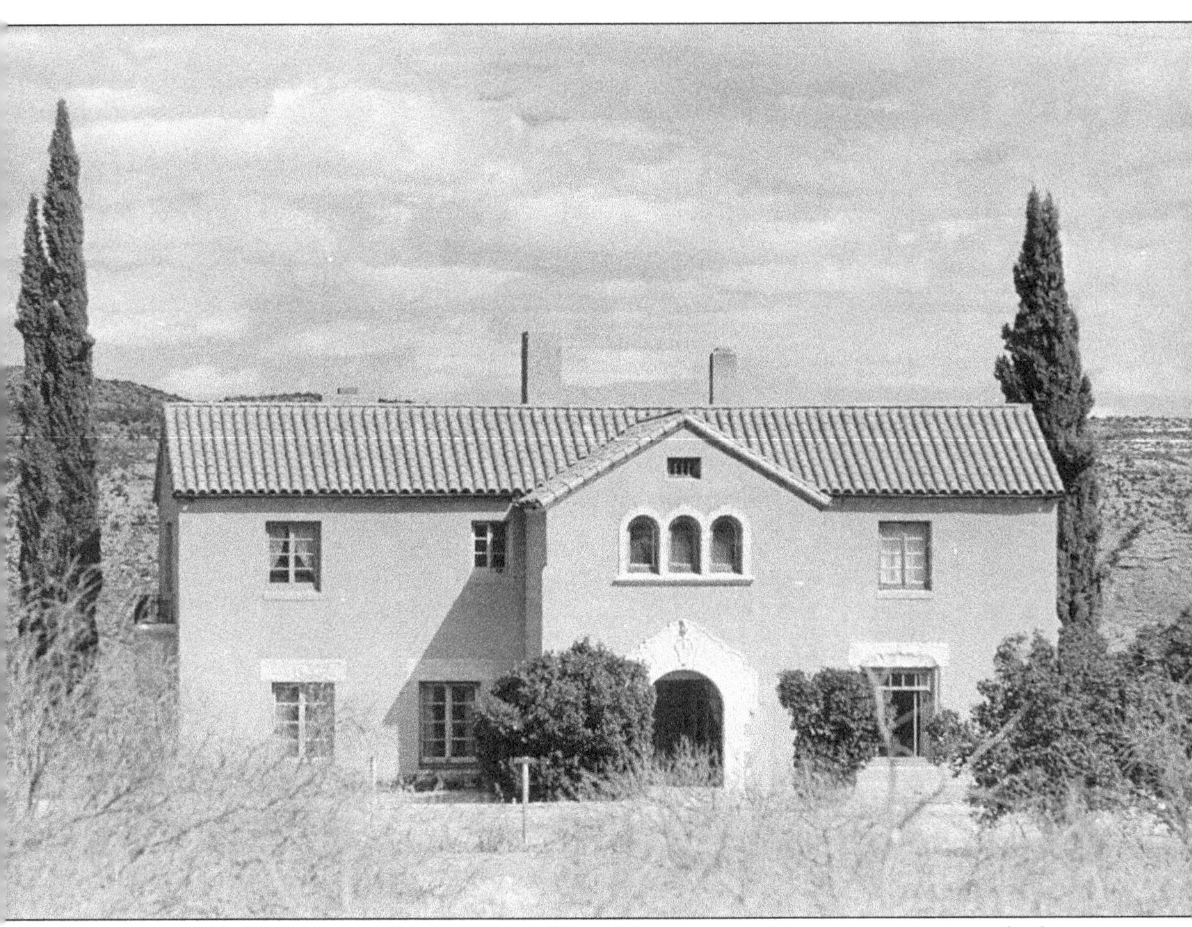

In August 1931, William A. "Tertius" Clark III and family moved into a mansion overlooking Clarkdale, the Verde River, and the golf course. Clark III, the grandson of Senator Clark, was designated to lead the UVCC. On May 15, 1932, at 29 years old, he died in a crash in his two-place, open-cockpit biplane just east of Clarkdale within sight of his home. (Courtesy John Bell Collection.)

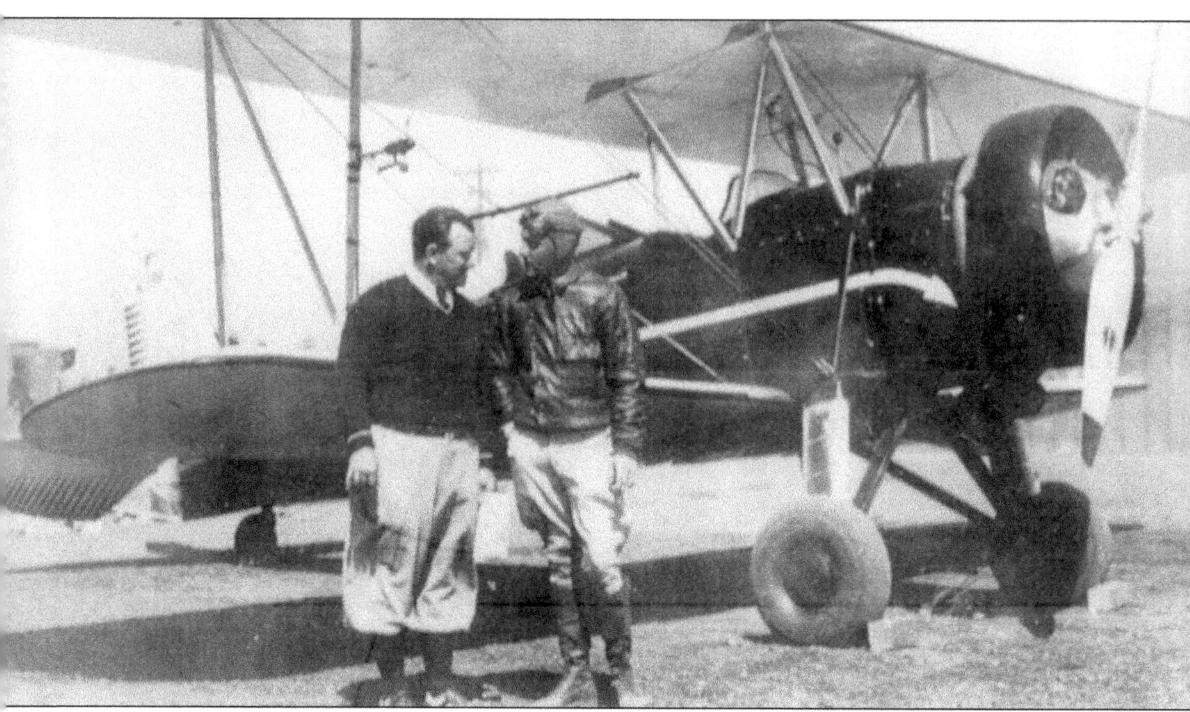

On the fatal flight, Clark (left) was practicing instrument flying, sometimes called blind flying because the pilot cannot see outside the cockpit. Flying with Clark as the safety pilot who could see outside was instructor Jack Lynch, an experienced 18-year pilot who had been Charles Lindbergh's copilot, had instructed more than 200 students, and was holder of the world record of 211 hours flying by instrument. (Courtesy John Bell Collection.)

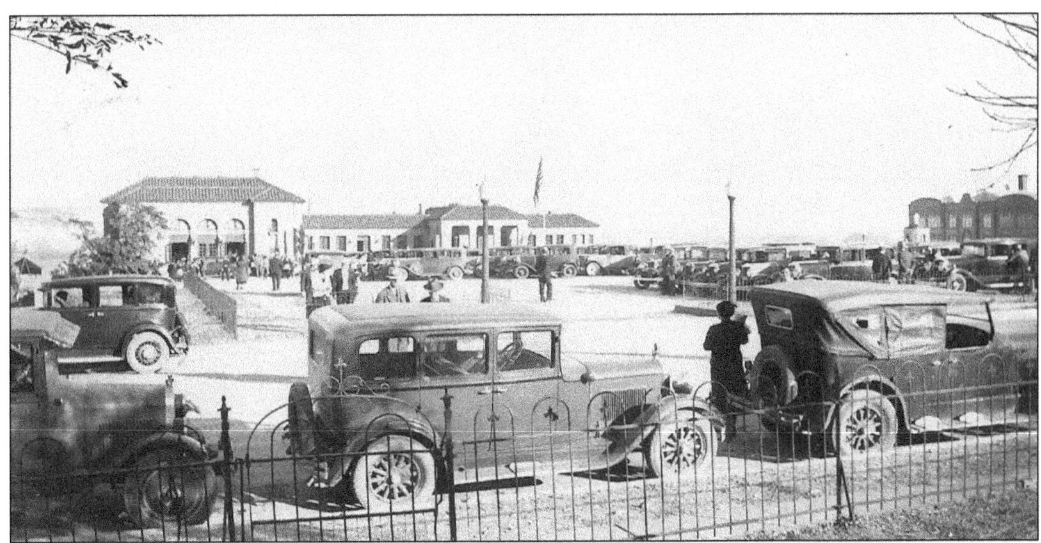

Clarkdale golfers saw the biplane go into a tailspin, followed by a brief pull up, then a final spin into the ground. Both men wore unused parachutes. It is an aviation mystery as to how this stall-spin accident happened in fair weather with an instructor safety pilot as experienced as Lynch. The funeral service was held at the Clark Memorial Clubhouse. (Courtesy Nancy James Baetz.)

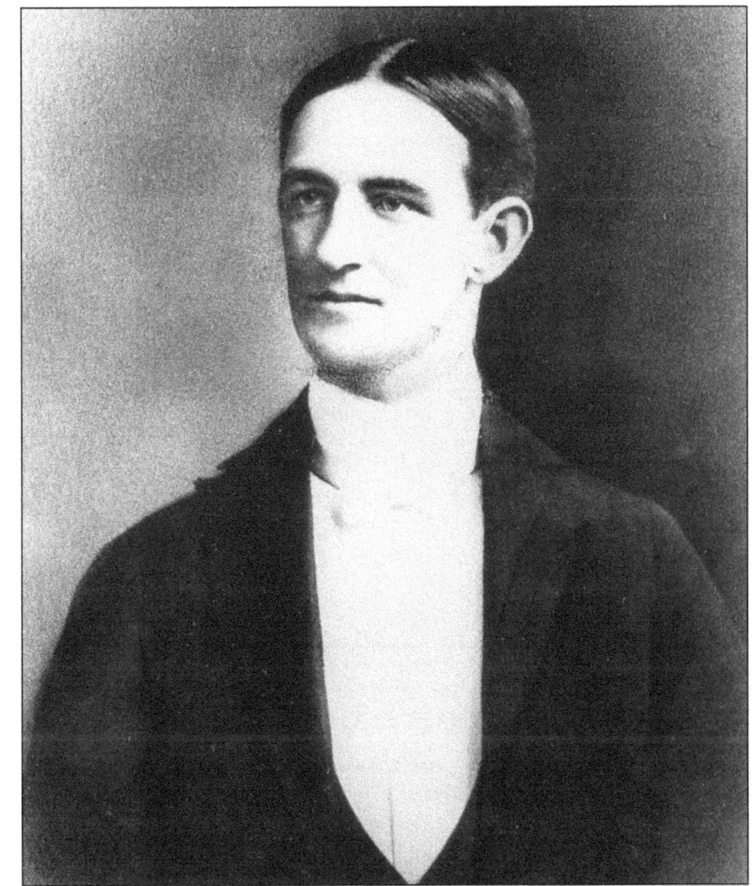

Within three years of the fatal crash, Senator Clark's two remaining sons died: Charles Walker Clark (pictured) in 1933 and William A. Clark Jr. in 1934. The deaths of these last two Clark male heirs proved to be a major turning point in the story of Clarkdale. After alleged family squabbles about the estate, the three female heirs agreed to sell out. (Courtesy Jerome State Historic Park.)

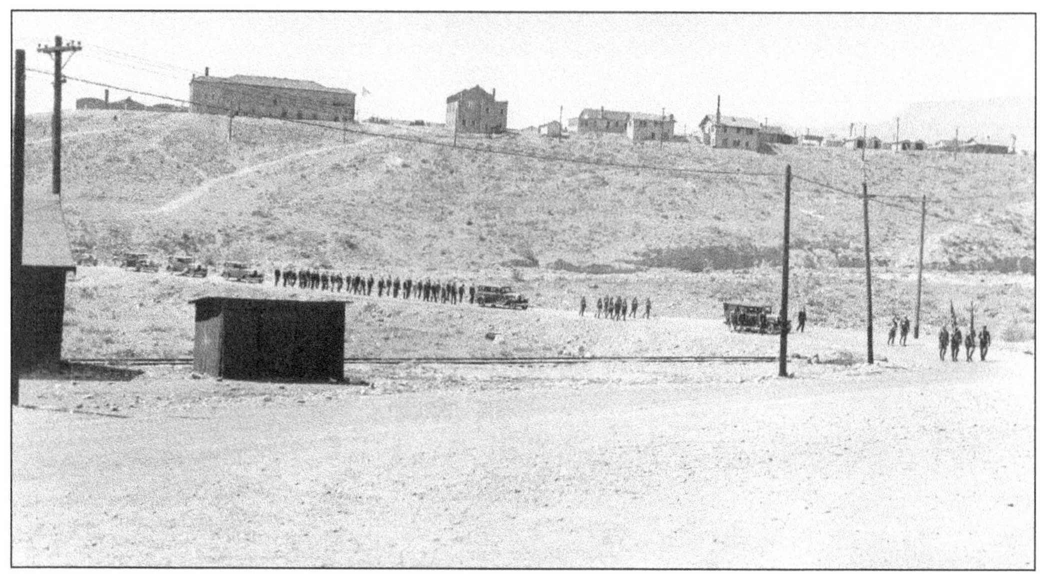

In 1935, Clark's three daughters sold Clarkdale and its smelter, mine, and lands to Phelps Dodge for a reported $20.8 million. The assets included stockpiled copper ingots worth $10.5 million, leaving a final cash cost to Phelps Dodge of $10.3 million. Over the remaining 18 years, the smelter generated over $40 million in profit. The Clark III funeral procession to the train shown here symbolically represents the ending of the family's influence in Clarkdale's affairs. (Courtesy John Bell Collection.)

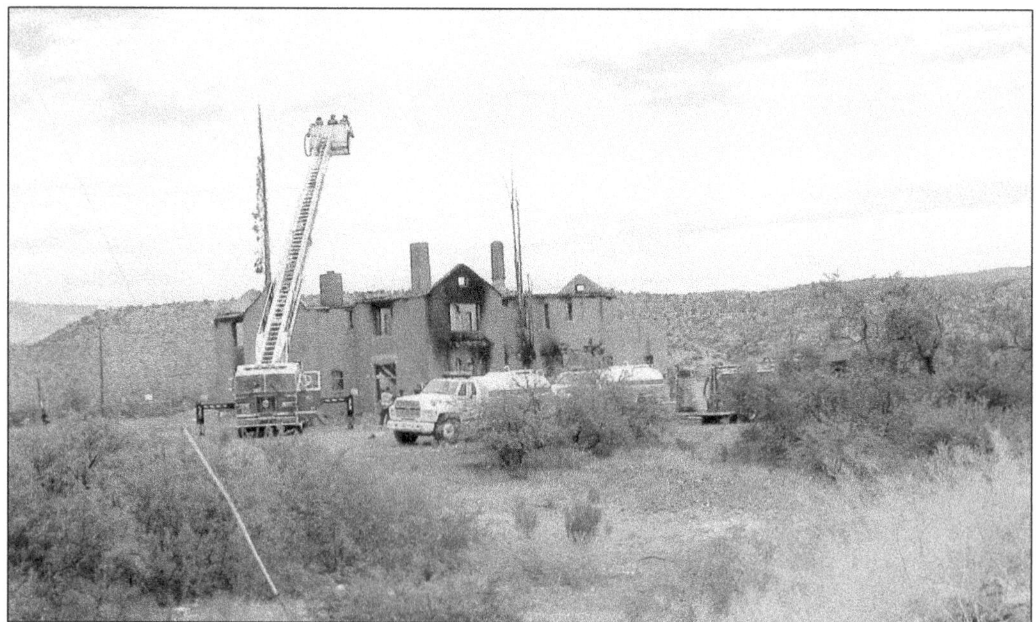

Following the death of William A. Clark III, his mansion was used through the decades as a residence, restaurant, golf clubhouse, and hay barn, and at times sat abandoned. In the latter state, fire destroyed the ill-fated Clark III mansion in 2010. Other historical UVCC buildings that have burned since the smelter closed include the smelter administration building, the 1914 school building, the dance pavilion, and the dairy homestead at Peck's Lake. (Courtesy Patricia Williams.)

Six

1912–1953
Clarkdale, the Smelter Town

By 1900, the UVCC output was limited by several factors: no flat land to expand operations, the small 1885 smelter could not increase ore production, the UVCC smelter in Jerome sat upon ore-rich ground preventing proposed open pit mining, the sulfide ores in the upper mine levels had caught on fire prohibiting mining that ore, and the UVCC needed a mainline railroad to ship out copper and transport in supplies. These early productive years of Clark's UVCC mine led to Jerome becoming Arizona's fourth most populous city in 1899 behind Tucson, Phoenix, and Prescott.

Starting in 1910, at an age (71) when most have retired, Clark began planning a large smelter, mainline railroad, and an attractive workers' community beside the Verde River. Clark conceived owning and controlling everything, including the everyday lives of the inhabitants.

The smelter/town project had to meet the following planning and design criteria: "Adequate water supply for potable and industrial uses; good drainage; ample sand and gravel river deposits for construction purposes; a clay deposit suitable for building brick; access to the proposed railroad; sufficient area at a satisfactory elevation for operations and waste disposal; a flat town location adjacent to the plant capable of expansion."

In 1912, the smelter and town construction began on 1,200 acres that Clark had bought for his proposed company town of Clarkdale. The Clark-financed AT&SF railroad arrived the same year. The smelter went into operation on May 26, 1915. The smelter process is described in the following pages.

By 1920, the Clarkdale smelter was one of the largest in the world, producing more than 150,000 pounds of copper per day. At the same time, the smelter was spewing out 935 tons of sulfur dioxide daily and more than 100 tons of metal-laden smoke that killed the vegetation around Clarkdale.

Sixty-eight years after Clark acquired the UVCC, Phelps Dodge closed the Jerome mine and Clarkdale smelter in May 1953. This world famous mine produced profitable ores from over 81 miles of tunnels with some workings as deep as 4,630 feet below the surface.

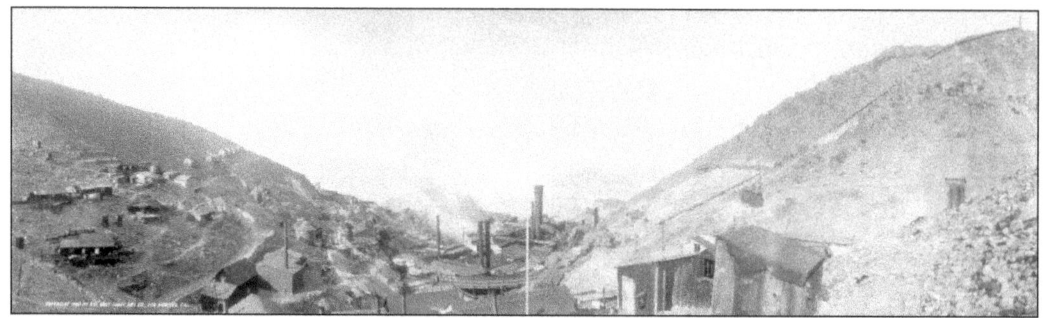

In 1888, Clark's smelter in Jerome annually processed 15,000 tons of ore; by 1915, that had increased to 400,000 tons. The new Clarkdale smelter in 1916 immediately doubled production to 800,000 tons. The topographic limitations for expanding the Jerome smelter are apparent in this photograph and the next. The UVCC ores initially averaged four percent to five percent copper that was rich enough to smelt directly on site. (Courtesy Verde Historical Society.)

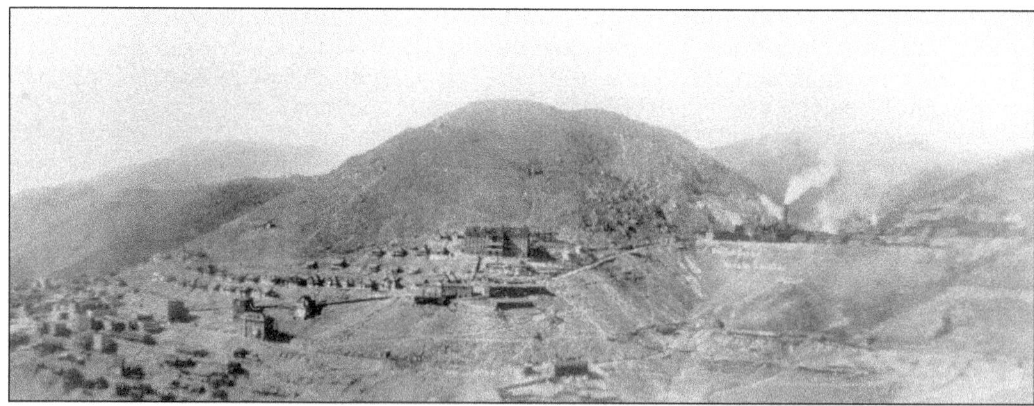

The ground under the Jerome smelter eventually was mined by means of the open pit seen today in Jerome. This pit was started in 1917, reaching the low-grade ore in 1922. This not only increased copper production, but also helped in finally extinguishing an underground fire in upper sulfide ore zones that had been burning since 1894. (Courtesy Robert Beltz.)

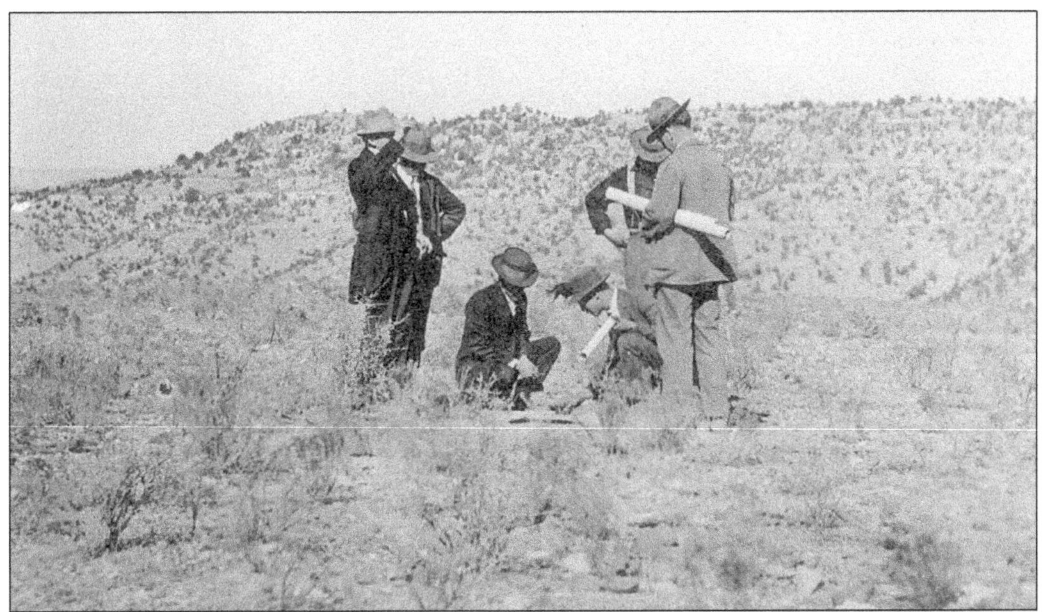

In 1910, Clark tasked his staff and engineers to begin detailed planning for a larger smelter and company town. This project would require flat land and abundant water resources. Clark had begun to acquire water resources in 1906 and the land acquisition began four years later. This 1910 photograph shows Clark, Roberts, Repath, Hopkins, Taylor, and Talley at the future Clarkdale smelter site. (Courtesy Jerome Historical Society Archives.)

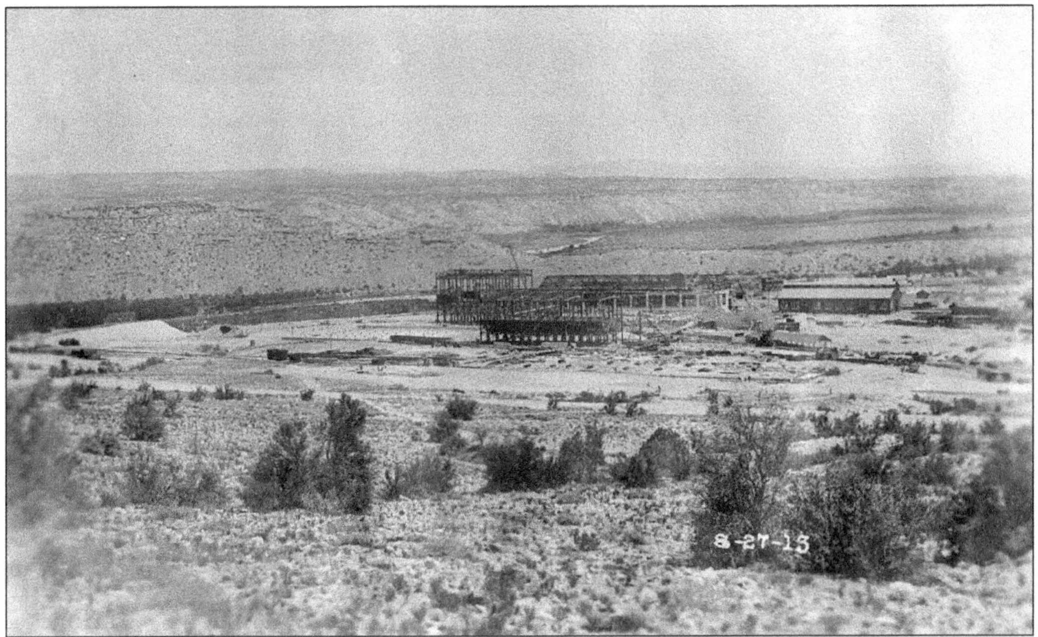

Smelter construction began in 1912, with operations starting in May 1915 and continuing until 1931, when the smelter shut down due to the Depression. In 1935, Phelps Dodge bought the UVCC and resumed operations in 1937 as economic conditions improved. The smelting of high-grade ore stopped in 1951, and on March 30, 1953, the plant closed when the converter processing of lower-grade ore ended. (Courtesy Drake Meinke.)

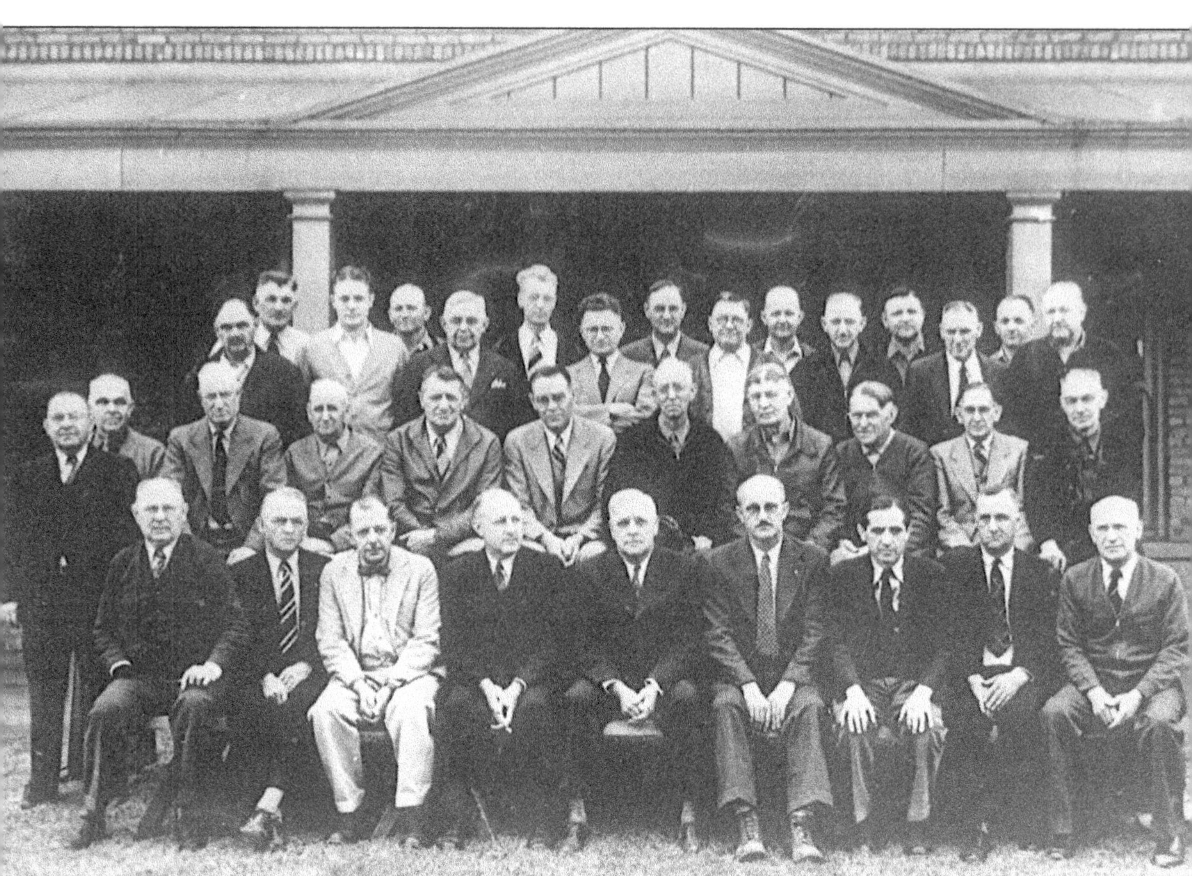

The Clarkdale smelter, under the senior management pictured here, became one of the largest metal producers in the world, delivering 1,142,690 tons of copper, 30.8 tons of gold, 1,160 tons of silver, 22,750 tons of zinc, and 295 tons of lead between 1915 and 1953. The total value of these metals at today's prices would exceed $8.5 billion. (Courtesy Verde Historical Society.)

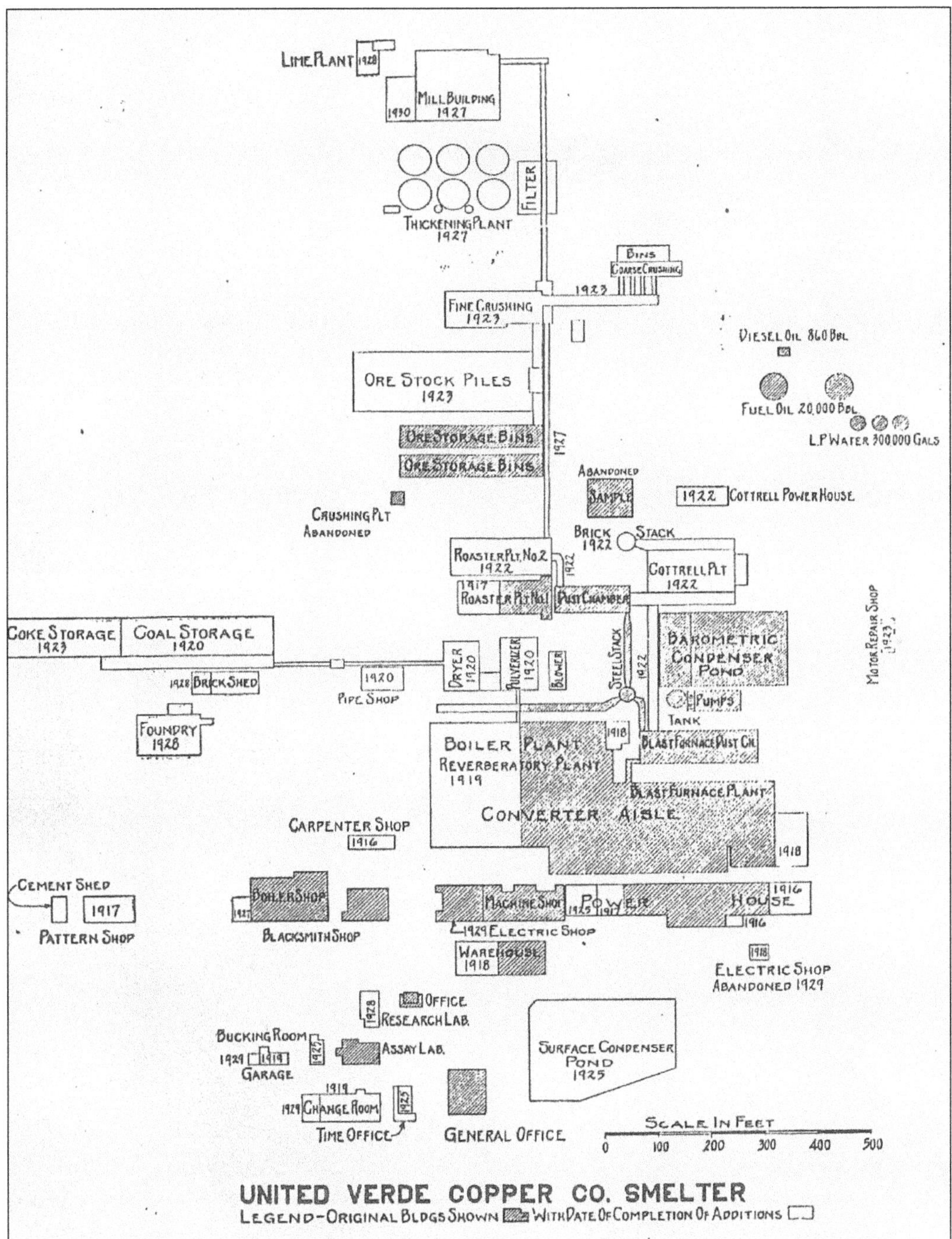

The 196-acre Clarkdale smelter yard contained 37 buildings plus water towers, fuel tanks, and storage facilities. The buildings were connected by miles of conveyor belts, pipes, wire, roads, and track. There were 13.2 miles of railroad track in the smelter yard including the roundhouse, with another two miles on the slag pile and a spur to the gravel plant at the river. (Courtesy Clarkdale Historical Society and Museum.)

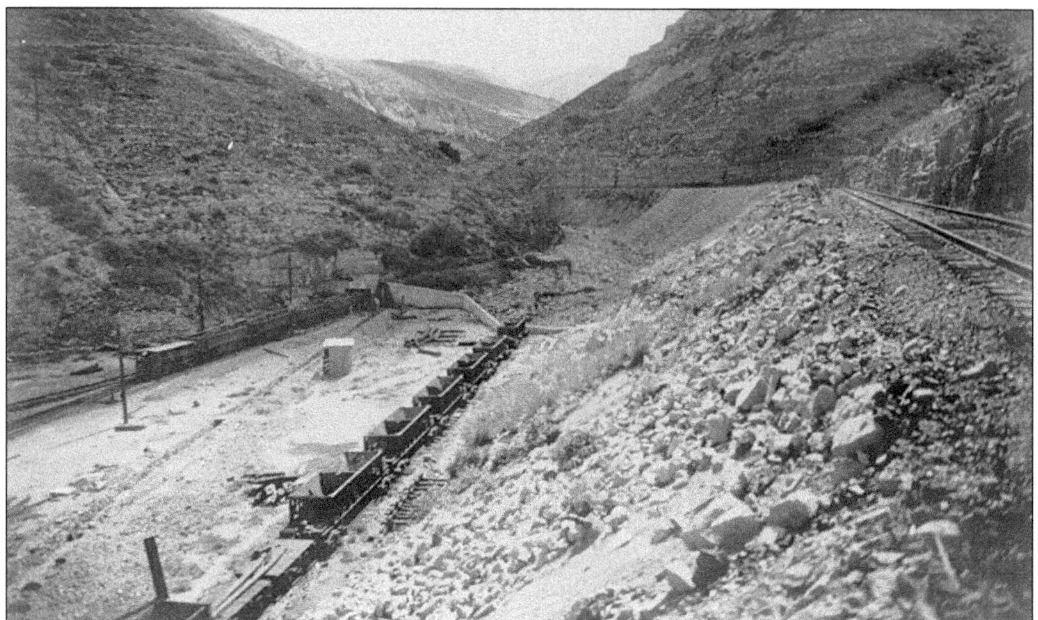

A seven-mile, serpent-like Verde Tunnel & Smelter standard-gauge railroad track connected the Clarkdale smelter with the Hopewell Tunnel mouth. An additional four miles of the VT&S surface track ended at the UVCC 500 level surface plant at Jerome. Due to the rugged terrain, it took 11 miles of track to go the four miles between the smelter and the mine. The photograph shows an electric engine pulling ore cars out of the tunnel. (Courtesy John Bell Collection.)

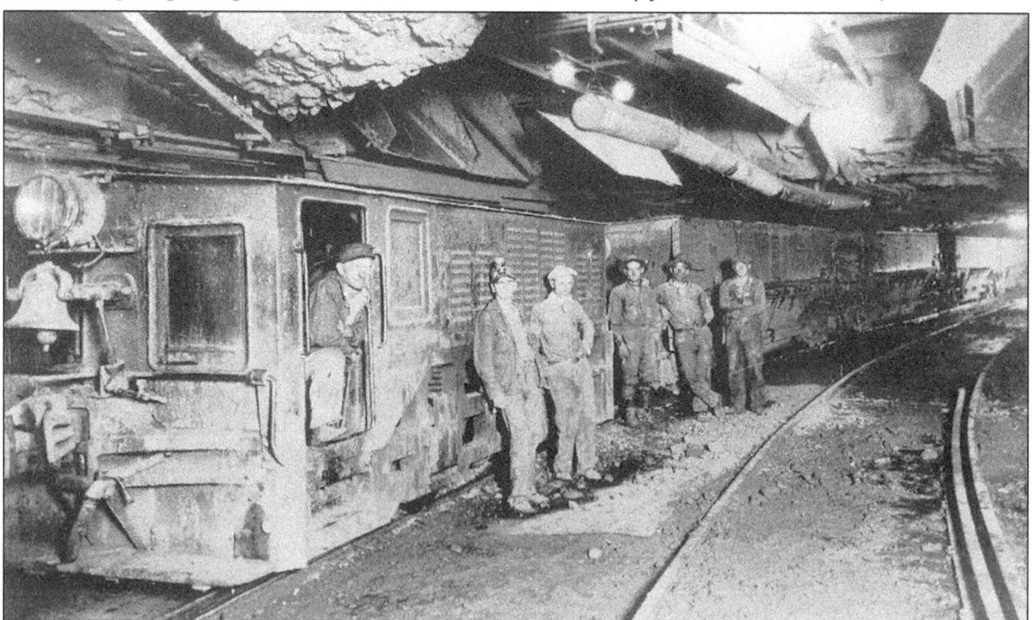

The UVCC smelting process began in the mine, where the raw ore was dumped into underground railroad cars. Electric engines hauled the loaded ore cars from the 1000 mine level through the 7,200-foot-long Hopewell Tunnel, from which a VT&S steam engine moved the cars down to the smelter. The ore was dumped into the crusher facility located at the highest level of the smelter buildings, as seen in the previous photograph. (Courtesy John Bell Collection.)

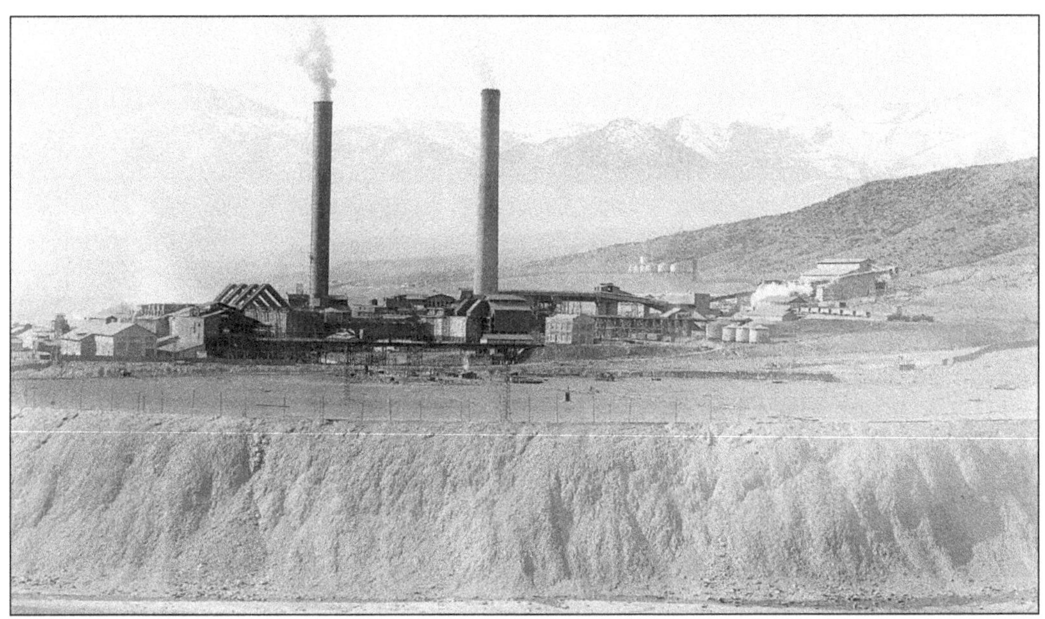

The UVCC mining, ore hauling, and smelter operations utilized gravity as much as possible to reduce energy costs in producing copper out of the raw ore. The ore was processed beginning at the highest buildings, shown here, and ending at the lowest structures where the copper anodes were made and the waste products were removed. (Courtesy Jerry Wombacher.)

The ore was a mixture of 3–5 percent copper, 10–35 percent silica, 11–40 percent iron, 10–38 percent sulfur, and other elements. The raw ore was first crushed, screened, and sent through the roasting process at 850–900 degrees Fahrenheit to drive off some sulfur as sulfur dioxides and to form copper oxides called calcines. The sulfur dioxide gas went up the stack into the atmosphere, becoming a vegetation-killing sulfurous acid. (Courtesy John Bell Collection.)

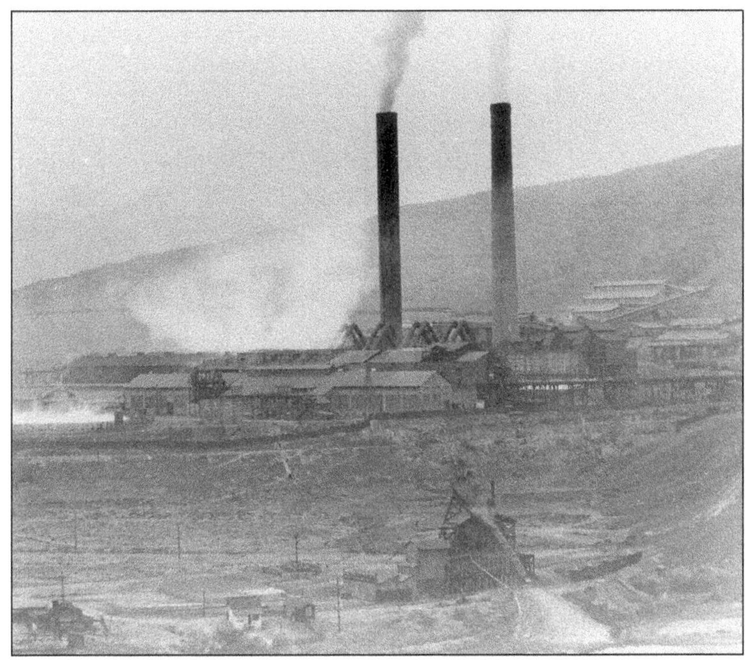

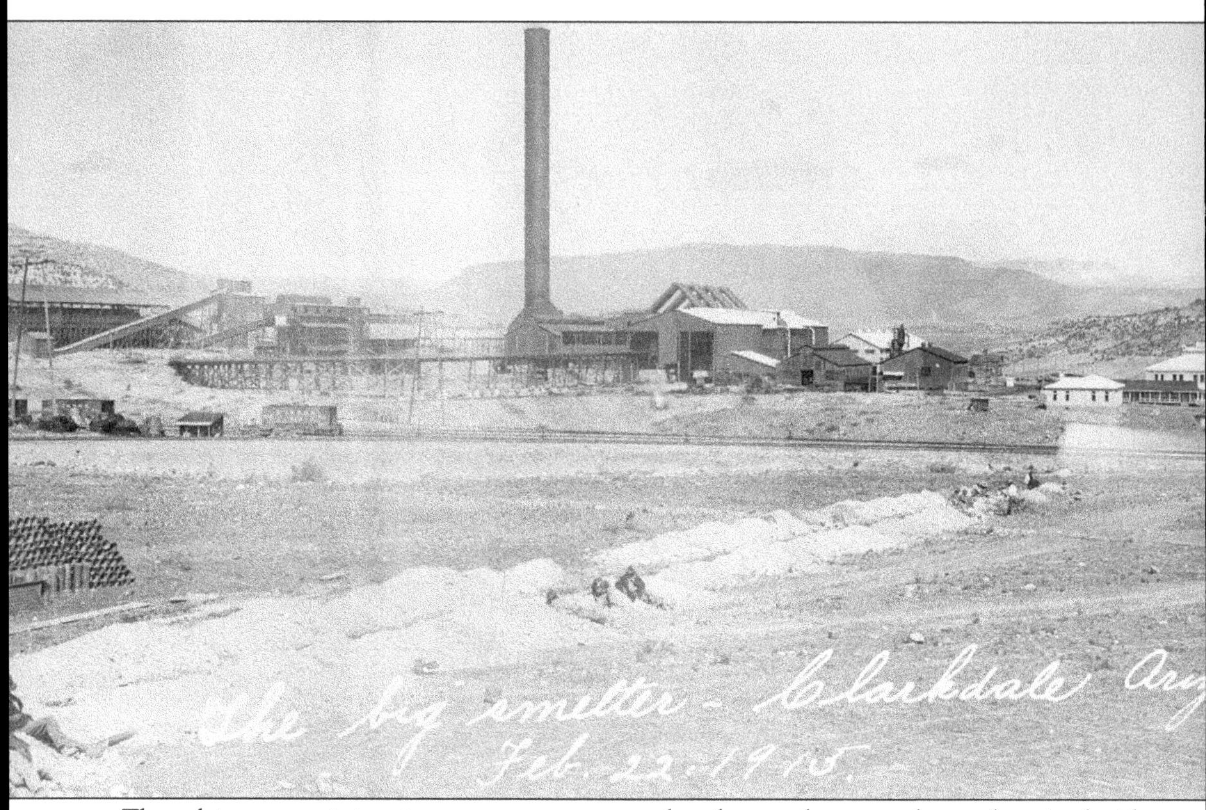

The calcines, containing six percent copper, moved to the reverberatory plant to be mixed with limestone flux and heated above 2,000 degrees Fahrenheit. The reverberatory process separated the calcines into an oxide-silicate slag that floated on top of a heavier metal-bearing matte. The oxide-silicate slag was skimmed off, and the copper-iron matte, averaging 28–35 percent copper, was tapped out from the bottom of the reverberatory and moved to the converters. (Courtesy Clarkdale Historical Society and Museum.)

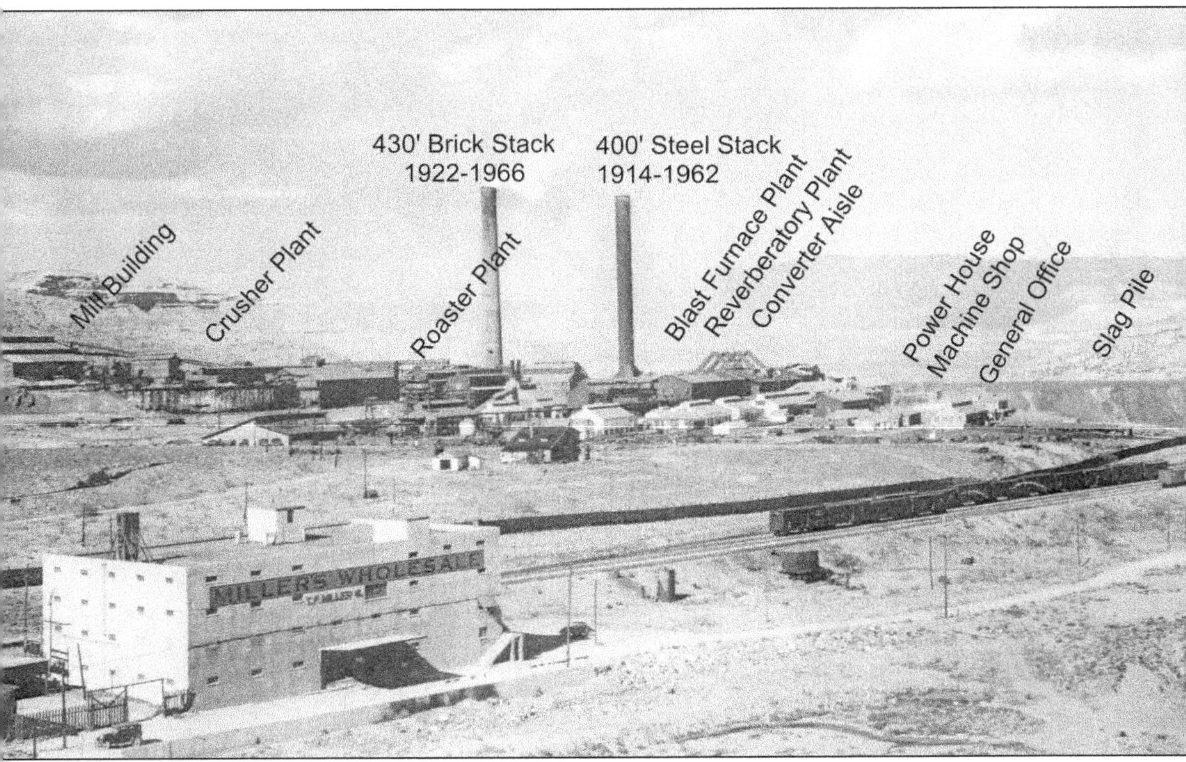

The converter process enriched the molten copper-iron matte by fluxing, heating, and hot air blasts into a 96–99 percent pure blister copper. In the molten state, this blister copper was cast into 700-pound anodes. These were shipped out by railroad for the final process of electrolytic refining that produced pure copper, gold, and silver. (Courtesy Robert Beltz.)

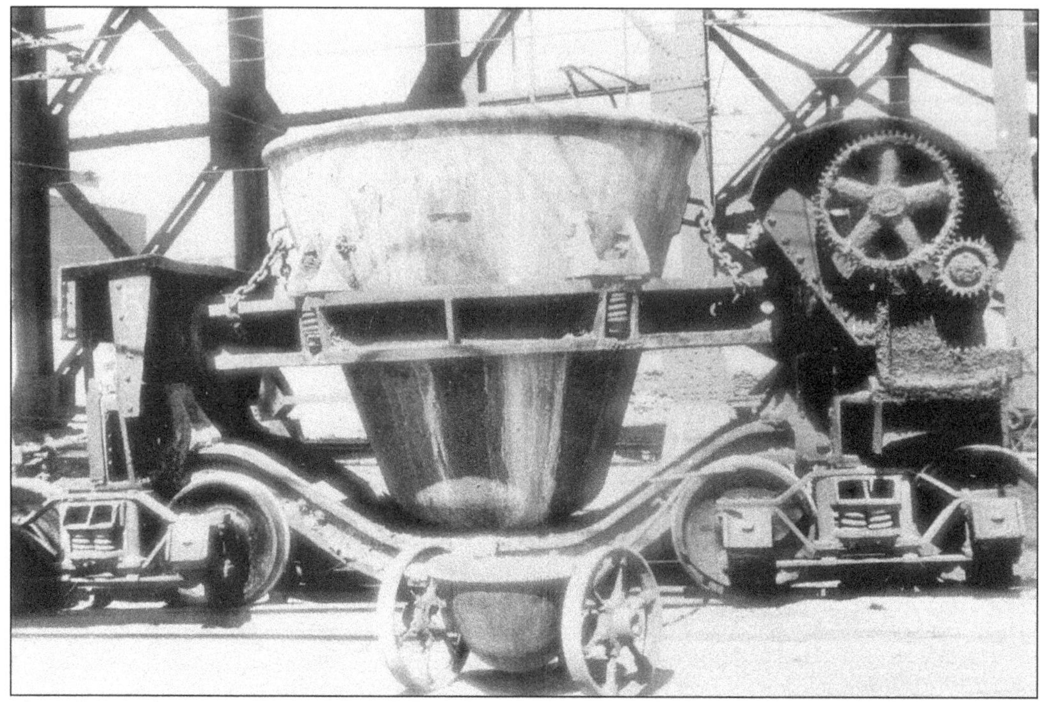

Slag, the smelter waste, was an iron silicate mixed with other elements. The transportation by dump car of yellow-red molten slag to the dumpsite made a spectacular visual display at night when the fiery liquid rock poured out onto the slag pile. The 32-acre dump contains more than 17 million tons of slag. The dump changed Clarkdale's landscape and even the course of the Verde River. (Courtesy Jerome State Historic Park.)

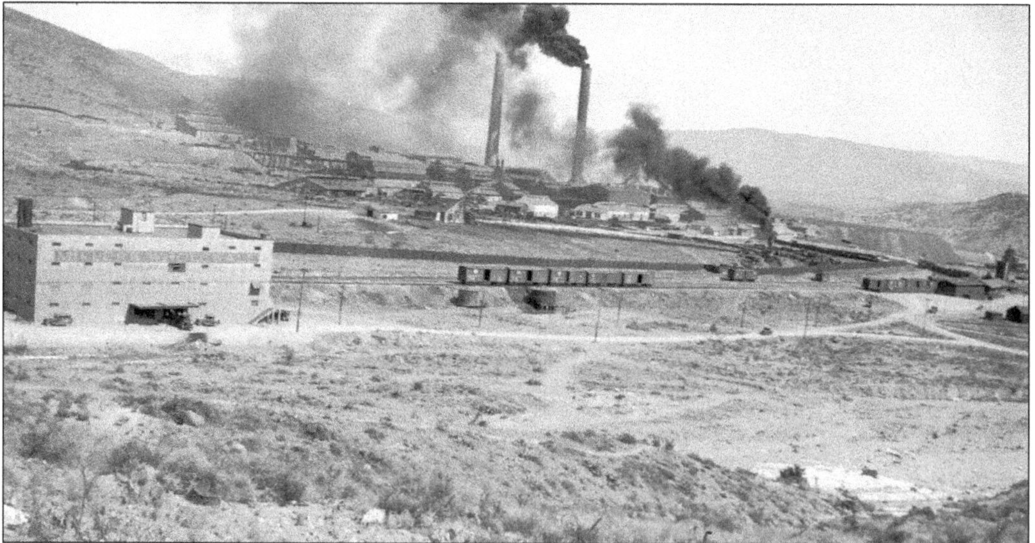

Clarkdale residents describe how the smelter smoke was seen, heard, smelled, tasted, and even felt. In 1918, the daily smoke emissions contained 100 tons of dust that included 1 ton of arsenic, 2.5 tons of lead, 12 tons of zinc, 5.5 tons of copper, and 935 tons of sulfur oxide as gas. Today, based on national averages, Clarkdale's 4,000 citizens are responsible daily for producing about 200 tons of carbon dioxide plus methane and nitrous oxide gases. (Courtesy John Bell Collection.)

The first smoke stack, 400 feet high, was constructed of steel in 1914. Due to the metal loss carried off by smoke, the Cottrell metal-trapping plant was added in 1922; this required a separate 430-foot-high brick and cement stack. The Cottrell facility daily recovered from the smoke more than 90 percent of the formerly lost copper, plus gold and silver values. (Courtesy Clarkdale Historical Society and Museum.)

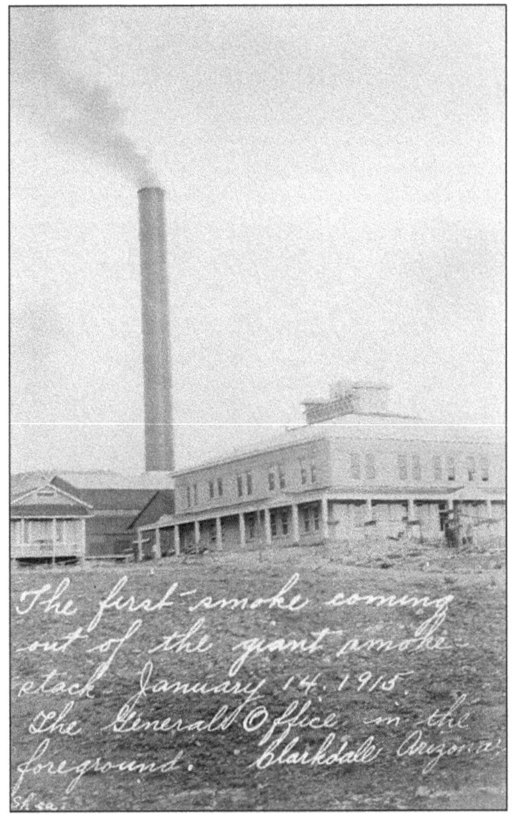

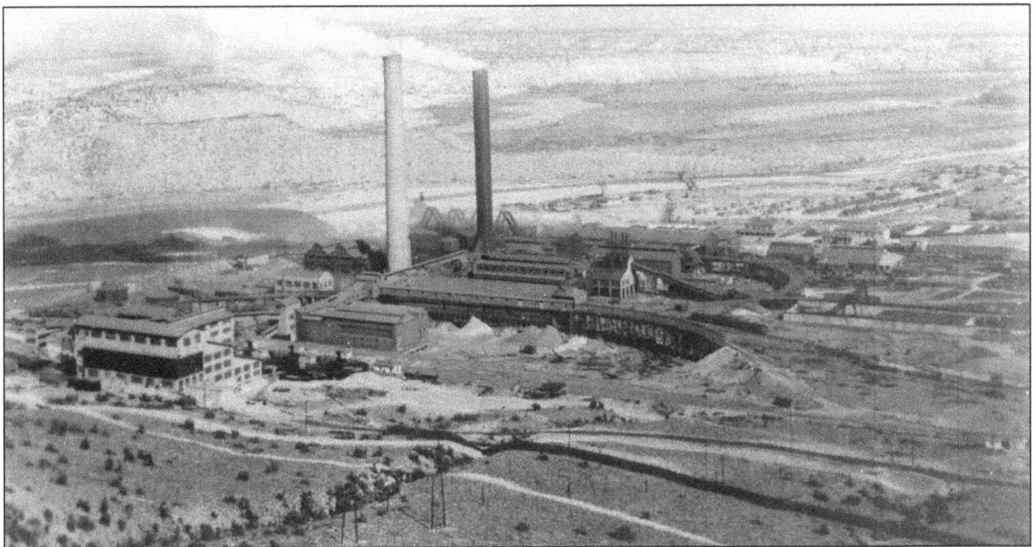

By 1920, smoke pollution from the Clarkdale and Clemenceau smelters and the Tapco power plant had destroyed the area's once bountiful farm production and the surrounding natural vegetation. The gases also exterminated bed bugs and fleas. The copper companies bought out many Upper Verde farms, some from voluntary sellers, and others in court proceedings. This acreage was ultimately resold to the public, but with smoke and flood easements that remain today. (Courtesy Jerome State Historic Park.)

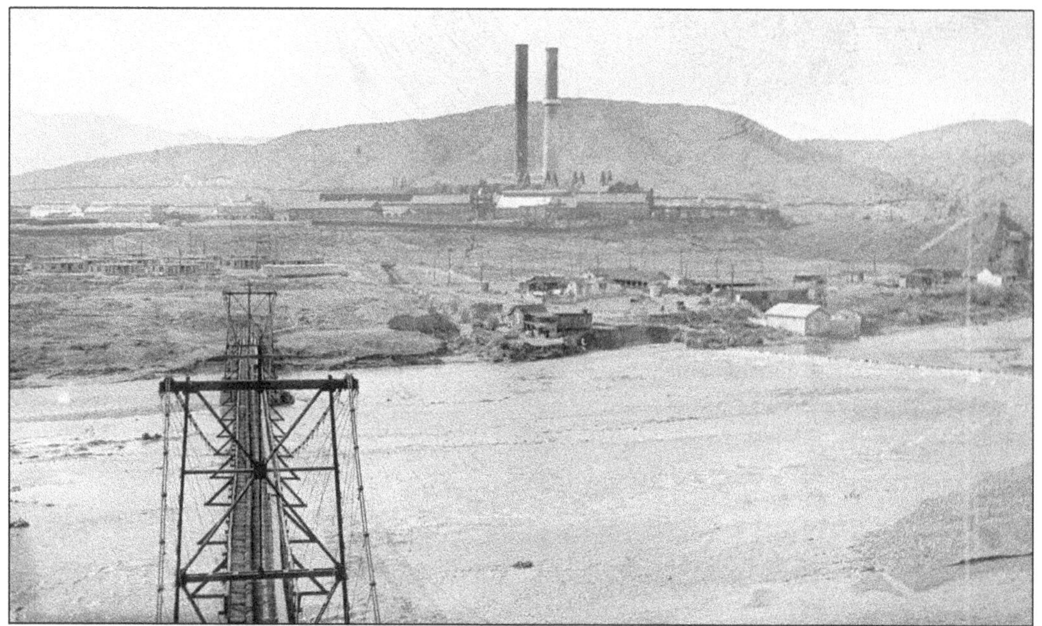

Lower-grade one percent to three percent copper rock was uneconomical to directly smelt. In 1927, a concentrator mill utilizing wet chemical processes was added to the Clarkdale plant to upgrade the lower-grade ores to a 16 percent copper product that could then be profitably smelted. The concentrator tailing waste, as a water-saturated slurry, was transported by pipeline across the river to a 65-acre canyon site near Tuzigoot. (Courtesy John Bell Collection.)

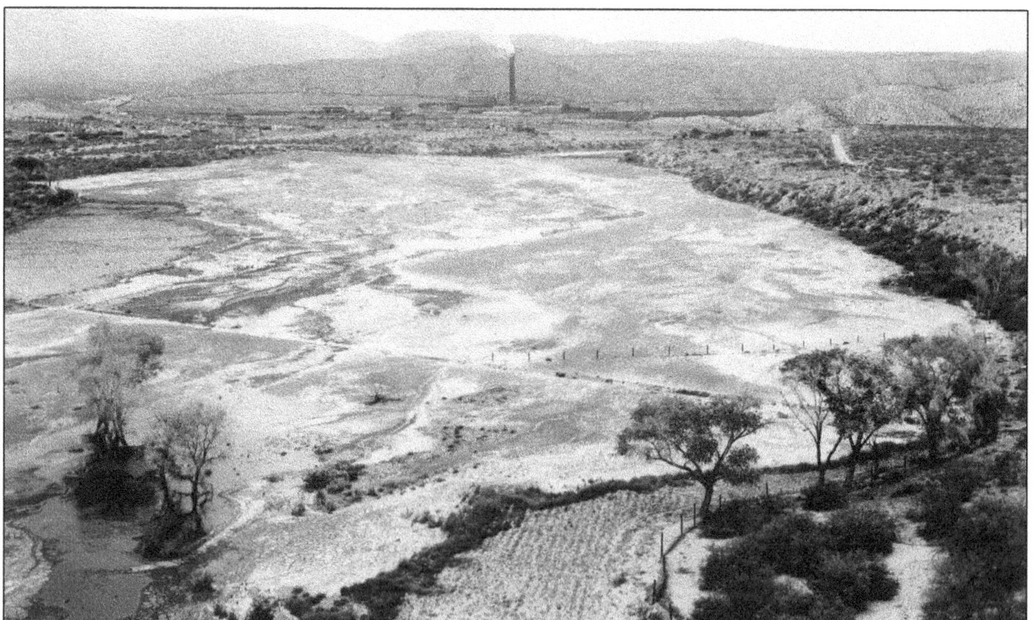

This tailings pond consisted of water-saturated silicates and iron sulfide wastes from the concentrating process. The concentrator operated until 1953, three years after the smelter closed. The 50-foot-deep tailings dump became a rusty-colored, flat area filling an ancient Verde River canyon. The Hawkins irrigation ditch lies beneath the tailings. This site has been reclaimed to prevent water pollution and eliminate dust pollution. (Courtesy National Park Service.)

The smelter workers were grouped into crews by job classifications. The crews worked under a foreman or manager. This pipe crew, bossed by A. James Kent, maintained the miles of piping in the smelter operation. They were also responsible for maintaining the water system from Haskell Spring to Clarkdale. Safety competitions were conducted between the crews with recognition, bonuses, and awards to the winning team members. (Courtesy Verde Historical Society.)

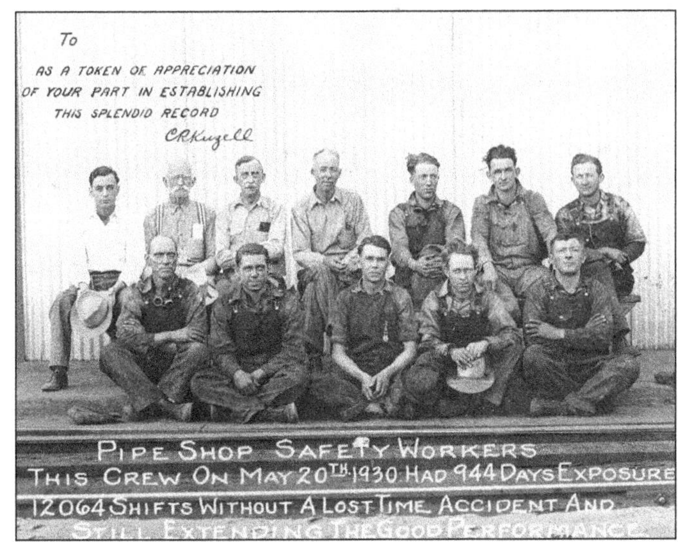

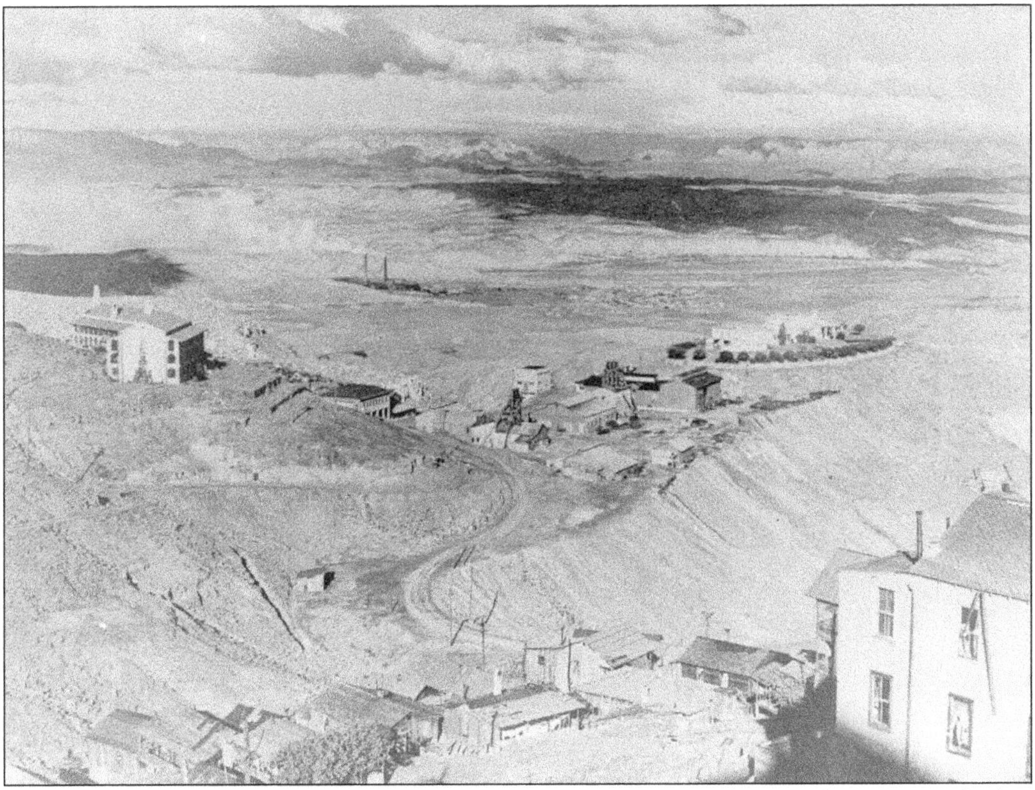

In 1914, James "Rawhide" Douglas discovered one of the world's highest-grade copper ore bodies 1,000 feet below Jerome. This became the United Verde Extension (UVX) mine. It operated through 1938, averaging more than 10 percent copper per ton during its lifetime. This view of the UVX mine is toward Clarkdale from Jerome. The building adjoining and just beyond the mine yard was Douglas's home. It is now the Jerome State Historic Park mining museum. (Courtesy Robert Beltz.)

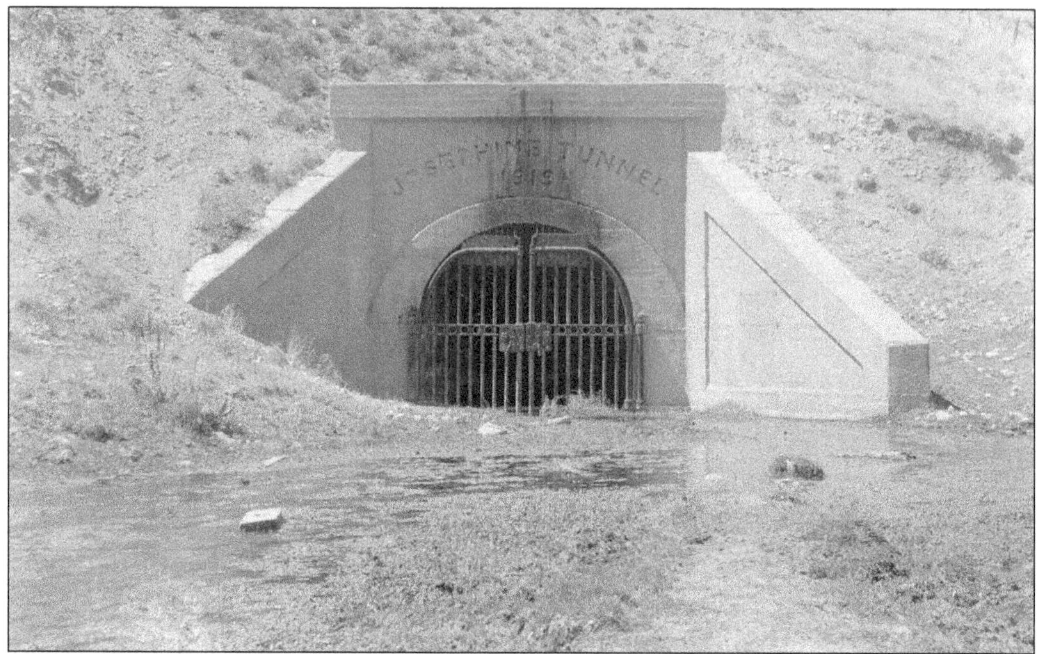

On Clarkdale's west border is the concrete portal of the Josephine Tunnel, named for Douglas's wife. This haulage tunnel went 2.5 miles underground to the 1300 level Audrey Shaft station in the UVX mine. This redwood shaft headframe stands below Jerome State Historic Park. Here tourists can peer down to the haulage tunnel's beginning. (Courtesy Robert Beltz.)

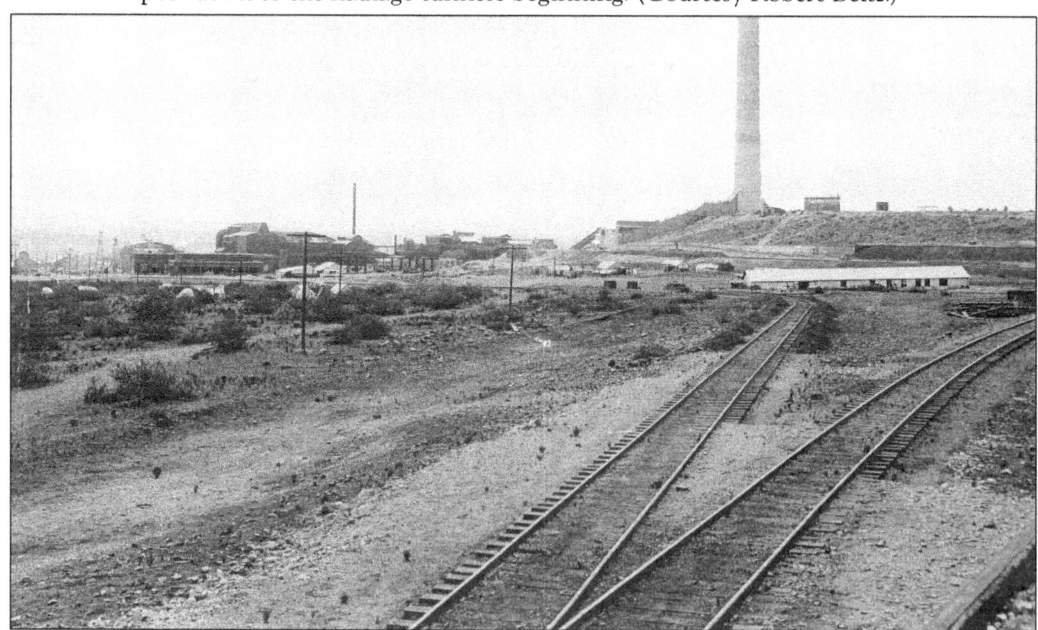

Electric engines hauled full-sized railroad ore cars from the 1300 level UVX underground workings through the Josephine Tunnel to the valley floor on Clarkdale's border. From there, steam engines hauled the ore cars across Clarkdale to the UVX Clemenceau smelter. Remains of this railroad bed and several wash-crossing bridges are visible today within Clarkdale. (Courtesy Verde Historical Society.)

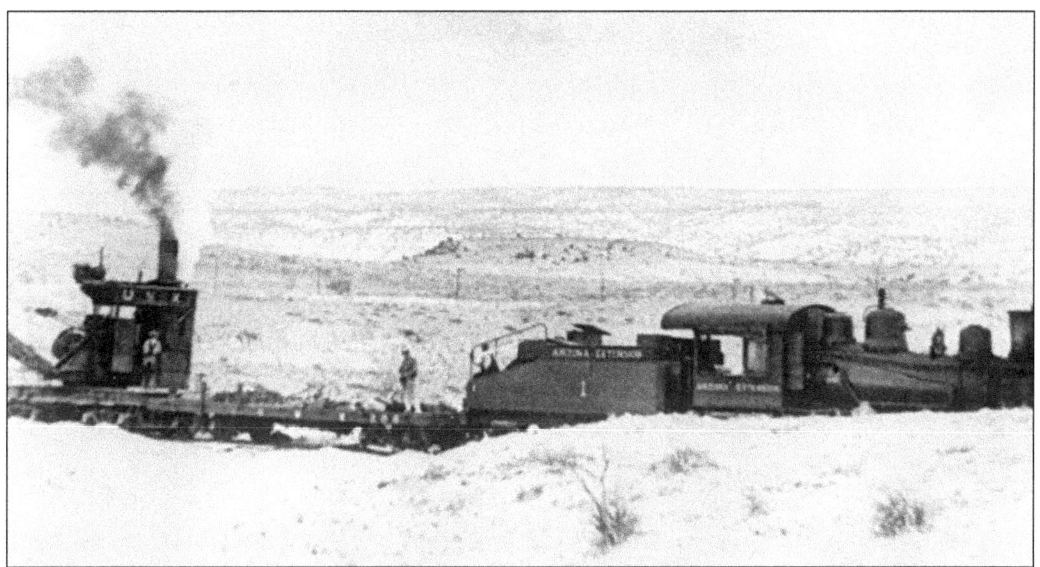

The UVX had a second surface railroad track across Clarkdale that connected the Clemenceau smelter to the Clarkdale AT&SF depot, providing access to the mainline tracks out of the valley. The railroad shipped coal in from UVX mines in New Mexico to fuel the Clemenceau smelter and shipped 99 percent copper out for the refining process at Douglas, Arizona. (Courtesy Thomas Handverger.)

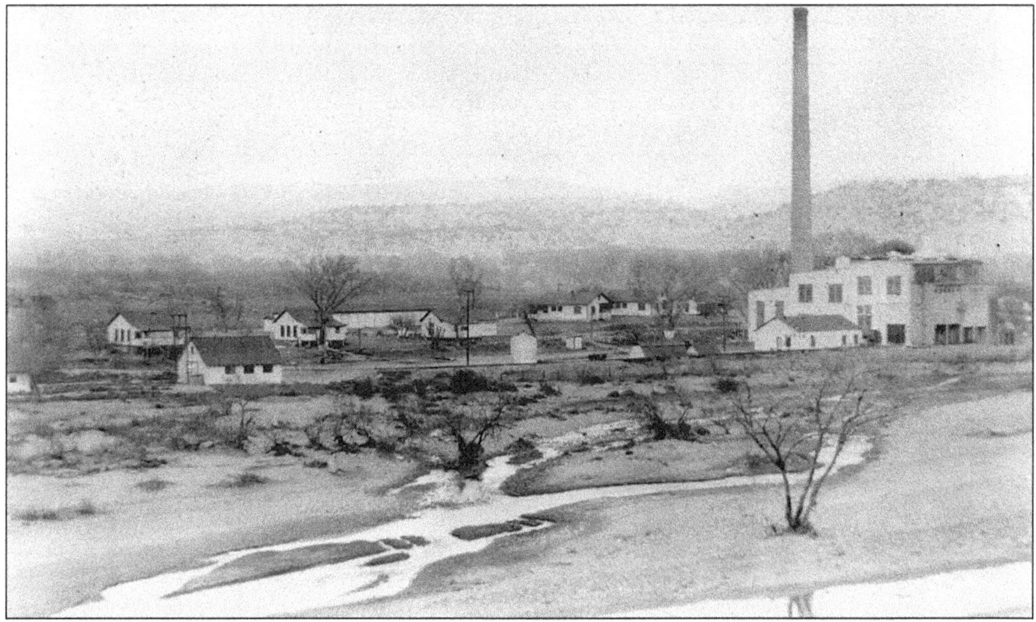

The Arizona Power Company built the Tapco electrical generating plant just north of Clarkdale, which opened in 1917. Twenty employees, some of whom lived in Tapco's 14 company houses, operated the power plant. Tapco generated electricity leading to Clarkdale becoming one of the first completely electrified communities in Arizona. This plant generated electricity for the UVCC, UVX, other small mines, and Cottonwood and Clemenceau. (Courtesy Clarkdale Historical Society and Museum.)

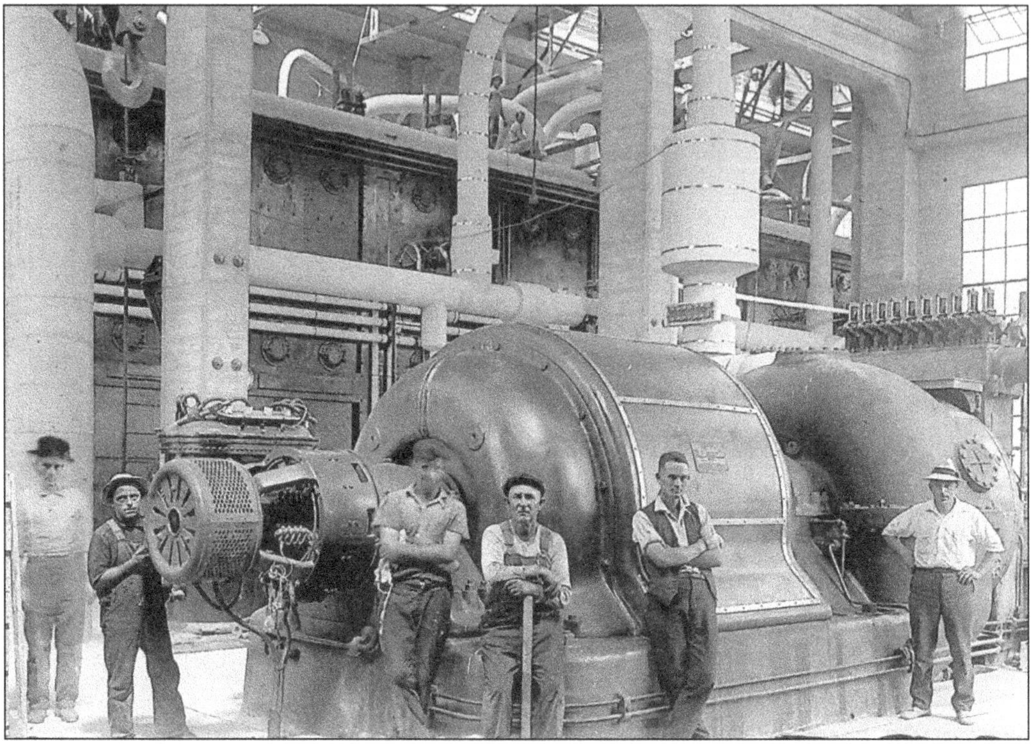

The Tapco plant used oil-fueled boilers to power steam-driven generators that provided 8.5 megawatts of electrical energy. Water for steam and cooling came from a flume off the Verde River supplemented by well water. The railroad brought in crude oil that was consumed at the rate of one tank car per day. The 220-foot stack continually billowed smoke day and night. (Courtesy Tim Coons.)

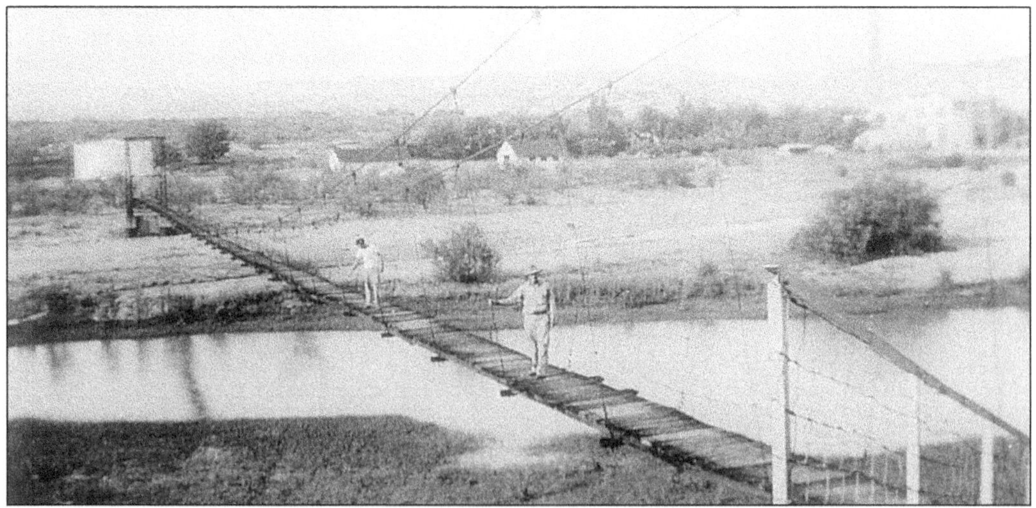

Road access to Tapco was subject to closure by flooding. A 450-foot suspension walking bridge was built across the river, allowing employees access during high water. In 1917, the Tapco section of the river was considered the town's swimming pool. This "Swinging Bridge" became a place for local people of all ages to playfully sway and bounce over the river. It was removed in 1982. (Courtesy Tim Coons.)

Seven

1912–1953
Clarkdale Homes and Buildings

Clark planned Clarkdale to be a model town in every way. UVCC engineers designed the houses after asking employees in Jerome what they desired for homes. Unlike other industrial towns, the community had brick houses of multiple designs with central heat, indoor plumbing, wood floors, and all utilities including a town sewer system. Individual fenced yards kept out the wandering burros. The construction of Clarkdale began in 1912. It took about two decades and $1 million to complete the town. It is Arizona's first planned community.

The UVCC designed Clarkdale as a walking town with sidewalks and streetlights lining wide streets. The roads paralleling Main Street were named North and South whereas the cross streets were named First to Seventeenth from Lower Town to Upper Town. Attractive yards were encouraged by an annual contest for the prettiest grounds. Governed by company regulations, Clarkdale Improvement Company officials regularly inspected the houses and conducted all maintenance and repairs unless caused by the occupant's negligence.

In July 1918, federal mediators and Arizona mine owners discussed the quality of the Clarkdale houses during a labor negotiation. One mediator said, "I frankly say to you that they [the homes] are too good for the uses of a mining camp . . . somebody blundered in building that exceptionally fine camp . . . splendidly equipped, bath tubs, shower baths, toilets; good enough for any one of us to live in; I would not hesitate to live in them." Robert Talley, the UVCC assistant general manager replied, "I agree with you that we made a mistake in building too good a town in Clarkdale."

Clarkdale had neighborhoods called Upper Town, Lower Town, Patio Town, Rio Vista, and seven numbered districts that together defined and also segregated the community economically and ethnically. Even surnames had a bearing on where one lived. Additional neighborhoods outside the main town further separated the residents. People in districts outside Upper Town, Lower Town, and Patio Town could lease UVCC land and construct private homes.

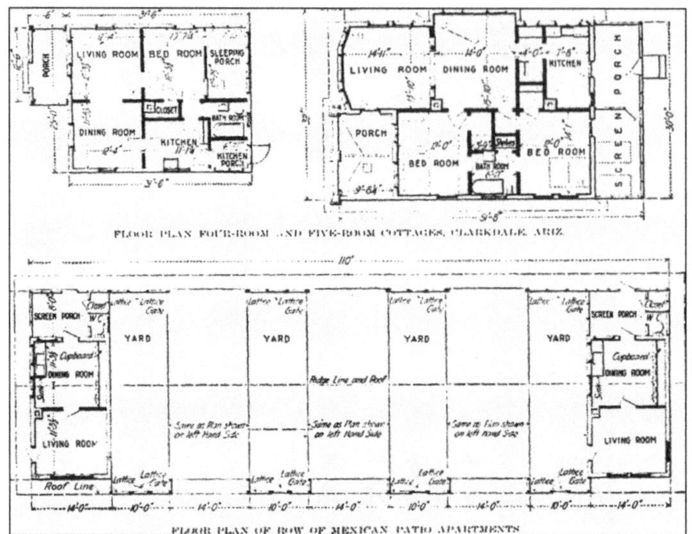

UVCC engineer T.C. Roberts designed Clarkdale as a model community with brick houses of various appealing designs. The planners interviewed workers who would live in the new smelter town as to what they wanted in a home and then mine engineers designed the town and houses based upon the results of that survey. Clarkdale's construction began June 1912 and was eventually completed for about $1 million. (Courtesy Clarkdale Historical Society and Museum.)

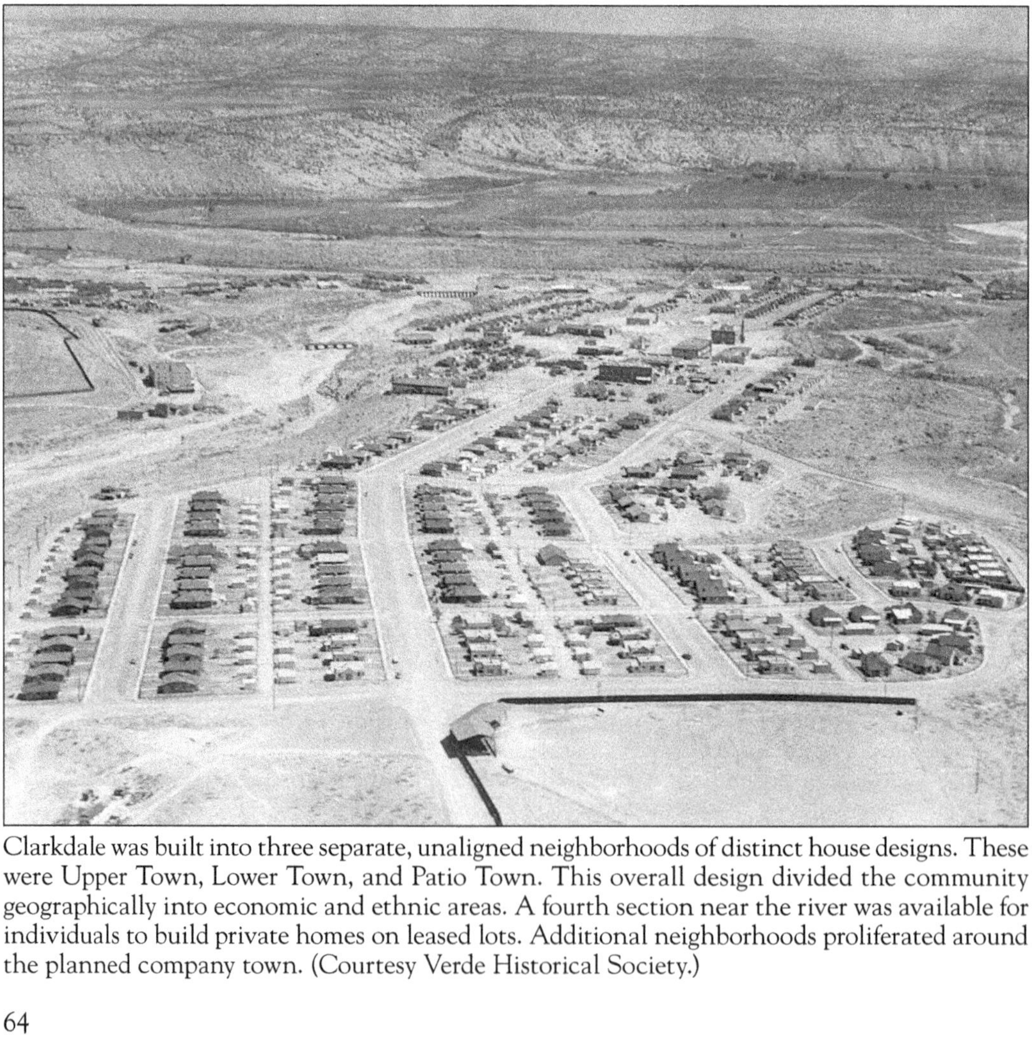

Clarkdale was built into three separate, unaligned neighborhoods of distinct house designs. These were Upper Town, Lower Town, and Patio Town. This overall design divided the community geographically into economic and ethnic areas. A fourth section near the river was available for individuals to build private homes on leased lots. Additional neighborhoods proliferated around the planned company town. (Courtesy Verde Historical Society.)

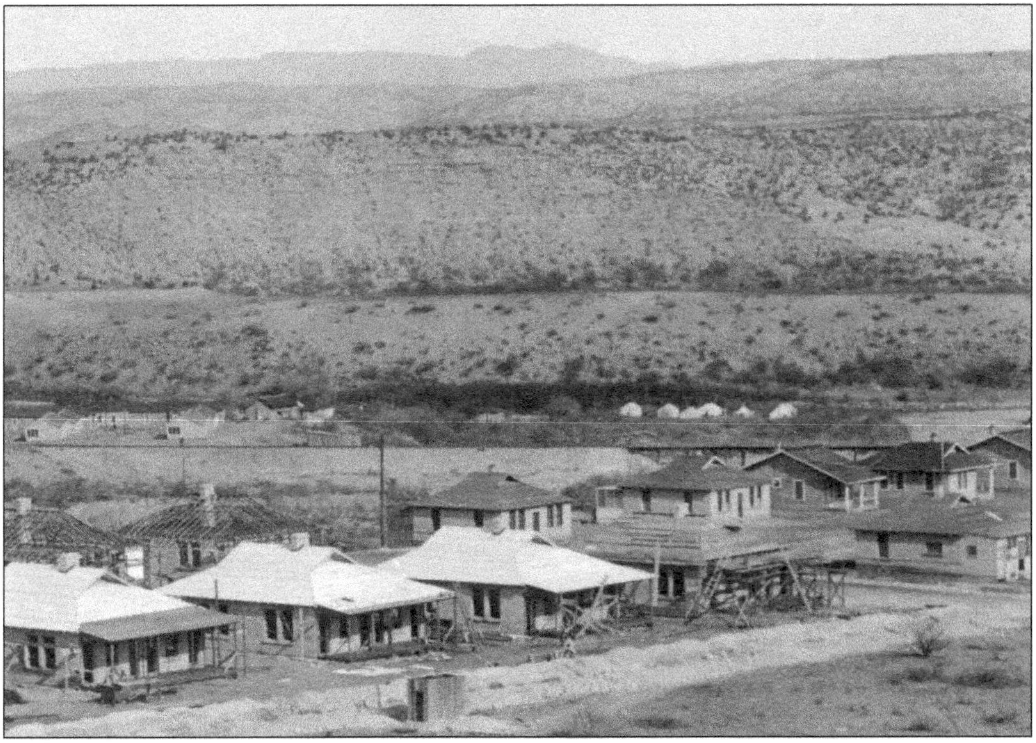

The construction of Clarkdale began in Lower Town. The construction workers lived in temporary dormitories and tents, visible in the background. Eventually, Clarkdale boasted wide streets, sidewalks, streetlights, water and sewer systems, underground electrical utilities, telephones, a plaza, churches, schools, library, post office, saloons, health clinic, dispensary, hotel, boarding house, restaurants, movie theater, and the Clark Memorial Clubhouse. (Courtesy B. Cimarolli.)

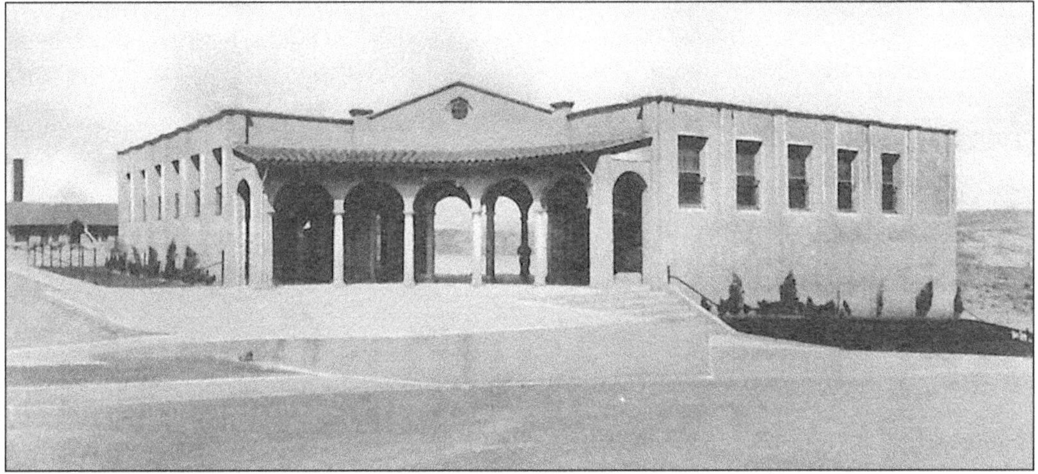

Most of Clarkdale's initial commercial, public, administrative, maintenance, religious, and educational facilities were centrally located between Upper Town and Lower Town. The Upper Verde Public Utilities Company (UVPUC) administration building and post office, now Clarkdale's town offices, were located at Main and Ninth Streets, as seen here. The Clarkdale Improvement Company maintained the town out of workshops along First South behind the main block. (Courtesy Drake Meinke.)

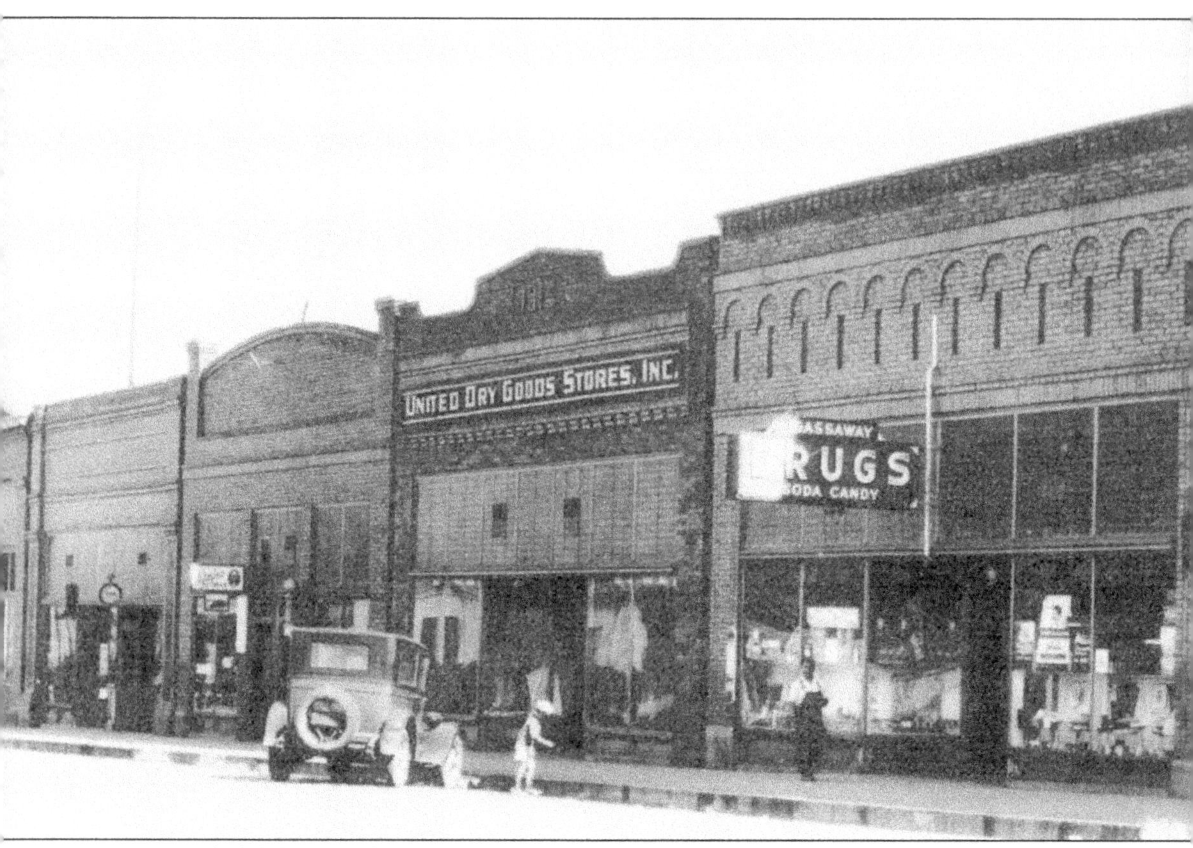

During Clarkdale's first decades, the central commercial block included a general store, dry goods store, bank, drug store, grocery, tailoring and cleaning establishment, jewelry store, music store, cigar stores, barber shop, pool halls, confectionery, movie theater, bakery, saloons, furniture store, and cafes. The upper floors of the commercial block housed dental offices, business offices, living apartments, and the Masonic lodge. The latter was used for church services and other meetings. (Courtesy D. Benatz and W. Conner families.)

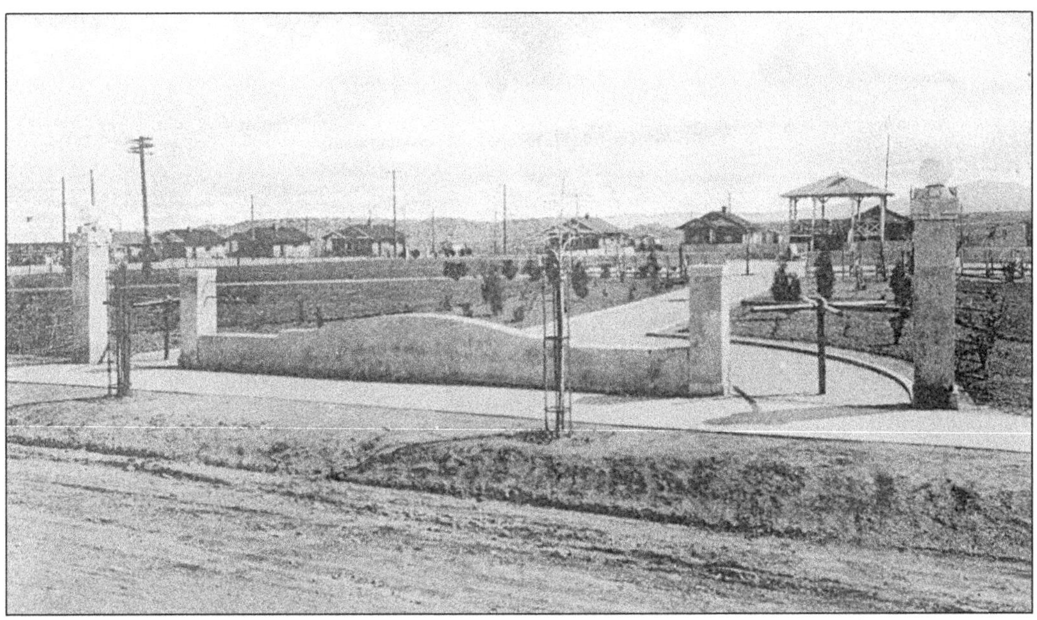

The Southwestern plaza–styled park was, and is today, the scene of family and town activities; many utilized the gazebo. The park was fenced off, with access by turnstile gates to prevent burros from entering. It was a place where marriages were celebrated, holiday speeches were delivered, parades were watched, children played, dances were held, concerts were offered, school activities occurred, politicians orated, and firemen contested. (Courtesy John Bell Collection.)

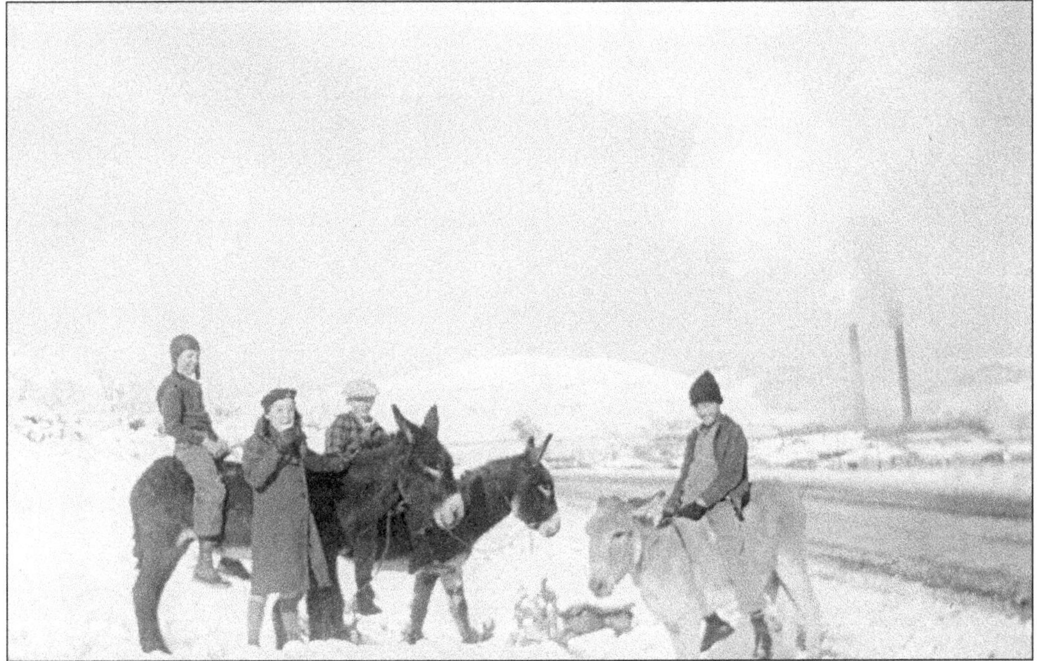

Roaming burros, many owned by the workers in Patio Town, freely wandered through Clarkdale. Children would often catch them and ride around town, and—if lucky—sometimes ride up the hill to school. All the homes had to have fences around their yards to keep the burros from eating the grass and gardens. (Courtesy Robert Beltz.)

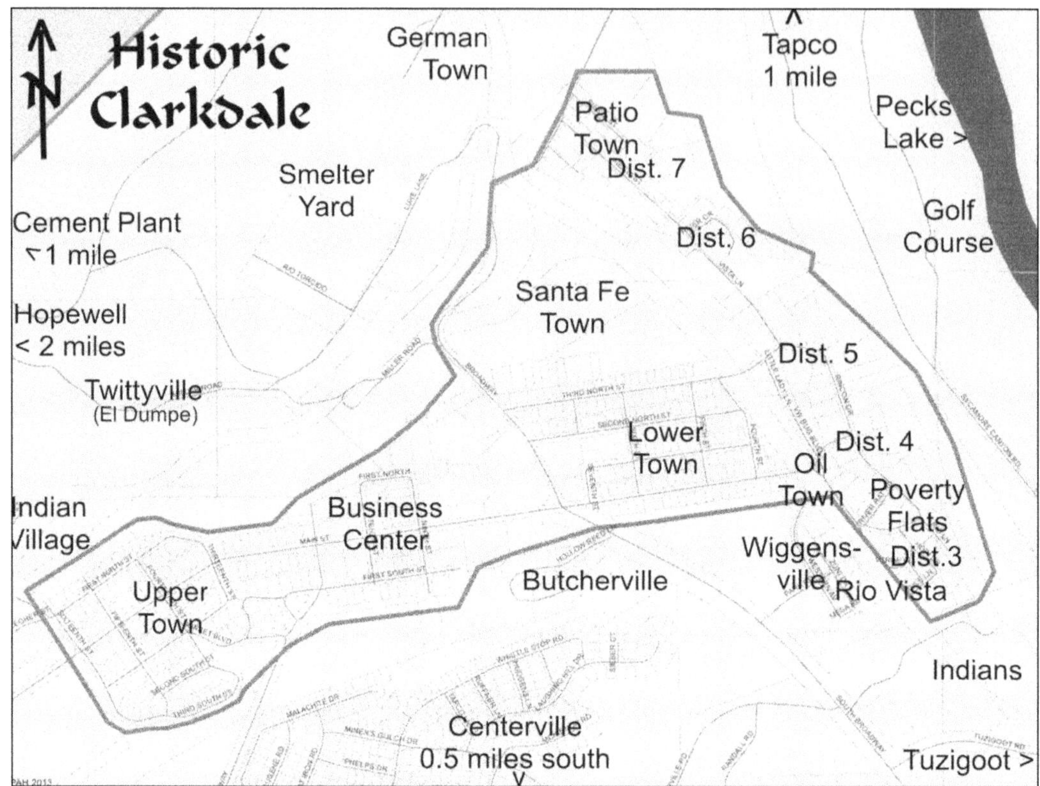

Upper Town was built for "the 400," also known as the managers, merchants, company officials, and professionals in town. Lower Town was rented to craftsmen and shift bosses, mostly Anglo in heritage. Patio Town was constructed for the Mexican laborers. Rio Vista, Poverty Flats, and Wigginsville were located between Lower Town and the river where employees could lease land and build their own homes. Oil Town was in the same area adjoining the tracks. (Courtesy Town of Clarkdale and PAH.)

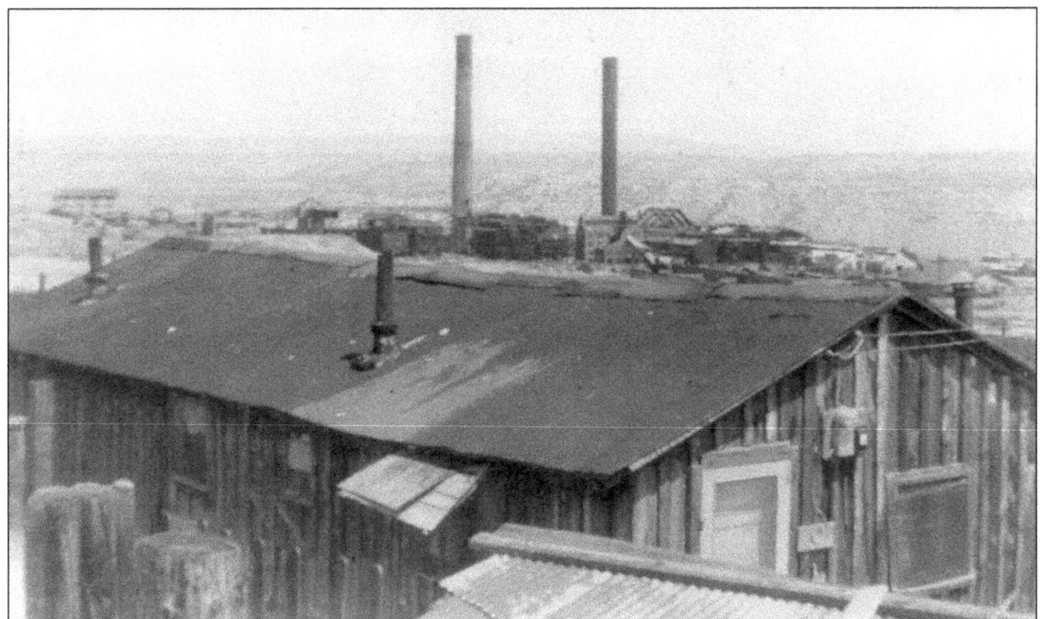

Railroad workers lived in Santa Fe Town near the depot. Twittyville, named for Fred Twitty, AT&SF yardmaster, was referred to as El Dumpe by the Mexican residents because of its proximity to the town dump near the tracks and the smelter border. The photograph is of the Uribe home. Butcherville was located near the stockyards close to today's Elks Lodge. Germantown was located beside the slag pile. (Courtesy Lupe Uribe.)

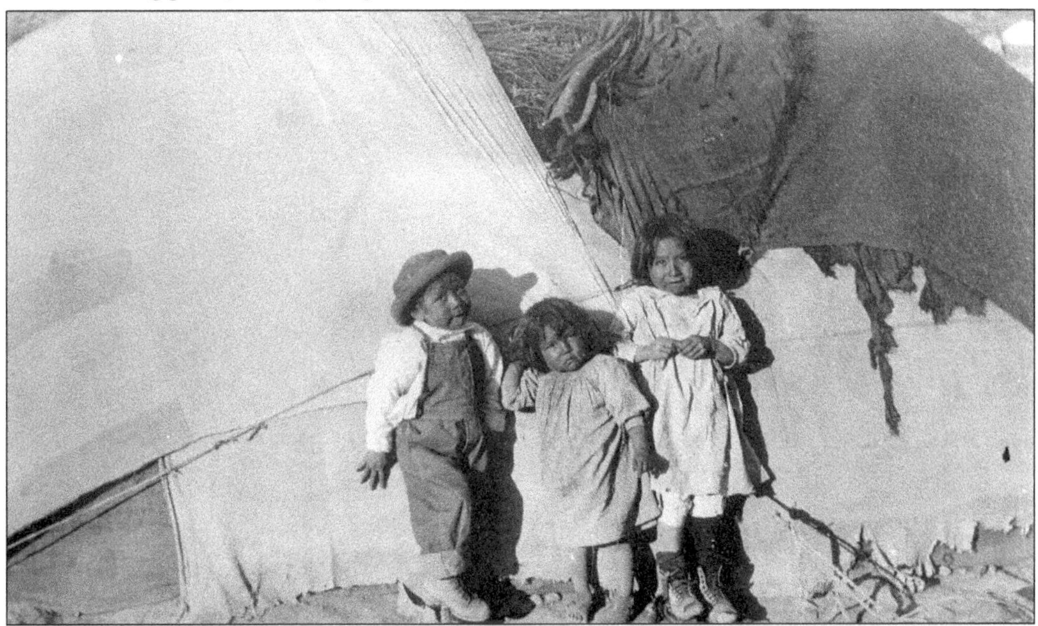

South of Lower Town, Indians, mostly Apache, lived on undeveloped UVCC land. One half mile south of Upper Town, a 40-acre parcel called Centerville (sometimes called Romita) was developed very early into a non-UVCC subdivision with its own general store, where Mexican workers could build homes. Centerville was thought to be the center of Arizona, but later surveys plotted the state's center about 16 miles south. (Courtesy John Bell.)

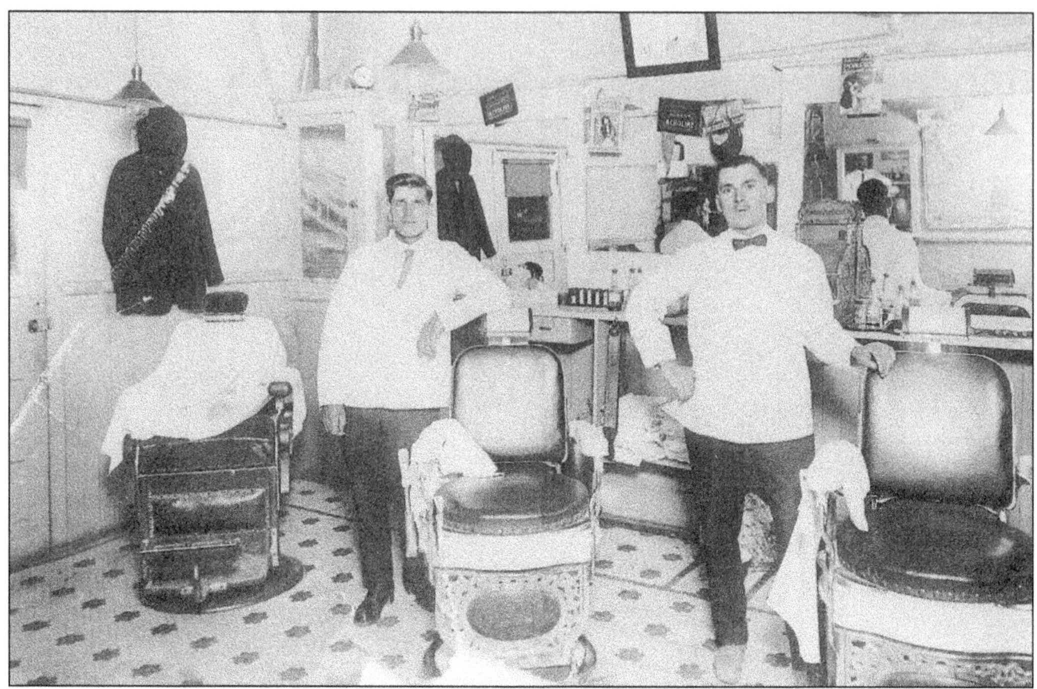

The UVCC wielded economic and moral control over all Clarkdale residents, whether working in the smelter or in private enterprises, such as these town barbers. Using company hiring procedures and property leasing policies, economic control was established and maintained according to company standards. If a worker broke rules, didn't pay bills, or even if his child misbehaved, the company could fire him and evict his family from their home. (Courtesy D. Benatz and W. Conner families.)

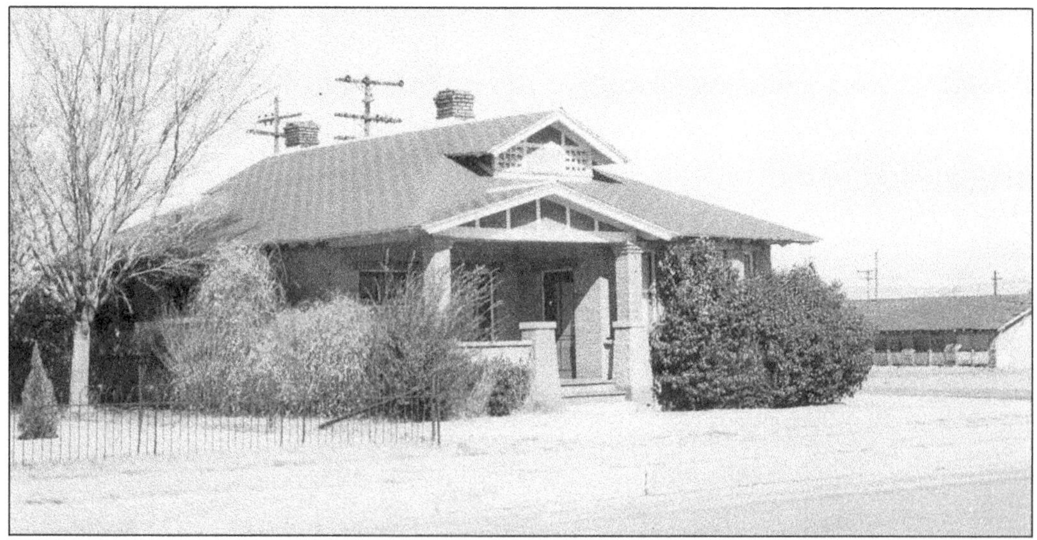

Clarkdale Improvement Company maintained all the town's buildings, streets, and utilities under established procedures and regulations. Leases stated that homes were to be inspected monthly inside and outside. Subletting rooms in a house, which was a common practice in mining camps of that era, was tightly regulated. Saloons were restricted in number, and red light districts were banned. A company-paid town marshal enforced law and order. (Courtesy M. Hill.)

Clarkdale's first company house, named the Pilot House, was completed in 1913 between Lower Town and the river. It was a two-story, concrete structure without architectural niceties. Clark did not like its appearance. He said he wanted "a model town . . . different in construction from the usual company-built towns in that all the buildings would not be of the same design." (Courtesy M. Hill.)

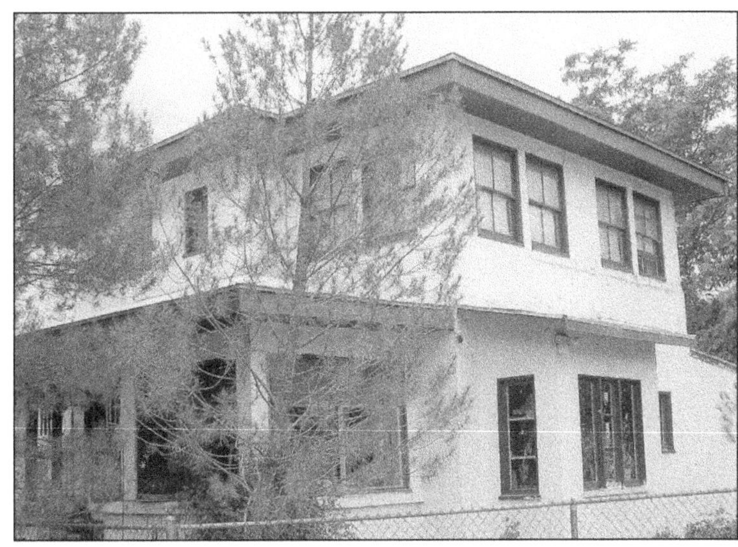

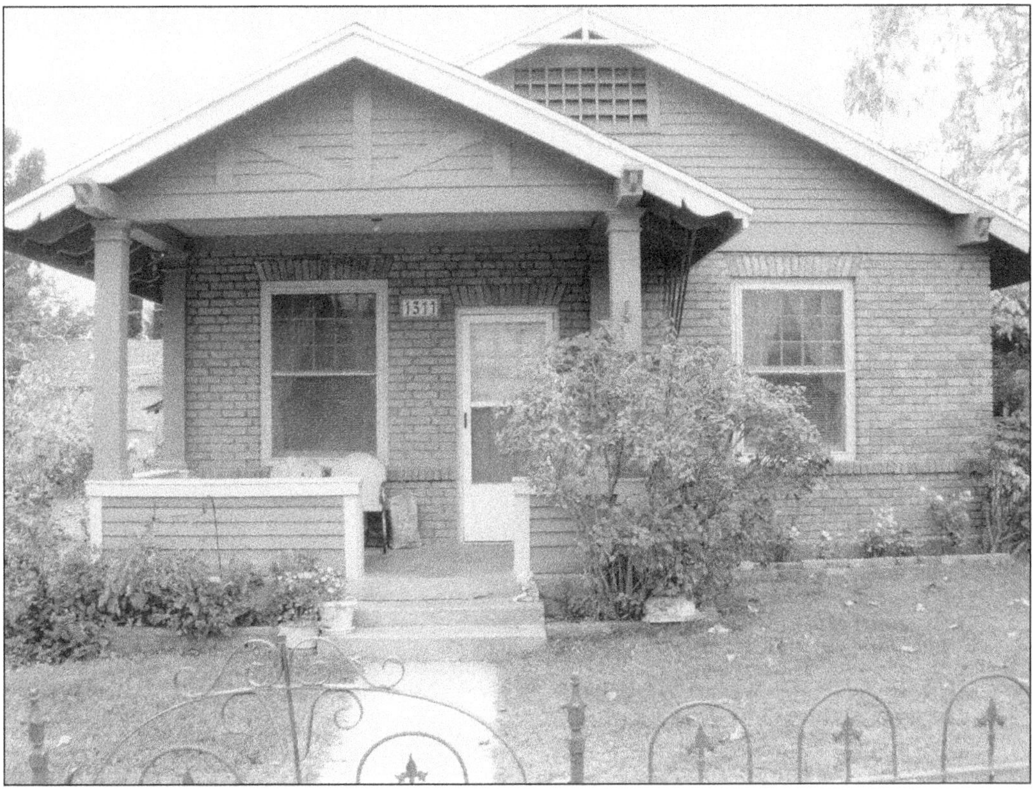

Upper Town houses had four or five rooms with maple wood floors, room dividers, a front porch, a rear sleeping porch, and a complete bathroom with tub or shower. Most had a 10-foot-wide back alley, with garages off the street. The houses were constructed of multi-toned bricks manufactured locally. Building costs were $1,700 for the four-room houses and $2,600 for the five-room houses. (Courtesy M. Hill.)

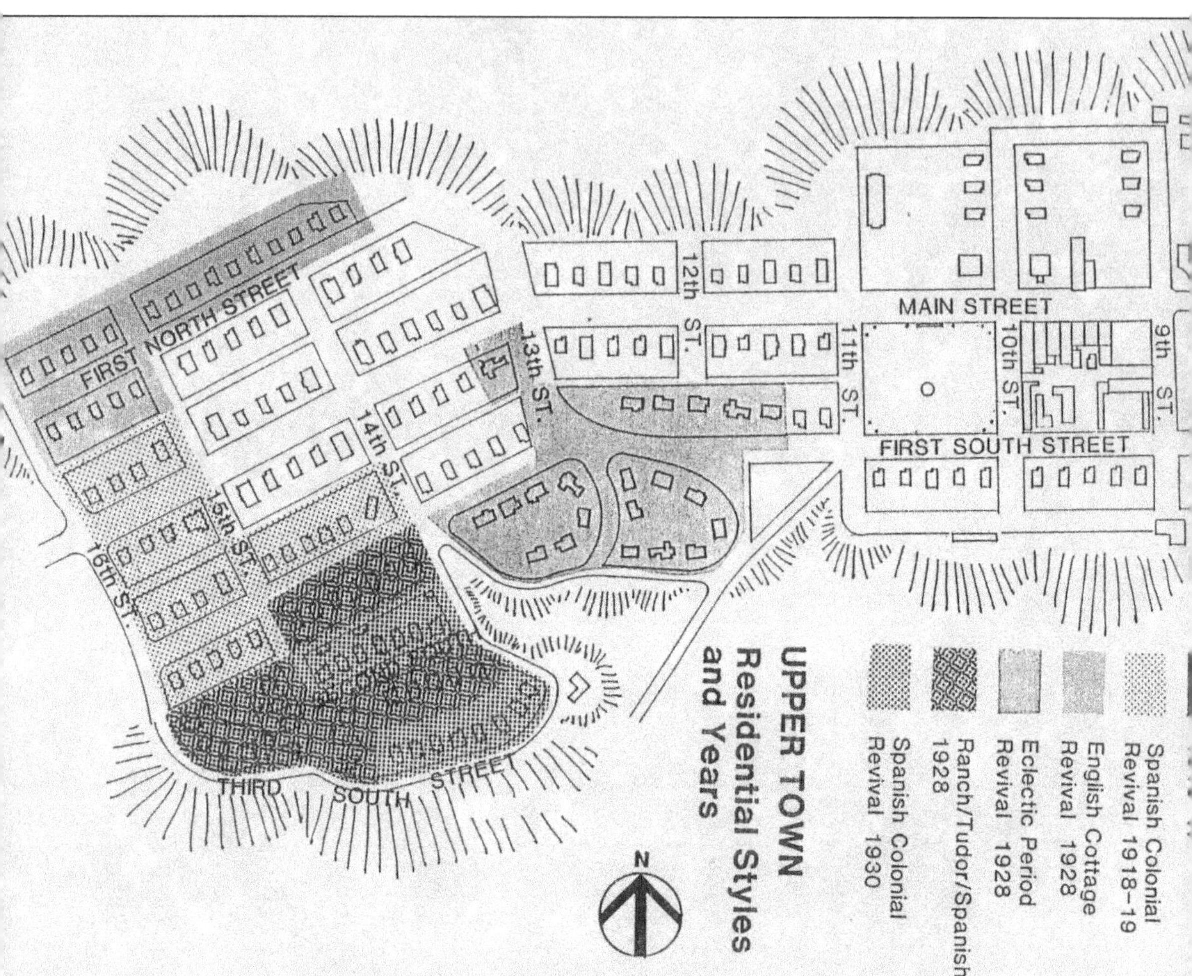

There were six models of Upper Town houses constructed between 1914 and 1930. The diagram shows when and where the different models were built on 32 by 120 foot lots. The stoutly built external brick walls are 8.5 inches thick. Today, many of the town's homes retain their original century-old exterior appearance. (Courtesy Clarkdale Historical Society and Museum.)

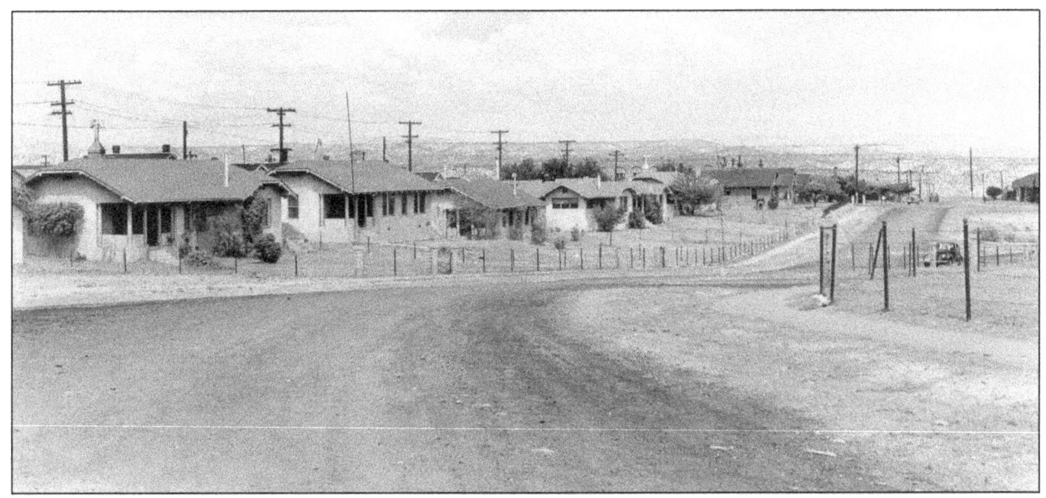

The UVPUC maintained the town, the public buildings and facilities, houses, streets, trash pickup, water, electrical, sewer system, and fire hydrants. Electricity produced from the Tapco generating plant was initially supplied to the homes through underground lines. However, the boom in household electrical usage in the 1920s exceeded the power-carrying capacity of the buried lines, and overhead lines had to be installed. (Courtesy John Bell Collection.)

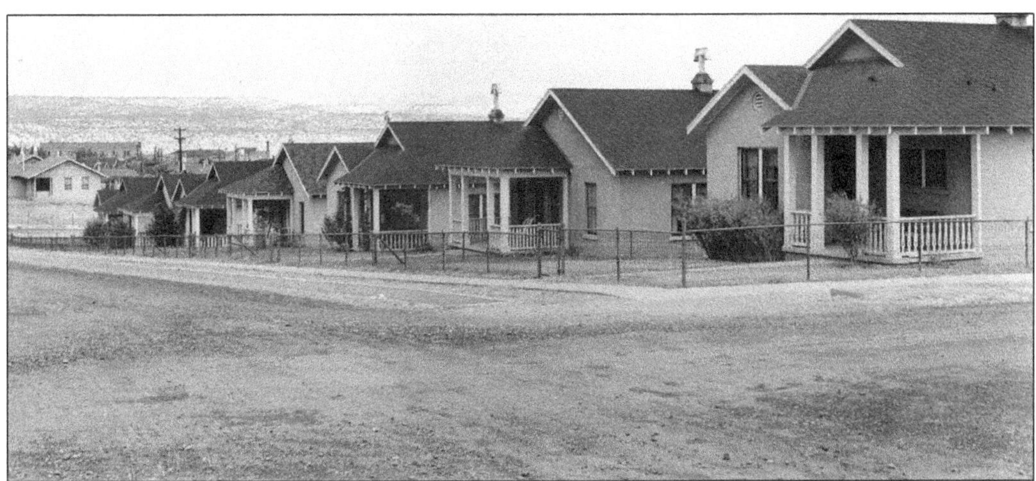

In 1918, the house rents were established according to job. Laborers paid $5.15 per month, muckers $5.50, miners $5.15 to $6.00, and mechanics $6.50. Monthly utilities were $1.00 for electricity, $2.00 for telephone, and $2.25 to $2.60 for water with 15,000 gallons of free water during the summer months to encourage yard beautification. Clarkdale Improvement Company collected about $7,000 monthly in building rents. (Courtesy John Bell Collection.)

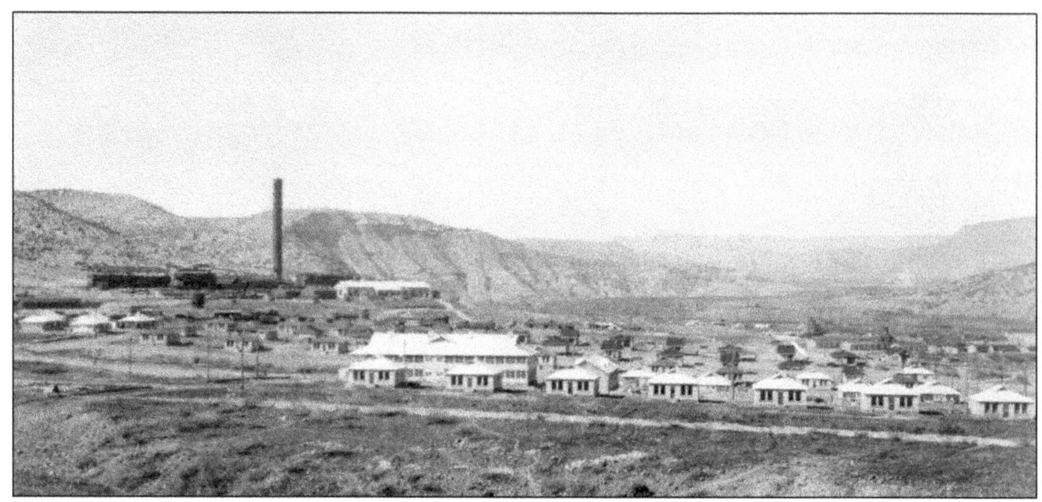

A major business located in Lower Town in the earliest years was the Verde Hotel, a 30-room boarding house built for the permanent workers. Attached to the hotel was Charley Hung's restaurant, which served meals to the single male inhabitants living in rooms without kitchens. The restaurant has been converted into living quarters today. (Courtesy Sedona Heritage Museum.)

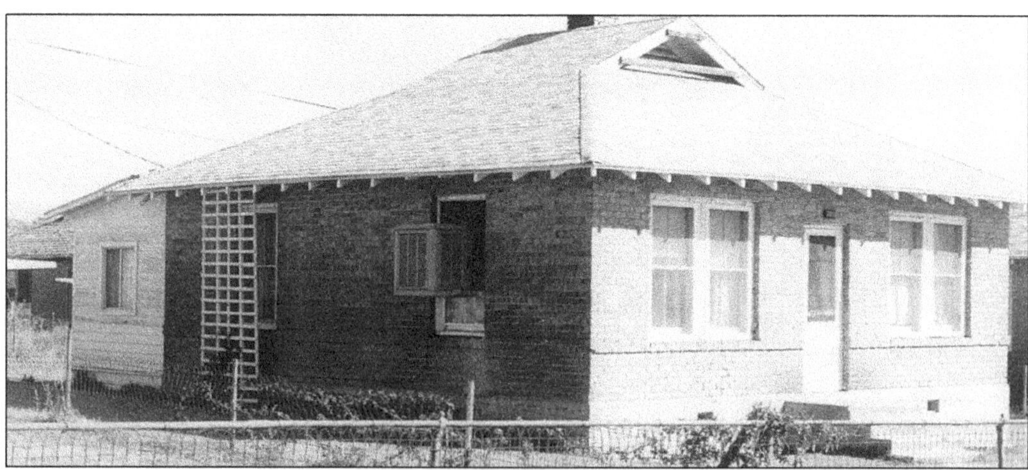

Lower Town houses were built simpler and smaller than Upper Town houses on fenced-in 30-by-90-foot lots. Most homes had four rooms: living, dining, bedroom, and kitchen with Oregon pine floors. A sleeping porch on the back contained the shower-equipped bathroom. The majority of occupants of these homes during the smelter years were culturally diverse. (Courtesy M. Hill.)

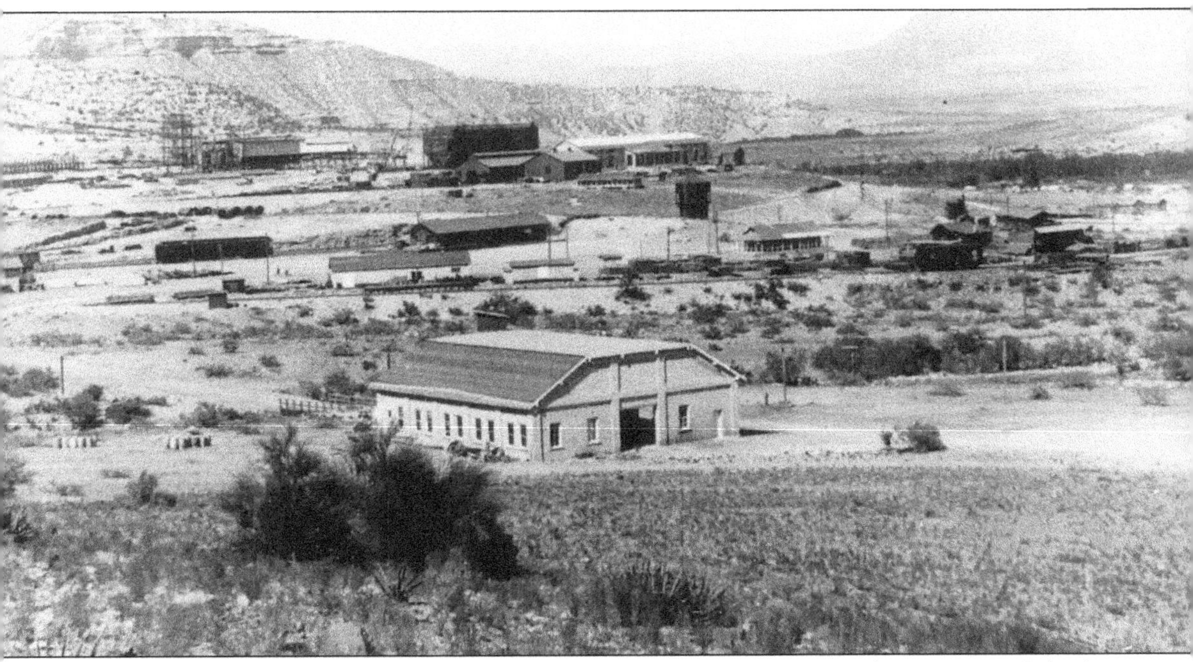

The UVCC cabinet shop, pictured in 1914, was where the carpentry work was accomplished during the construction phase of the town's buildings. After the town was built, the building became Lindner's automobile garage. Oil depots and freight terminals were located along railroad tracks in Lower Town. A laundry, livery stable, and stockyard were located close by Lower Town. (Courtesy Jerome State Historic Park.)

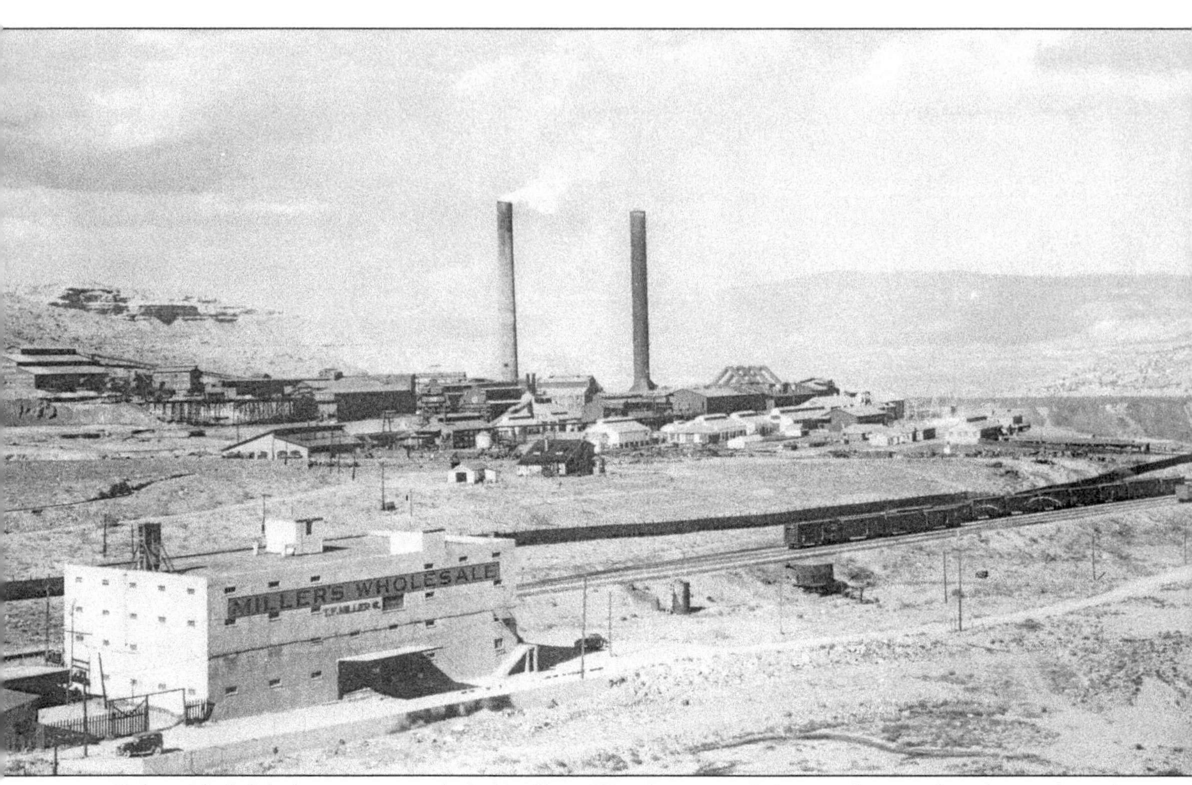

Other Clarkdale businesses included Miller's Warehouse and the nearby ice plant located on the railroad tracks below Upper Town next to Bitter Creek. A dairy and a turkey farm operated at Peck's Lake. The Upper Valley slaughterhouse was located in the Bitter Creek drainage on the extension of Clarkdale's Main Street, which was the main road between Clarkdale and Jerome. (Courtesy Robert Beltz.)

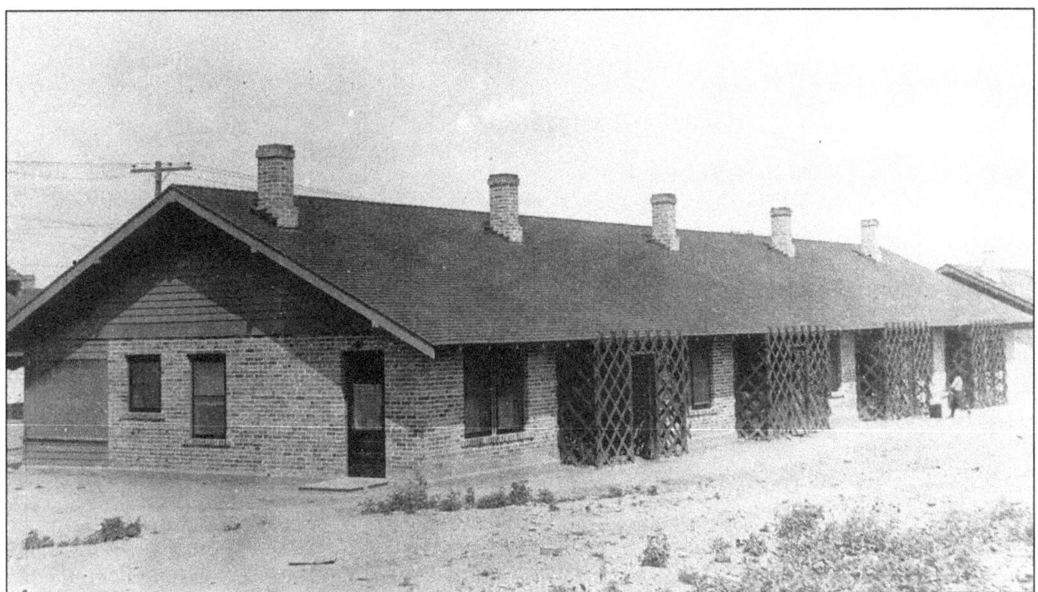

Patio Town housing consisted of five attached three-room apartments (each 32 by 14 feet). Each unit had a living room, dining room, and screened sleeping porch that had a toilet/shower/bath at one end. There was an open breezeway between each apartment. Garden space was available for the occupants. (Courtesy Jerome State Historic Park.)

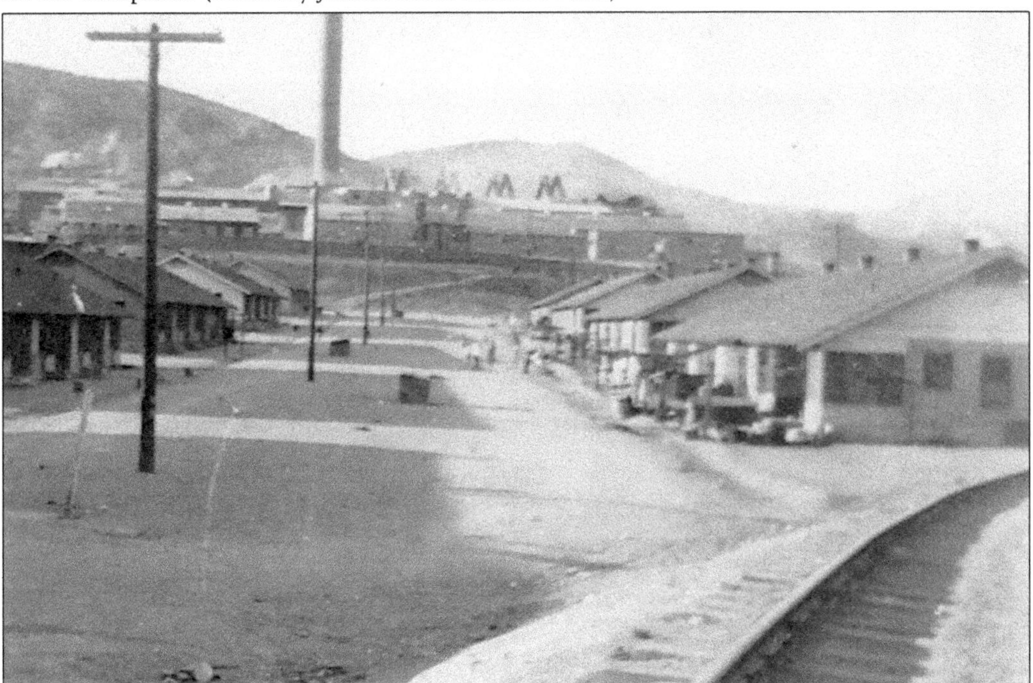

Patio Park (Fire District Seven) was the third planned and built neighborhood in Clarkdale. It became known as Patio Town. Sixteen patio-apartment complexes (each 110 by 32 feet) were built along two streets between the Verde River and the smelter. Miscellaneous structures in nearby District Six included Barragan's General Store, a dance hall, pool hall, card room, bar, swimming pool, and a small one-cell, three-bed jail. (Courtesy Jerome Historical Society Archives.)

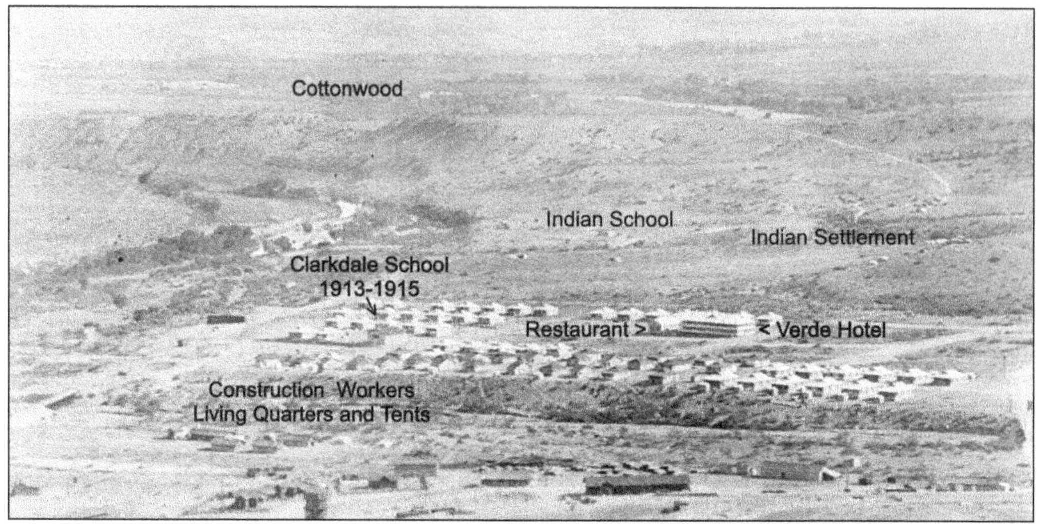

Three hundred men were employed to build Clark's town. Lower Town was built first to house the construction workers. Outside the main town, laborers and Indians occupied rent-free land. Many of the smelter construction laborers were Mexicans who ended up working in the smelter once it became operational and whose descendants live in Clarkdale today. (Courtesy C. Bohall and Robert Beltz.)

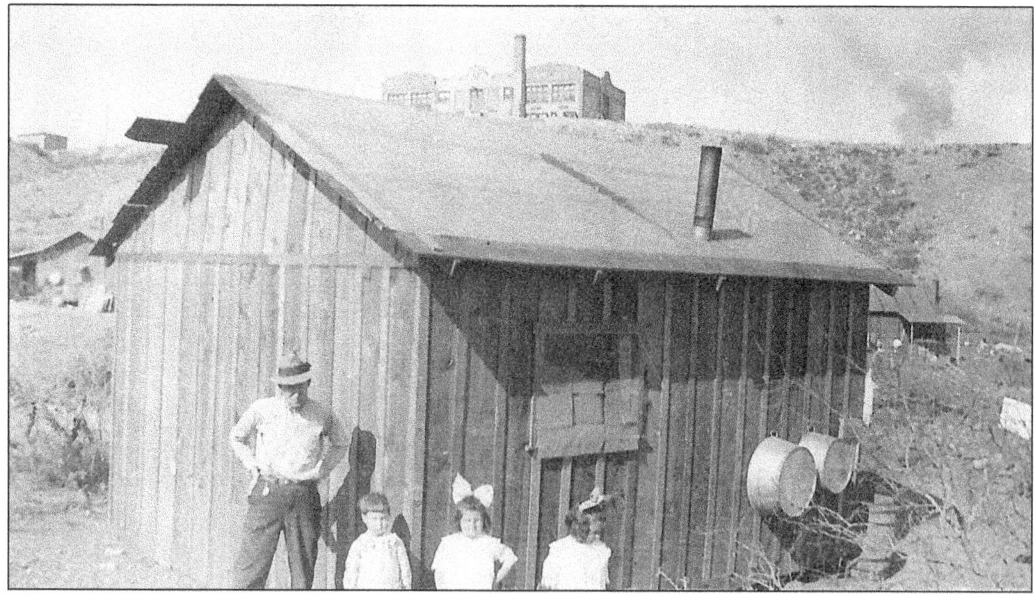

This is an example of a typical privately built house in the various neighborhoods surrounding Clarkdale's main subdivisions. The Rose home and others are located in the Butcherville neighborhood. Note the 12-grade school above and the ever-present smelter smoke in the background. During the town construction years, many workers lived in tents and temporary frame structures. (Courtesy the Rose family.)

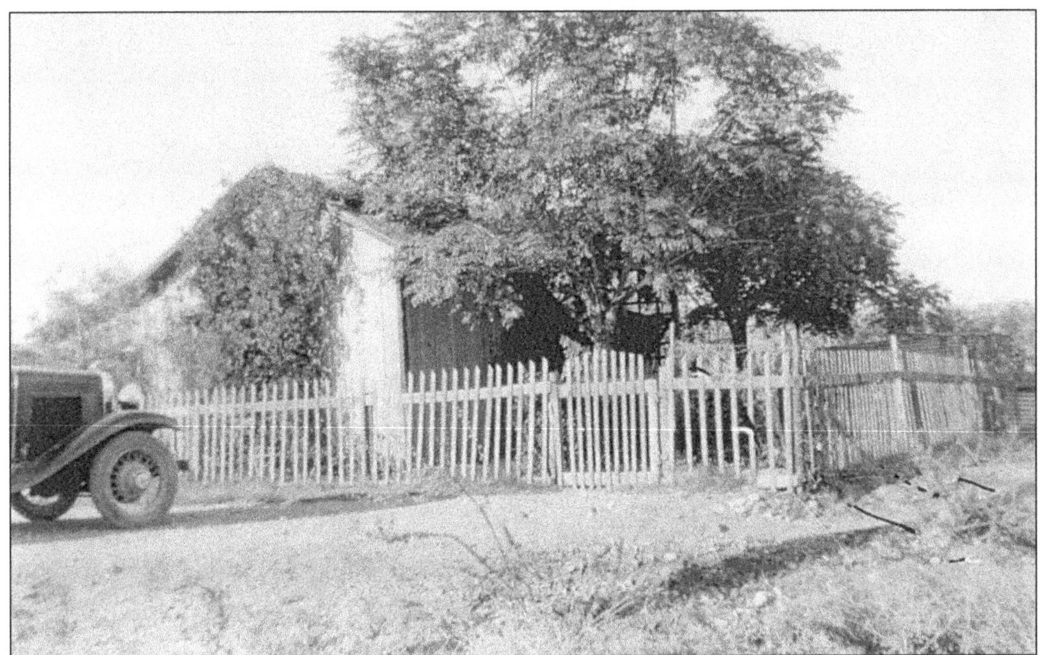

This is the Beltz home located in the Poverty Flats, or District Three neighborhood. This represents the typical wood frame homes of mining communities throughout the West during this era. Today, this home, like many of Clarkdale's historic homes (including the company brick houses) have been enlarged and remodeled inside and outside. (Courtesy Robert Beltz.)

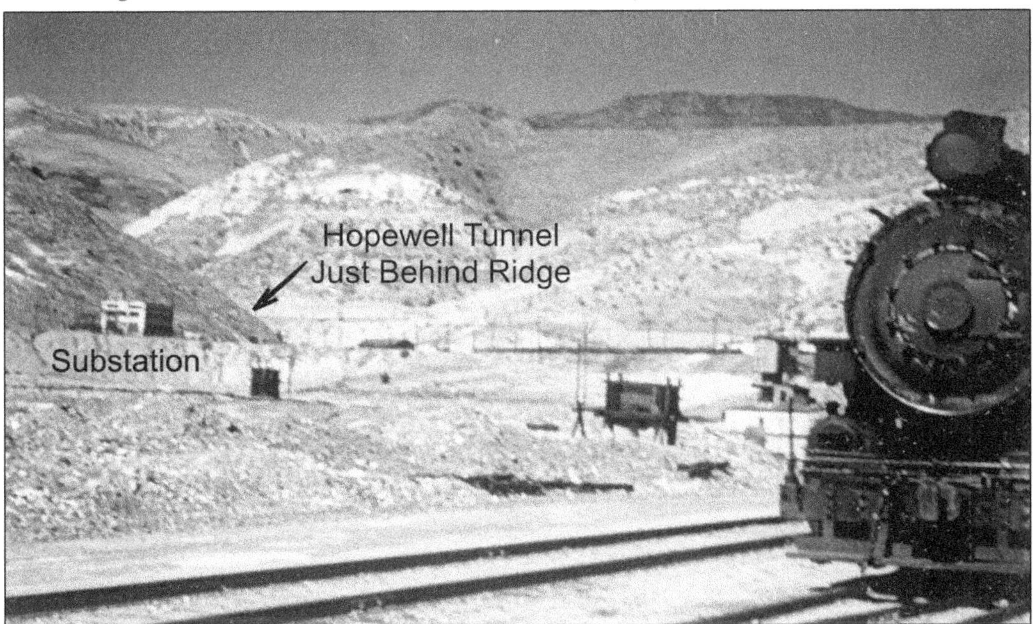

An outlying suburb of Clarkdale was constructed by the UVCC halfway between Clarkdale and Jerome at the mouth of the Hopewell Tunnel. In 1920, the community, named Hopewell, had 29 homes, a bunkhouse, a store for the 122 residents (according to the 1920 census), and a school for the children. The people of Hopewell went to Clarkdale by rail bus on the VT&S railroad, nicknamed the "Very Tired and Sleepy" railroad. (Courtesy Verde Historical Society.)

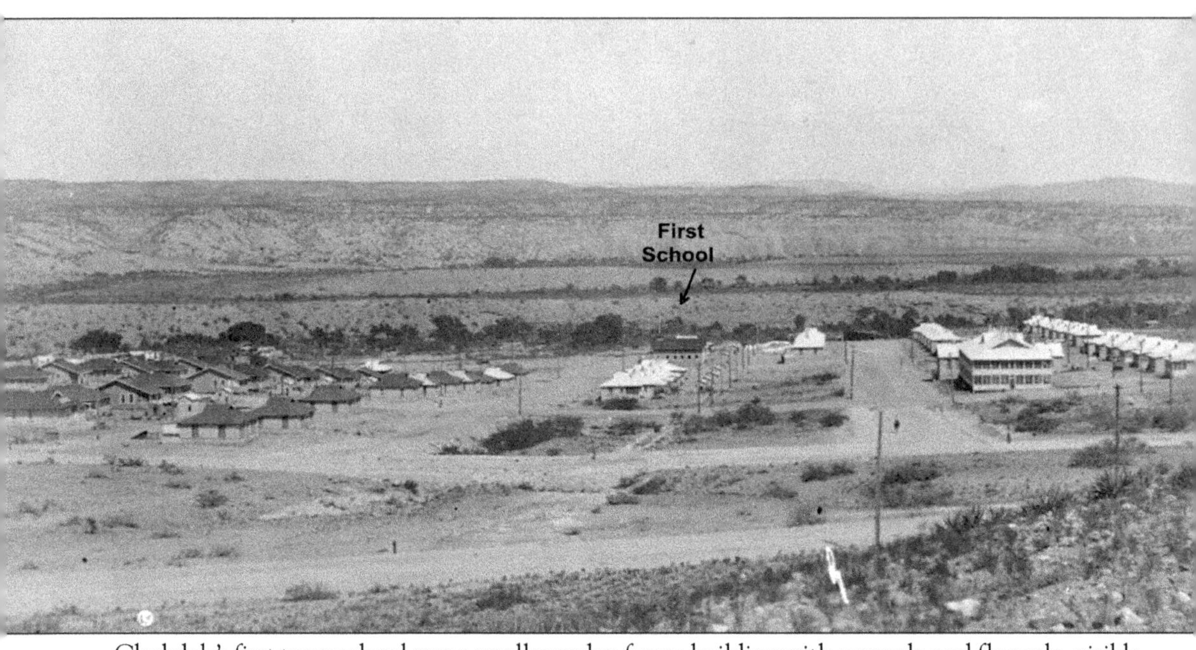

Clarkdale's first town school was a small wooden frame building with a cupola and flagpole, visible here at center with a dark roof at the end of Second North Street. It was constructed in 1913 to replace the Peck's Lake school at Second North and Fifth Street within the fast-growing part of early Clarkdale. This first school was used only two years until the 12-grade Upper Town brick school building was completed. (Courtesy Clarkdale Historical Society and Museum.)

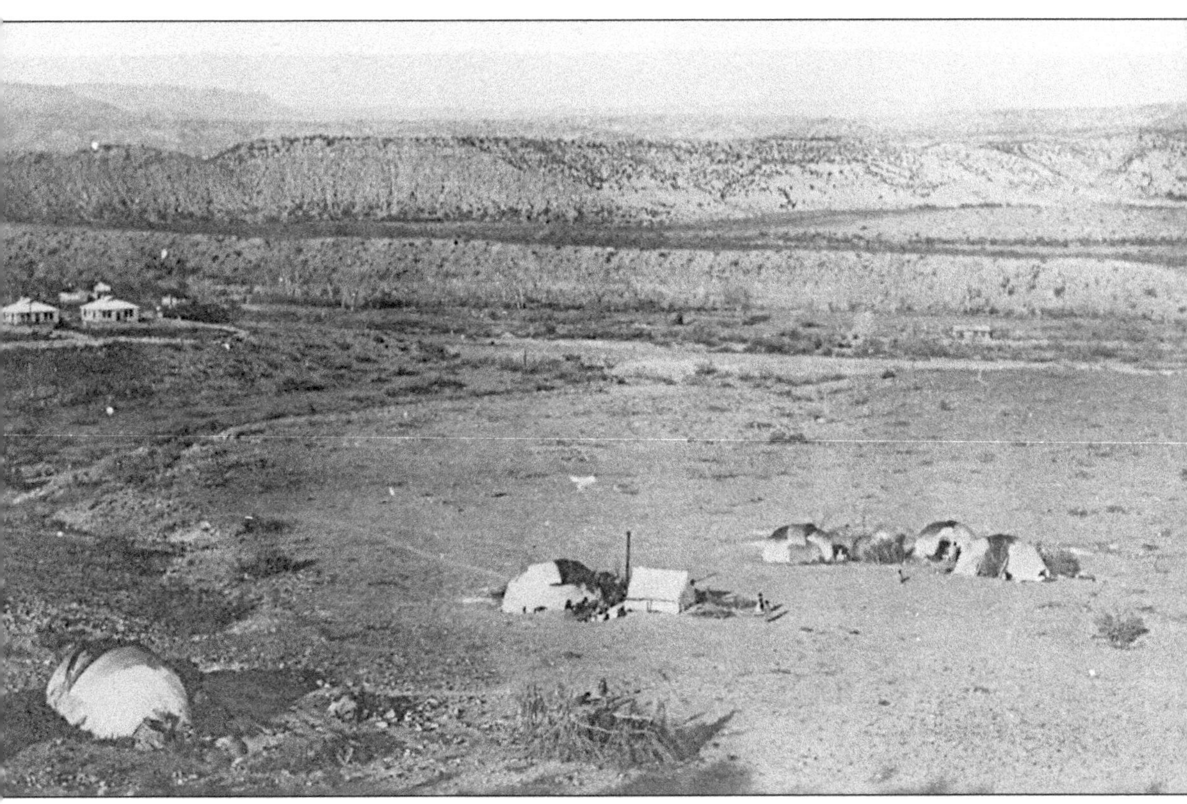

At the end of the 19th century, the Indians expelled in 1875 from the Rio Verde Reservation returned to Clarkdale after more than two decades of exile in San Carlos. Some Apache returnees established dwellings south of Clarkdale where several springs occurred between the Verde River and the Elks Lodge. Other returning Yavapais settled on land just west of Upper Town. (Courtesy John Bell Collection.)

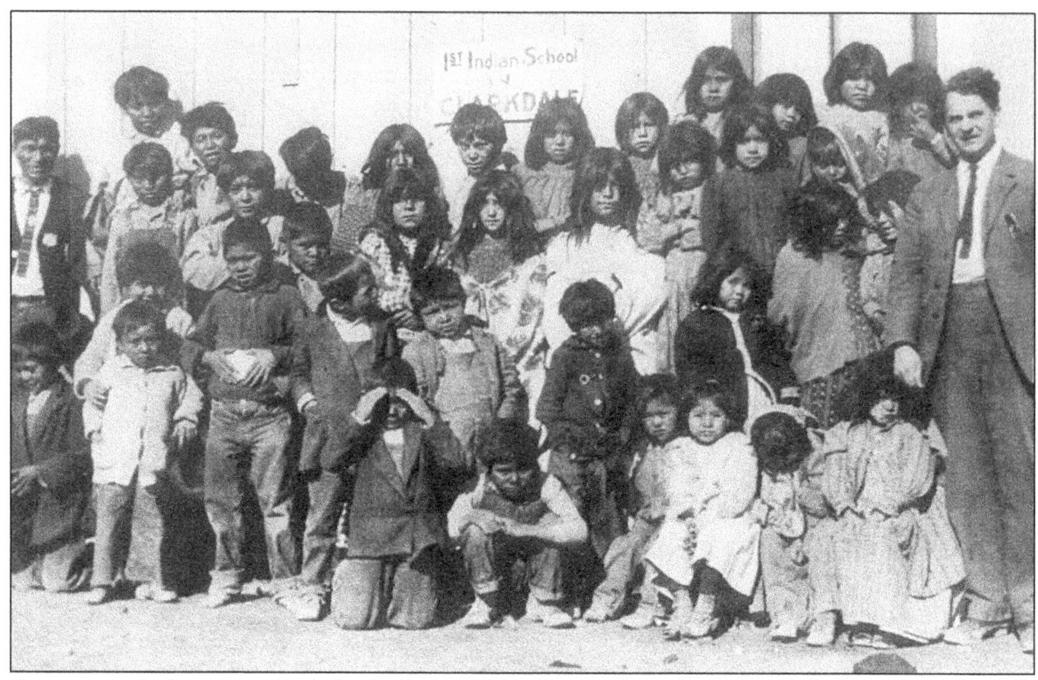

A one-room Indian day school, funded by the federal government, was established in 1914 just north of the Tuzigoot Road and south of Lower Town. This was in an area occupied by several Indian families living in tent structures. The school closed before the 1920s when the Indian children were integrated into Clarkdale's public schools. (Courtesy Clarkdale Historical Society and Museum.)

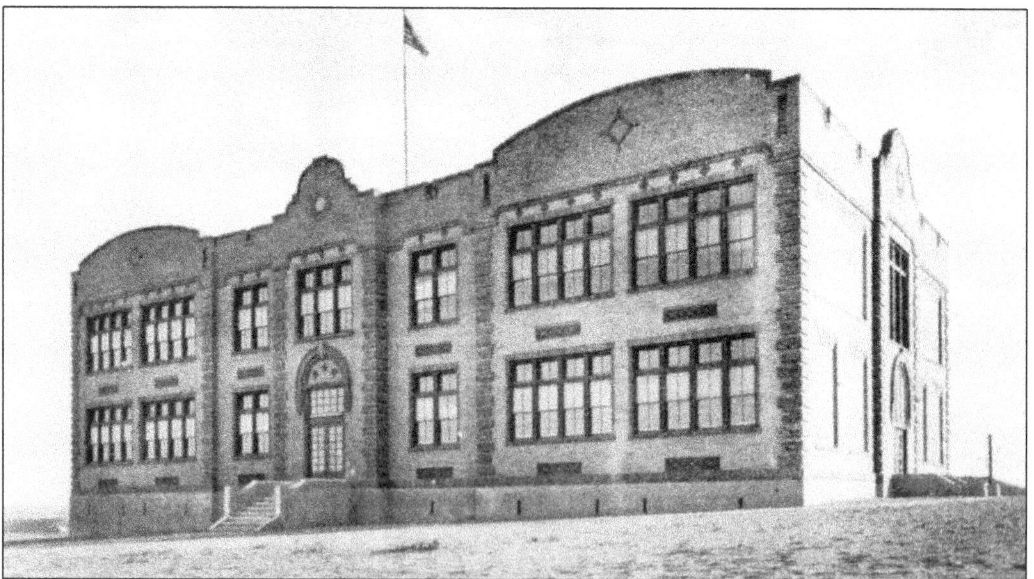

Clarkdale's first permanent school, built by the UVCC for all 12 grades, opened during the 1914–1915 school year with 110 students. This centrally located building was clad in Clarkdale's attractive multihued bricks. The playground included an outside dirt-floored high school basketball court. Following completion of the elementary school in 1924 and the adjoining high school in 1928, this building hosted grades 5–8 continuously until burning down in 1983. (Courtesy of Jerome State Historic Park.)

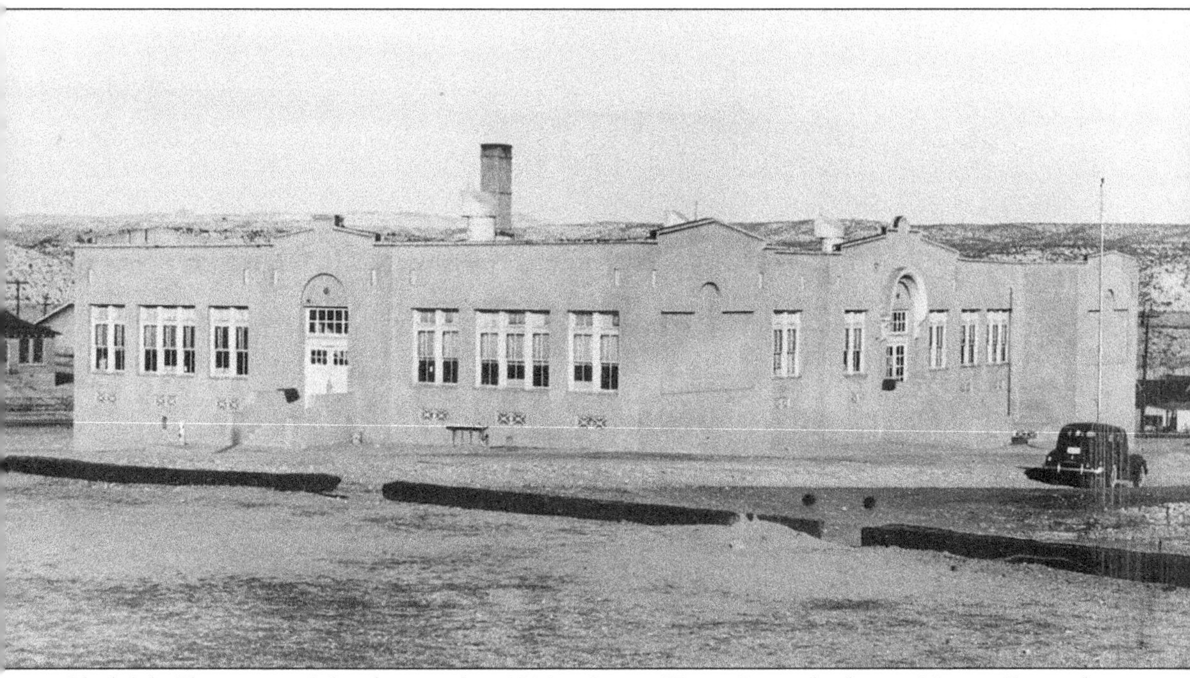

Clarkdale Elementary School opened in 1924 in Lower Town. It was built in a Mission Revival style with stucco exterior, six classrooms on the main floor, and two more below. It remained the community's kindergarten through fourth grade school until 1985. It became a privately owned commercial leasing facility. The former playground is a community ball field and park. (Courtesy Clarkdale Historical Society and Museum.)

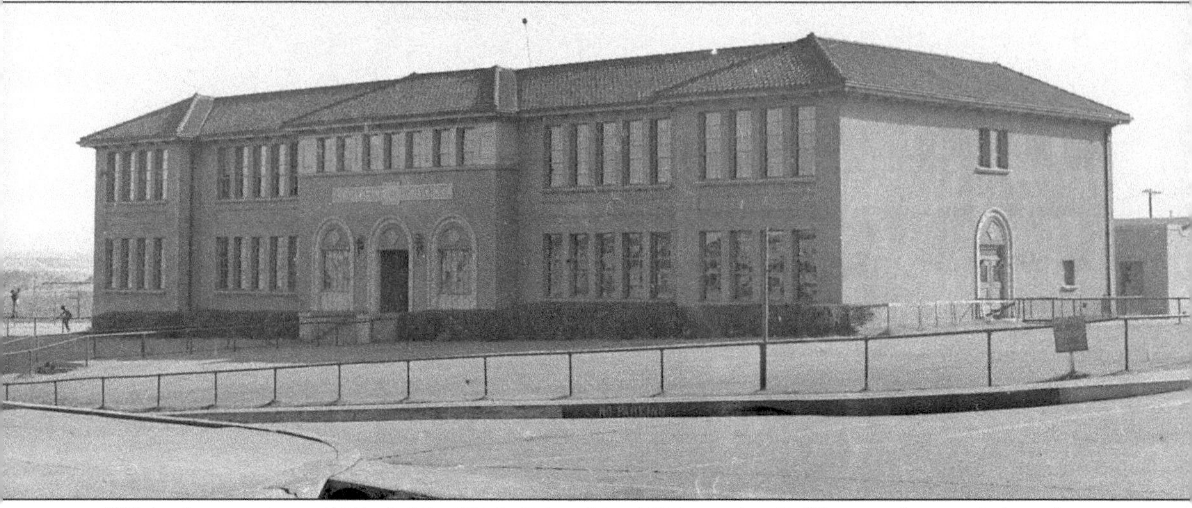

With the opening of Clarkdale High School in 1928, grades 9–12 moved out of the adjoining 1914 school, leaving that building to the middle grades. Secondary buildings were subsequently added. The stucco-clad structure held nine classrooms and a library, stage, and auditorium. All Upper Valley children, except those in Jerome, went to this high school from 1928 through 1960. (Courtesy John Bell Collection.)

Eight

1912–1953
Clarkdale Life in the Company Town

The early 20th century was a period of labor unrest nationally. Senator Clark wanted his employees to be content in Clarkdale. To this end, he built attractive, modern, utility-equipped, company-owned homes along with public facilities, commercial buildings, and recreational resources.

Clark had a reputation for keeping absolute control of his investments, and that included Clarkdale. Through hiring and leasing policies, Clark determined where employees could live based upon their white-collar or blue-collar job, nationality, and race. Owning the commercial buildings, Clark established and controlled the types of businesses and the managers through selective leasing policies.

The Clarkdale Improvement District, a UVCC subsidiary, constructed the town's buildings and houses and supported an administration office, hospital, clinic, marshal's office, jail, volunteer fire department, and recreational facilities. Commercial buildings, schools, and roads were maintained by the CID. The UVCC incorporated the UVPUC to supply water, electricity, sewage, and garbage services, and to collect rent and utility payments.

During these years, many Clarkdale men and women served in the armed forces during World War I, World War II, and the Korean War. The fatal influenza epidemic of 1918 hit the community hard, especially the Indian population. Labor unrest did come to Clarkdale in 1917, and in a strike that led to a shutdown in 1919. Residents disobeyed Prohibition along with the rest of the country. The UVCC ceased operations during the post–World War I recession of 1921–1922 and again during the Depression years of 1931–1937 that created economic hardships for Clarkdale's workers.

Clarkdale's residents were year-round outdoor enthusiasts, participating in hunting, fishing, camping, and hiking. Local schools made the first day of deer hunting season a school holiday because so many townspeople took to the hills. Fishing in the Verde River and Peck's Lake provided both pleasure and food. Youngsters hiked the hills or caught and rode the free-roaming burros or played ball in the park. Picnics from riverbanks to mountaintops were a commonly enjoyed family recreation. Sporting events, particularly the spirited school competition between the Clarkdale Wolves and the Jerome Muckers, entertained young and old.

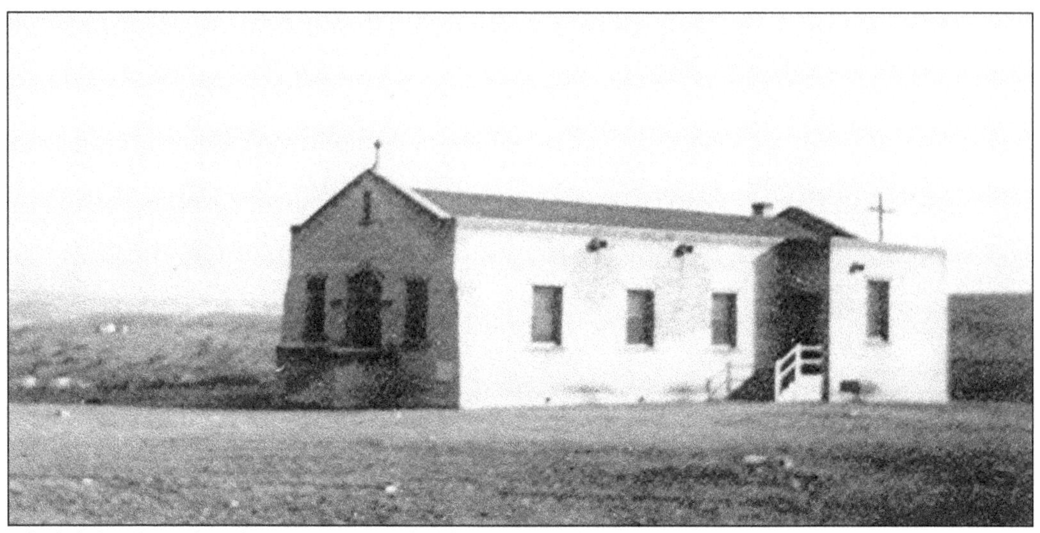

Clarkdale's first church services were held in private homes or in public rooms. Clarkdale's first church was St. Thomas Episcopal Church, completed in 1917. Clark's daughter, Mary Clark Kling, funded the Spanish mission–styled building, capped by a mine locomotive bell, in memory of her son, Gerald Kling. From 1913 until 1921, the Episcopal clergy often walked between Clarkdale and Jerome to conduct services. (Courtesy Jerome State Historic Park.)

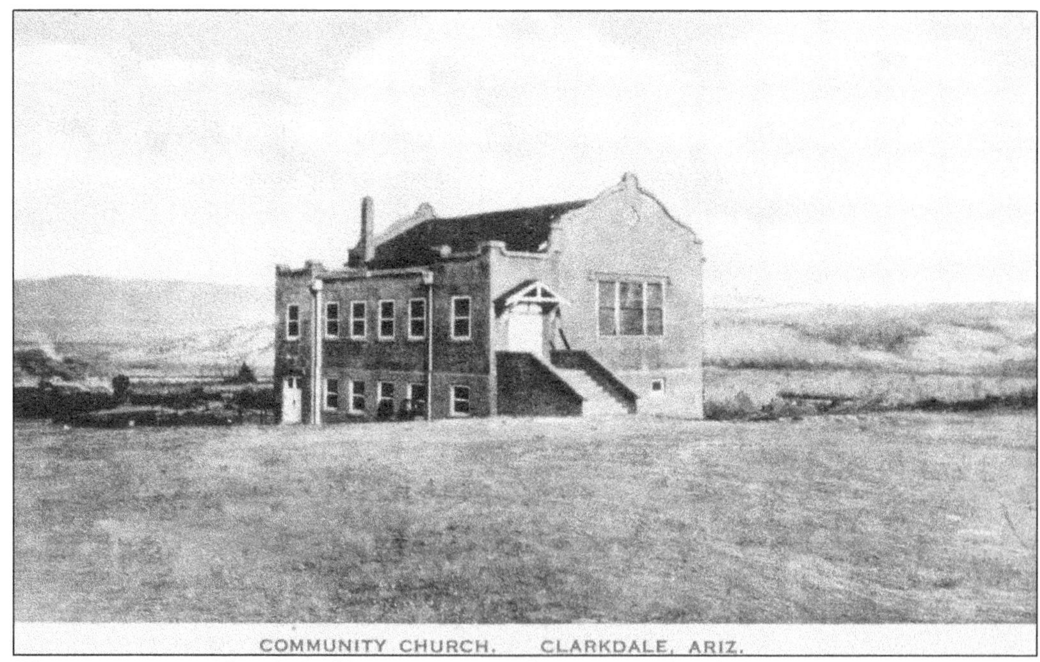

COMMUNITY CHURCH. CLARKDALE, ARIZ.

The Community Church building, constructed in 1921 with Clark family financial support, served as the Clarkdale United Methodist Church until 1990. The building's upper main floor now serves as the Town of Clarkdale's library and often presents a rotating citizen's art exhibit. The lower floor houses several town administrative offices. (Courtesy Janice Benatz.)

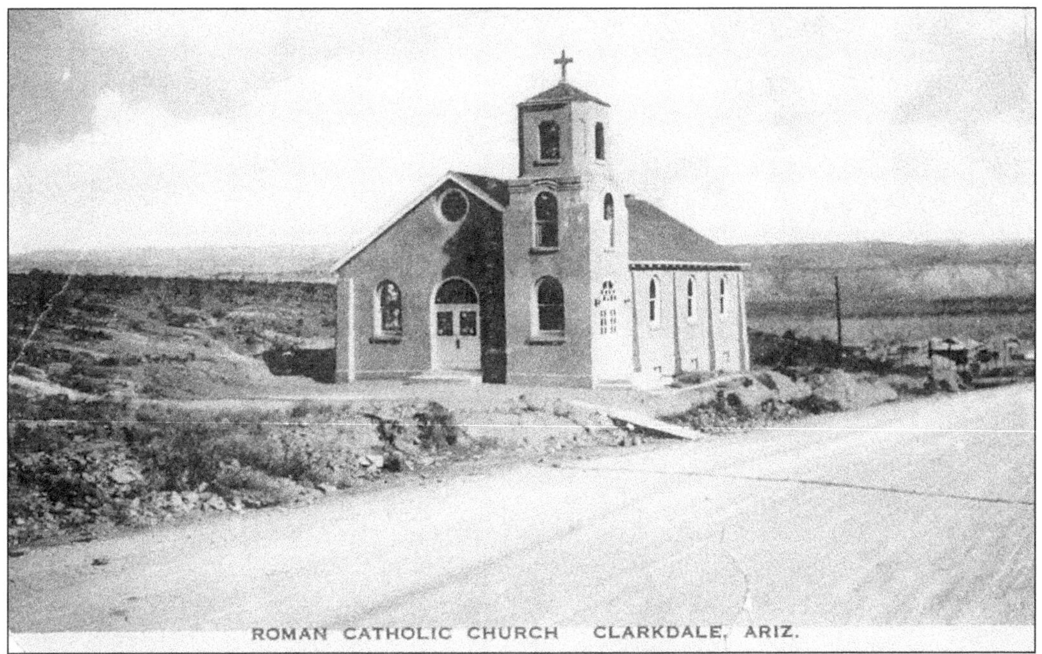

St. Cecelia's Catholic Church was built in 1920 in the mission style. Prior to this, services had been held in the town's Masonic hall. The Claretians conducted St. Cecilia's as a mission. It later became a parish, but when the mines faced closure in 1950, it again became a mission. It has been called the "White Dove of the Verde Valley." (Courtesy Janice Benatz.)

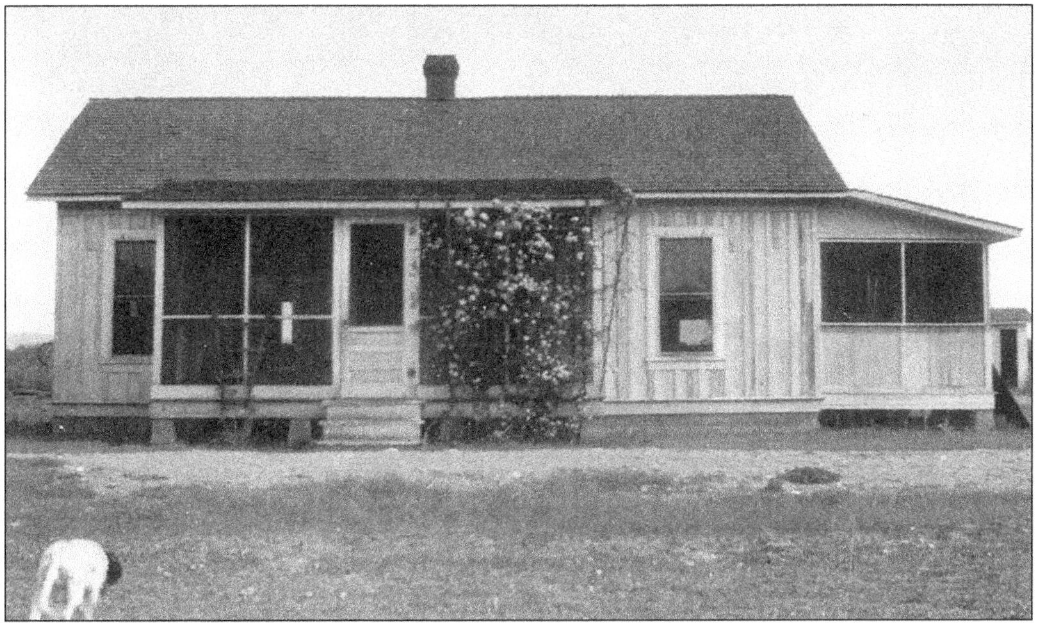

In 1923, two general meetings were held by 43 Mormons at the Tapco homes of Parley Bigelow and Edison Porter, resulting in establishment of the Jerome Branch of the Latter Day Saints. This photograph of the Moeny home shows an example of a Tapco house of that period. In 1927, the Mormons moved from Jerome to Clarkdale, where they met at Clarkdale's American Legion Hall until moving to Cottonwood in 1931. (Courtesy Tim Coons.)

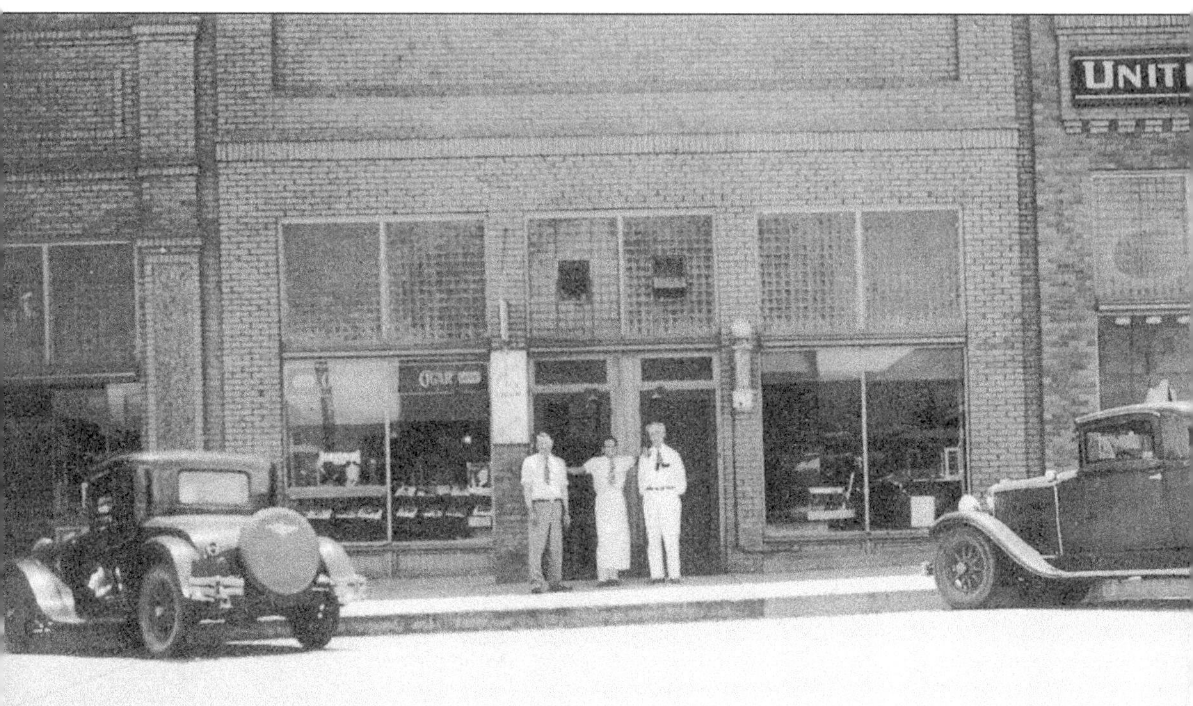

Clarkdale's early years reflect the community's diversity: 57 percent Anglo, 35 percent Hispanic, 7 percent Native American, 1 percent other. The fluctuations of Clarkdale's population through the decades relate to its up-and-down economic history: 1910 had 0, 1920 had 2,435, 1930 had 2,643, 1953 had 900, 1960 had 1,095, 1970 had 892, 1980 had 1,512, 1990 had 2,144, 2000 had 3,422, and 2013 had more than 4,000 residents. (Courtesy Janice Benatz.)

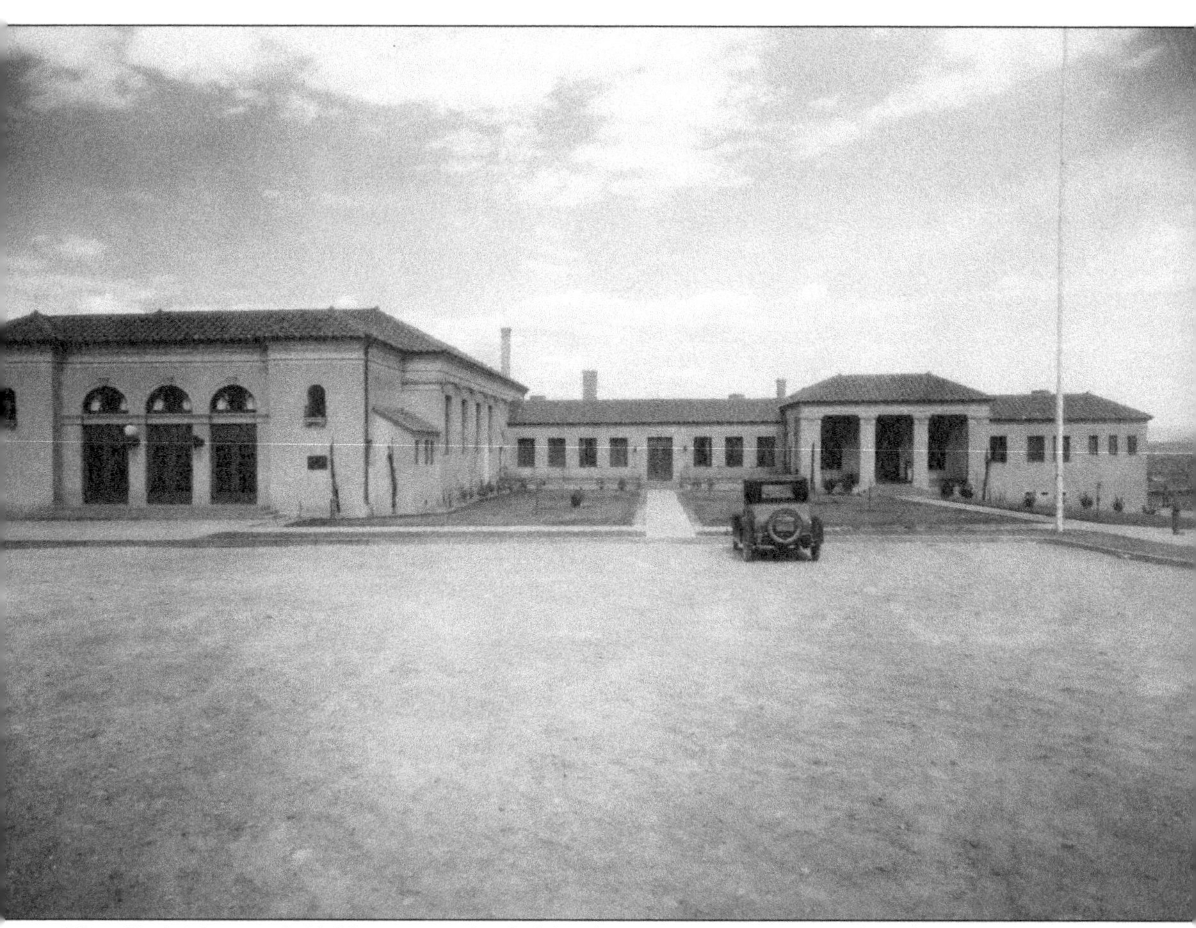

The Clark Memorial Clubhouse was funded for the community's citizens by a $100,000 bequest of Senator Clark's estate. The Clark family subsequently added another $50,000 for a swimming pool and for the special interior copper furnishings preserved there today. Since opening in 1927, it has been an important center for a variety of public activities and private gatherings. A second clubhouse was built for Patio Town residents. (Courtesy Clarkdale Historical Society and Museum.)

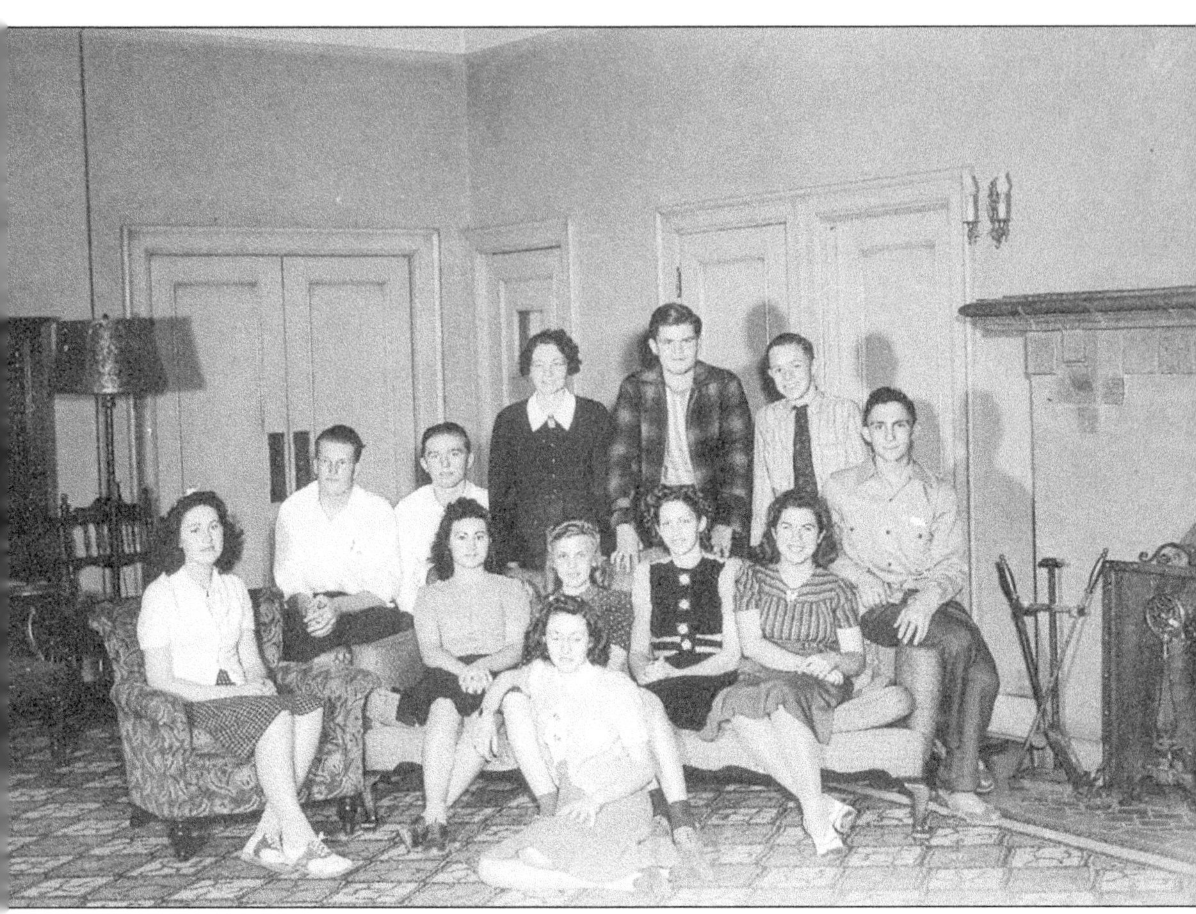

The Spanish colonial facility included a ladies' lounge, men's meeting or card room, kitchen, soda fountain, library, bowling alley, and a pool or billiards room. The 600-person auditorium and stage served as a theater, gymnasium, and voting place, and hosted music performances, dances, weddings, reunions, lectures, art exhibitions, and other events. Clarkdale's town council meetings have been held in the clubhouse for decades. The photograph shows a school English class in the ladies' lounge. (Courtesy Clarkdale Historical Society and Museum.)

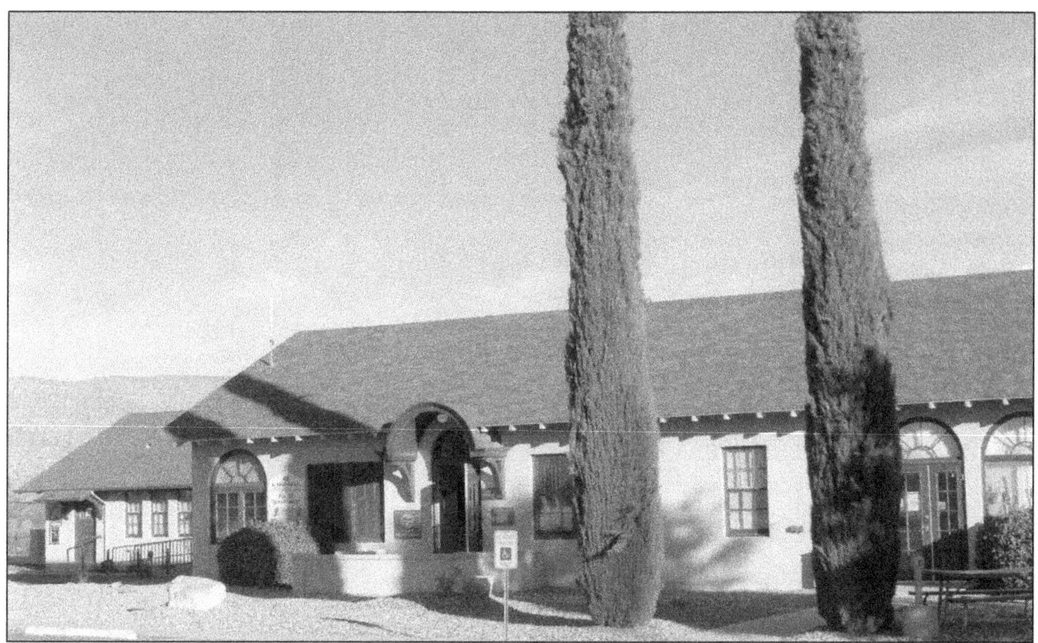

Beginning in 1919, the UVCC provided hospitalization in Clarkdale for workers and families. Employees paid a few dollars monthly for medical, hospitalization, and surgical care. Employees' families had free medical care up to $75, except for surgery charges. However, many Clarkdale children were born in their homes. In the 1930s, the building became the smelter superintendent's home, and later a family home. It is now the Clarkdale Police Department headquarters. (Author's collection.)

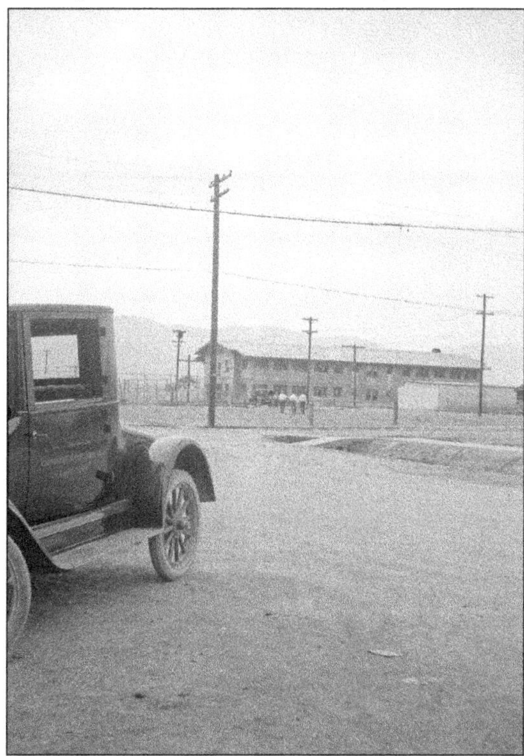

In 1919, the "dormitory" was built in Upper Town. There were 28 worker's rooms with common bathrooms in the hallways. At each hallway end was a two-room apartment with a private bathroom for visiting dignitaries. The windows had hinged sills under which, stored inside the walls, were storm windows for winter use and fabric-covered frames for summer use. The fabric in the latter was moistened for evaporative cooling. (Courtesy Sedona Heritage Museum.)

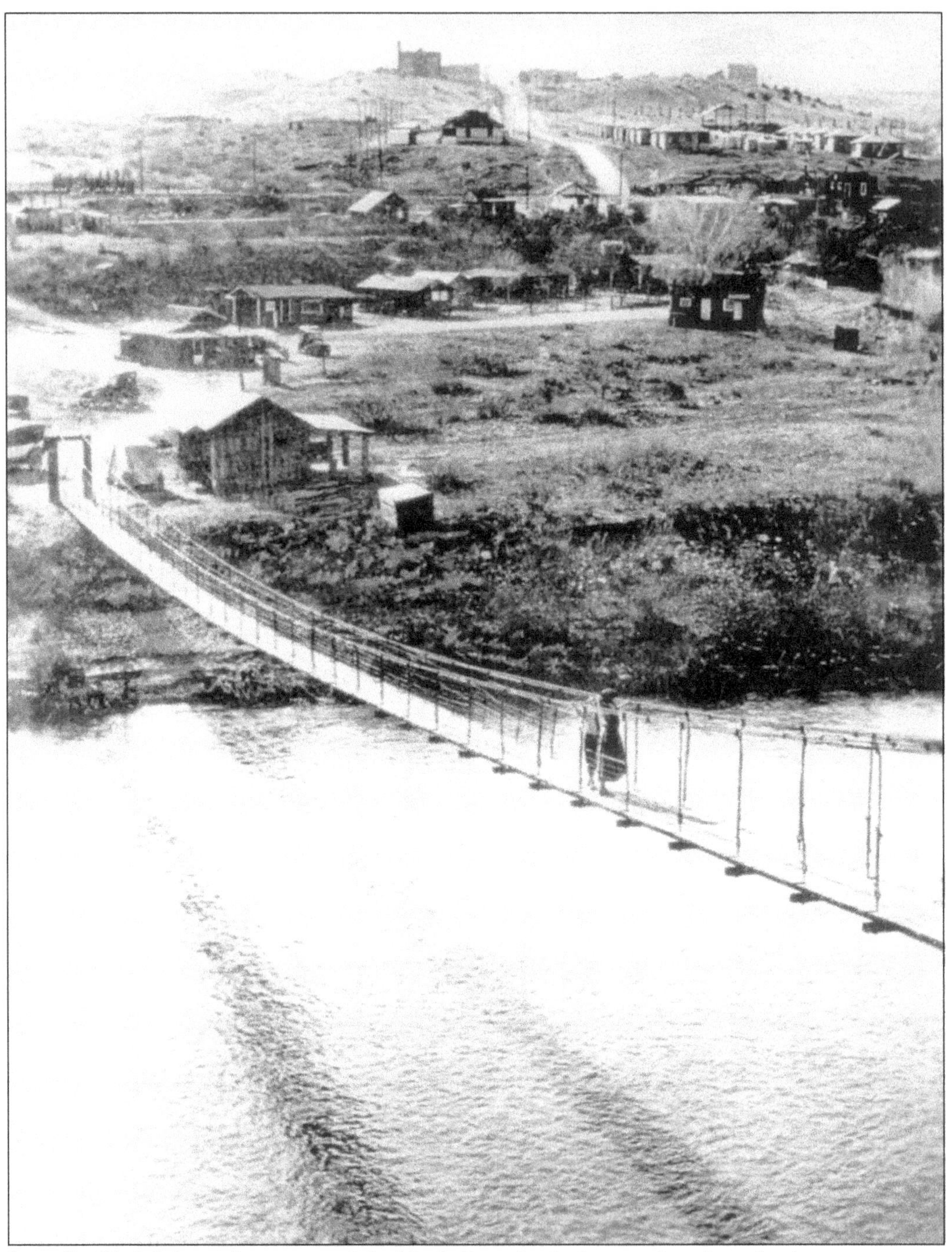

Initially, Clarkdale residents crossed the Verde River by fording on foot, horseback, or in wagons. This cable-strung walking bridge at the east end of Main Street provided people with dry and safe access to Peck's Lake at all times, especially during high water events as illustrated in the next photograph. The bridge was located in Poverty Flats. (Courtesy Jerome State Historic Park.)

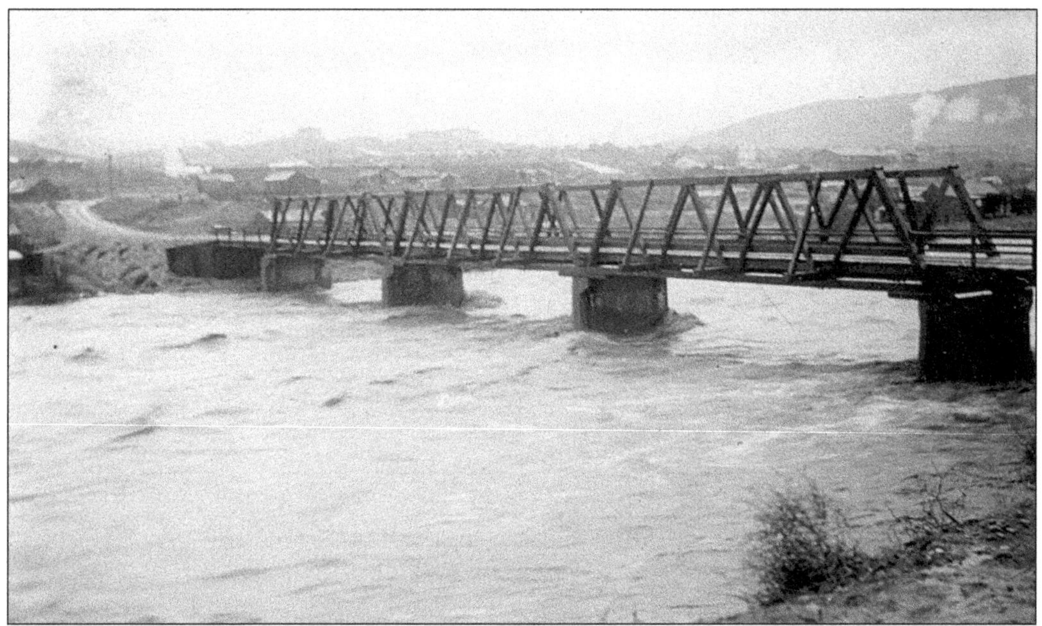

Clarkdale's first vehicle bridge, a plank-floored, single-lane structure built on concrete piers, was constructed in 1923. The bridge was used until 1966, when the Tuzigoot Road Bridge was built a few hundred yards downriver. The first bridge is preserved on celluloid in the 1947 movie *Desert Fury*, in which it has a starring role. (Courtesy Janice Benatz.)

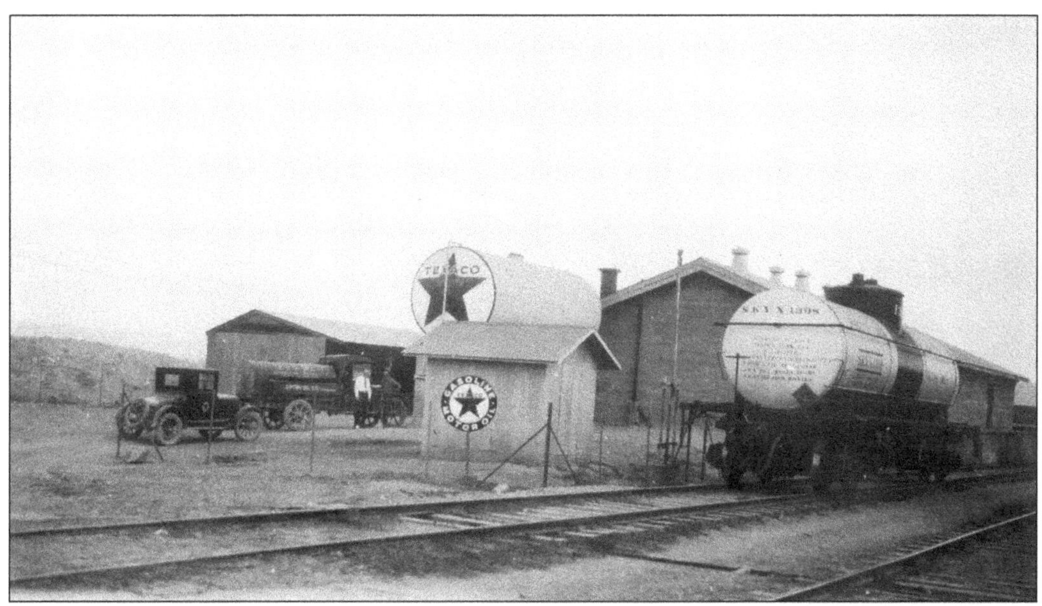

Clark gave the Atchison, Topeka, & Santa Fe Railroad money to build a 38-mile standard-gauge track from its main line at Drake to Clarkdale through the Verde River Canyon. The railroad, completed in March 1913, made Clarkdale the shipping point for outgoing metals, animal stock, and agricultural products, and the receiving hub for incoming fuels, food, general supplies, and construction materials. (Courtesy Jerome State Historic Park.)

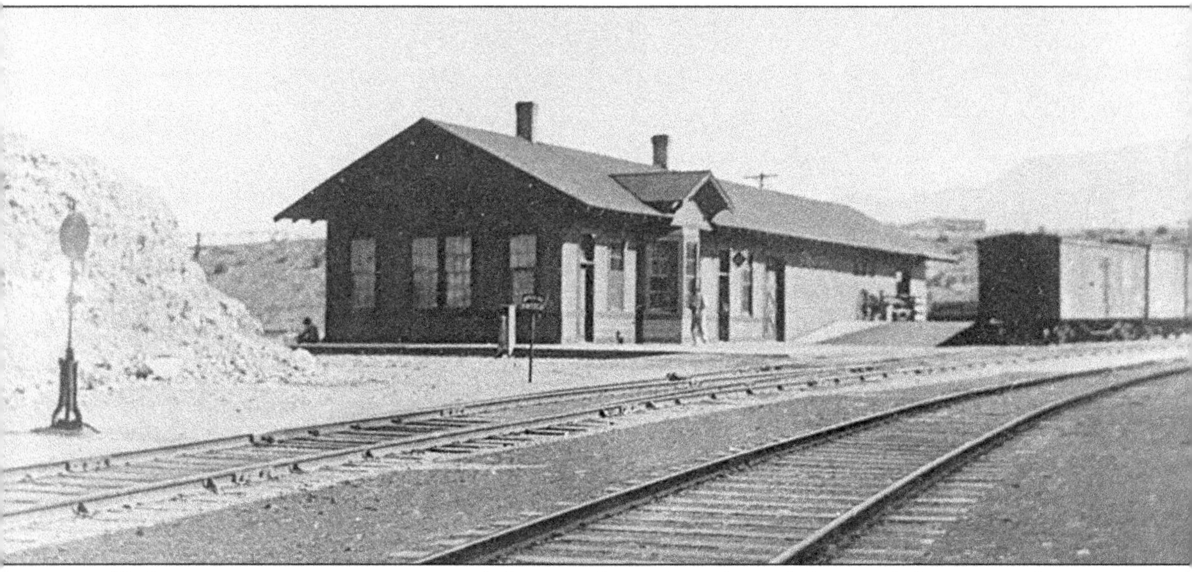

Daily train passenger service provided easy, safe, and rapid travel for people leaving and entering the then-remote Verde Valley. The railroad also provided daily excursions for the populace, including transporting youngsters up the river to swim, fish, picnic, and hike with custom delivery and pickup; it was a long hike home if you missed the pickup time. (Courtesy JB.)

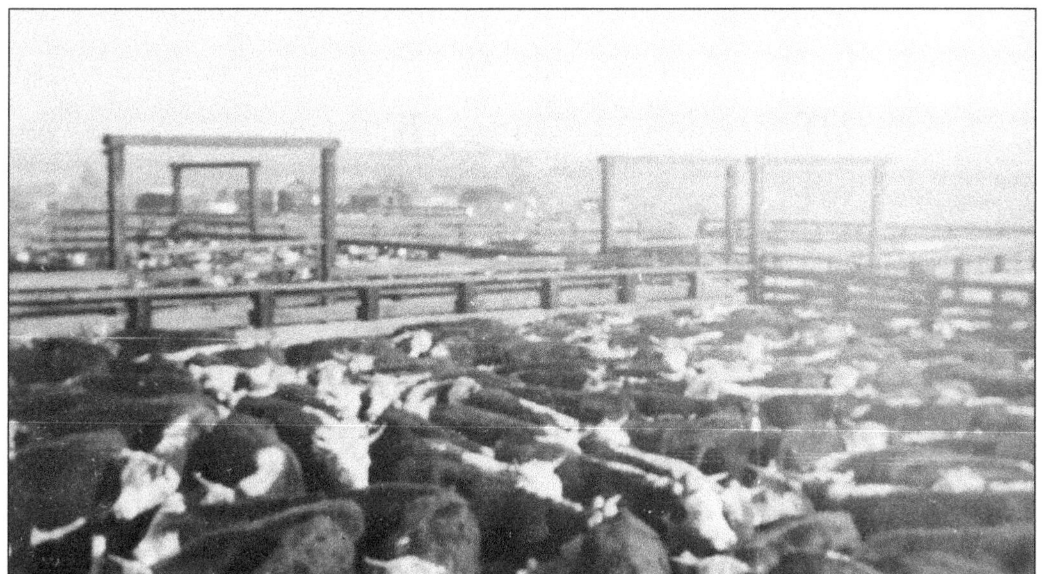

Verde Valley ranchers conducted cattle drives from the open range to the Clarkdale stockyard. A single rancher might herd a thousand head or more on one drive. Any winter shipments went through snow-free Clarkdale as opposed to Flagstaff. Tens of thousands of Verde Valley cattle were shipped out of Clarkdale's stockyard to the nation's markets. Residents would go down to see the excitement of the drives entering the stockyard. (Courtesy Jane Goddard.)

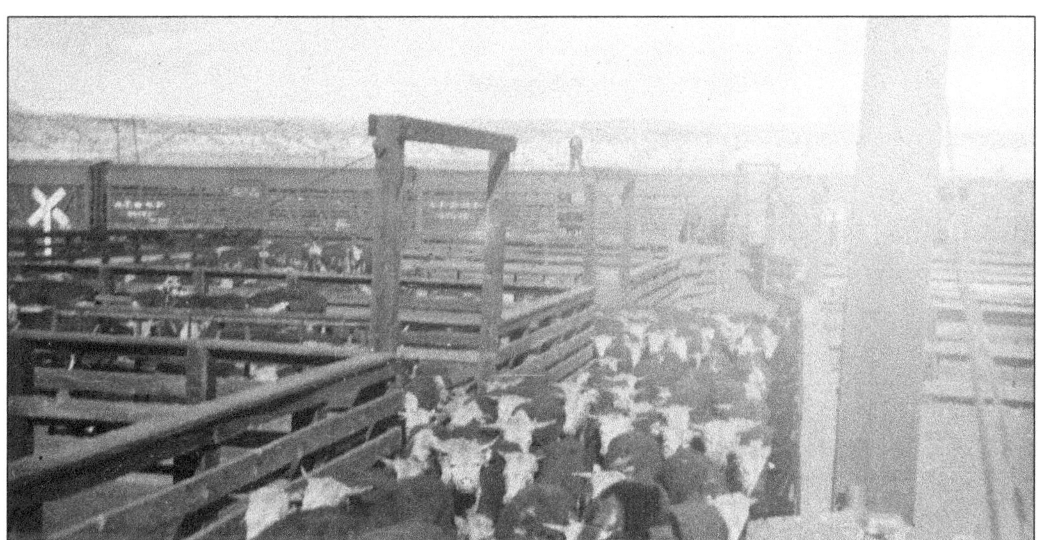

The stockyard was located alongside railroad tracks between Clarkdale's District Three and Tuzigoot Road. Cattle for local use were butchered in nearby aptly named Butcherville, just west of the stockyards. Most of the meat for the Upper Valley markets was prepared at the Jerome Meat Packing slaughterhouse halfway up the Clarkdale–Jerome main road that was the west extension of Clarkdale's Main Street. (Courtesy Jane Goddard.)

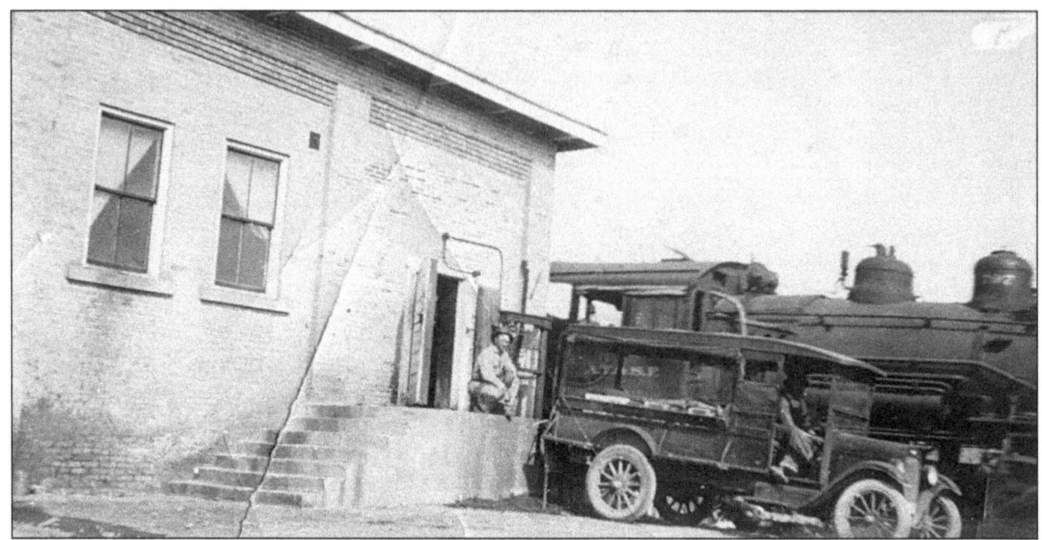

The UVCC built an ice plant with road and railroad access beside Bitter Creek below Upper Town. The plant produced 25 tons of ice daily in the summer and 5 tons daily in the winter. The VT&S railroad shipped ice daily to Jerome. It was delivered in Clarkdale by truck. J.A. Son, who lived next to the plant, leased the operation. (Courtesy Clarkdale Historical Society and Museum.)

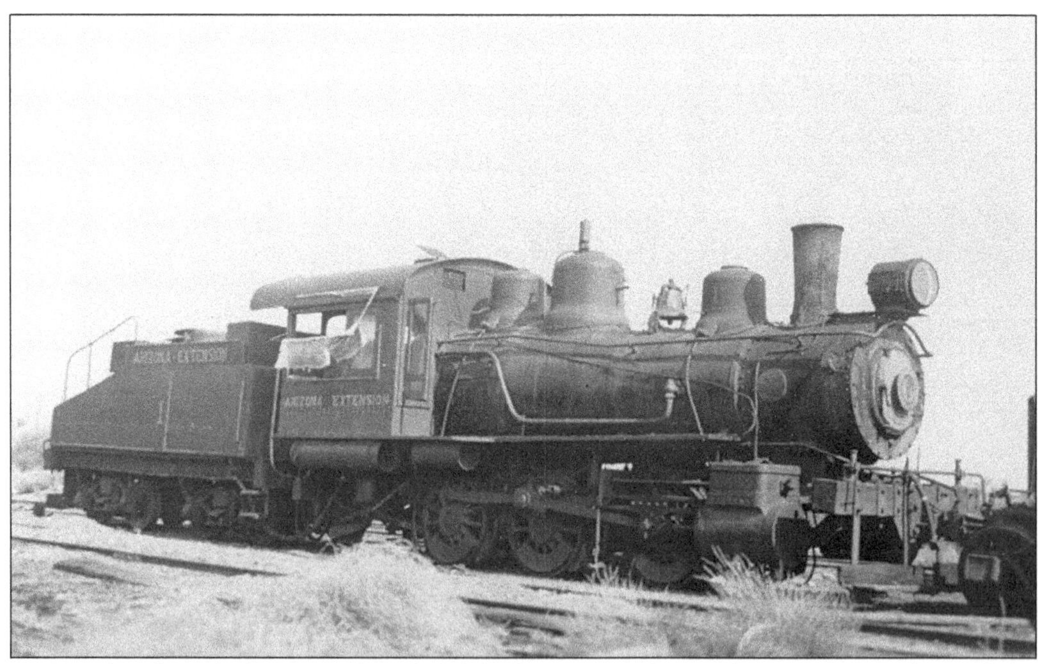

UVX railroad tracks began at the Clarkdale depot, passed near the Tuzigoot Bridge and the Clarkdale Moose lodge, and terminated at the Clemenceau smelter. This line hauled in the Clemenceau smelter's fuel mined from UVX coalmines in Gallup, New Mexico, and shipped out the copper anodes for the final electrolytic refining process. (Courtesy John Bell.)

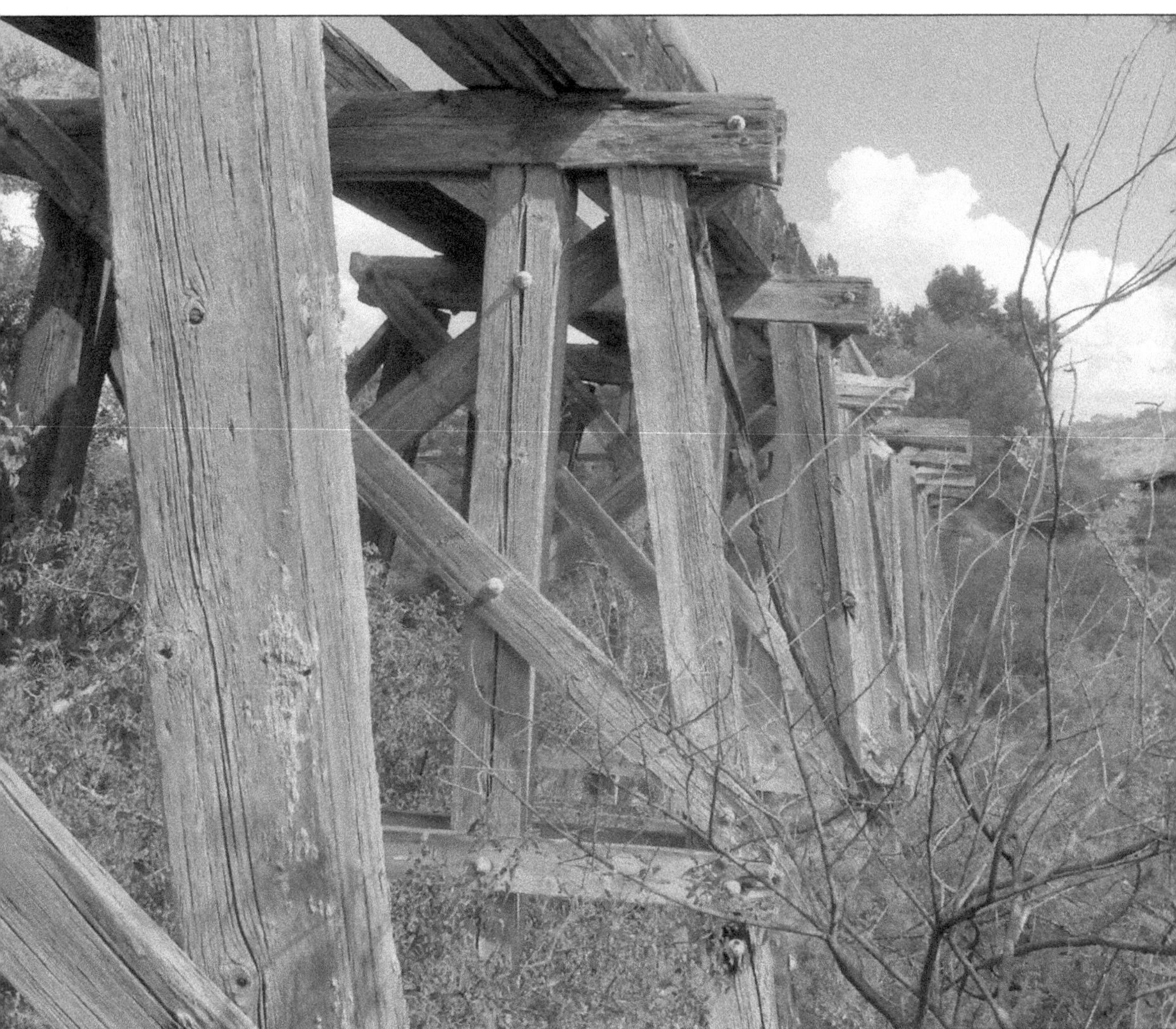

The UVX mine in Jerome closed in 1937 after 23 years of mining exceptionally rich copper ore. These trestle timbers supported a bridge across Bitter Creek used by the UVX ore-hauling railroad that ran from the Jerome mine's 1300 level through the Josephine Tunnel to the Clemenceau smelter. The slag used as track ballast, wood scraps, and rusted water pipes identify the abandoned track location across Clarkdale today. (Author's collection.)

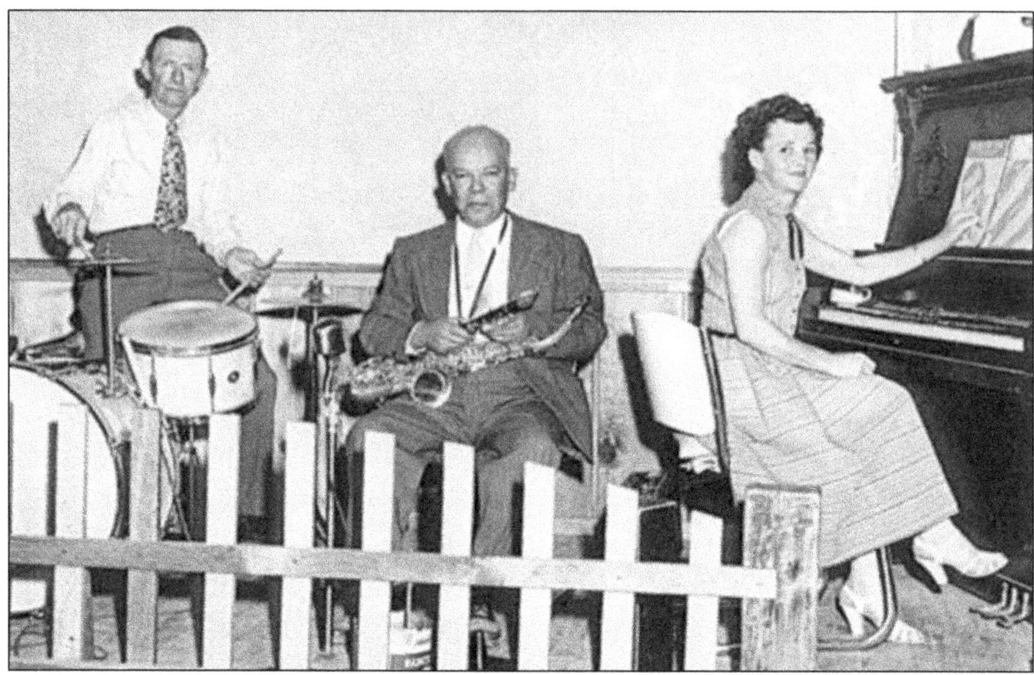

Clarkdale's residents were enthusiastic about dancing, an activity supported by the UVCC. In 1942 R. Duffey, utilities manager, heard the Moores (from left to right: Marshall, Perry Moore, and Petie Moore) playing in Flagstaff and hired them to come to Clarkdale. The UVCC put them in a company house, where they lived out their lives playing dances known for their smooth style. Petie continued playing into the 1960s with the local Lakesider's Band. (Courtesy James and Dinah Gemmill.)

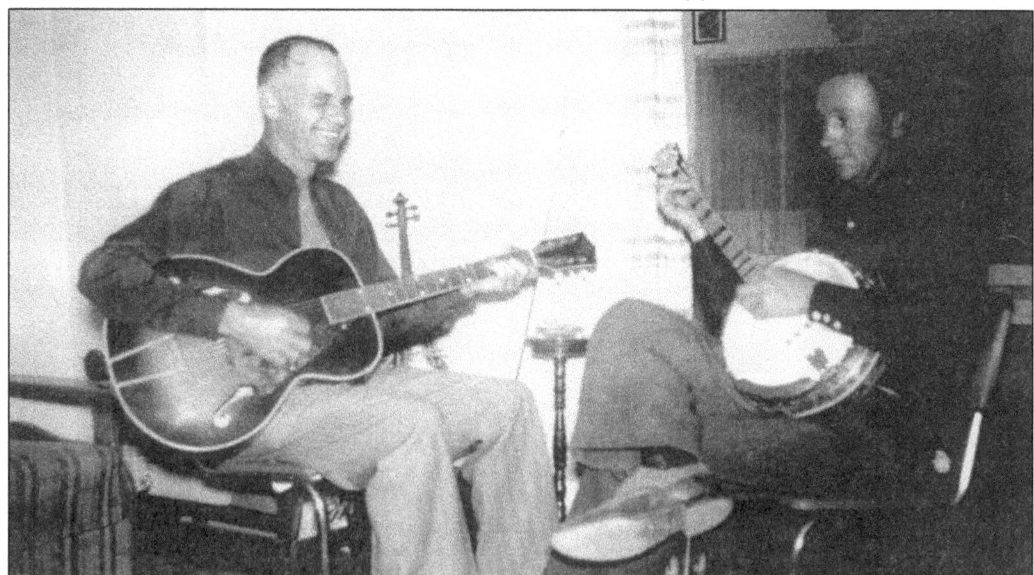

The Arizona Sand Pickers was composed of Clarkdale residents. Carl Beltz was the caller and fiddle player, Evan Derrick strummed the banjo, and Ben Kane picked the guitar. In addition to playing square dances throughout the Verde Valley, they had a weekly radio show on Jerome's radio station, KVRD. Clarkdale's enthusiastic dancers would go out of town to dances as far as Mormon Lake and the Prescott-Dewey area, arriving back home at 3:00 a.m. (Courtesy Bob Beltz.)

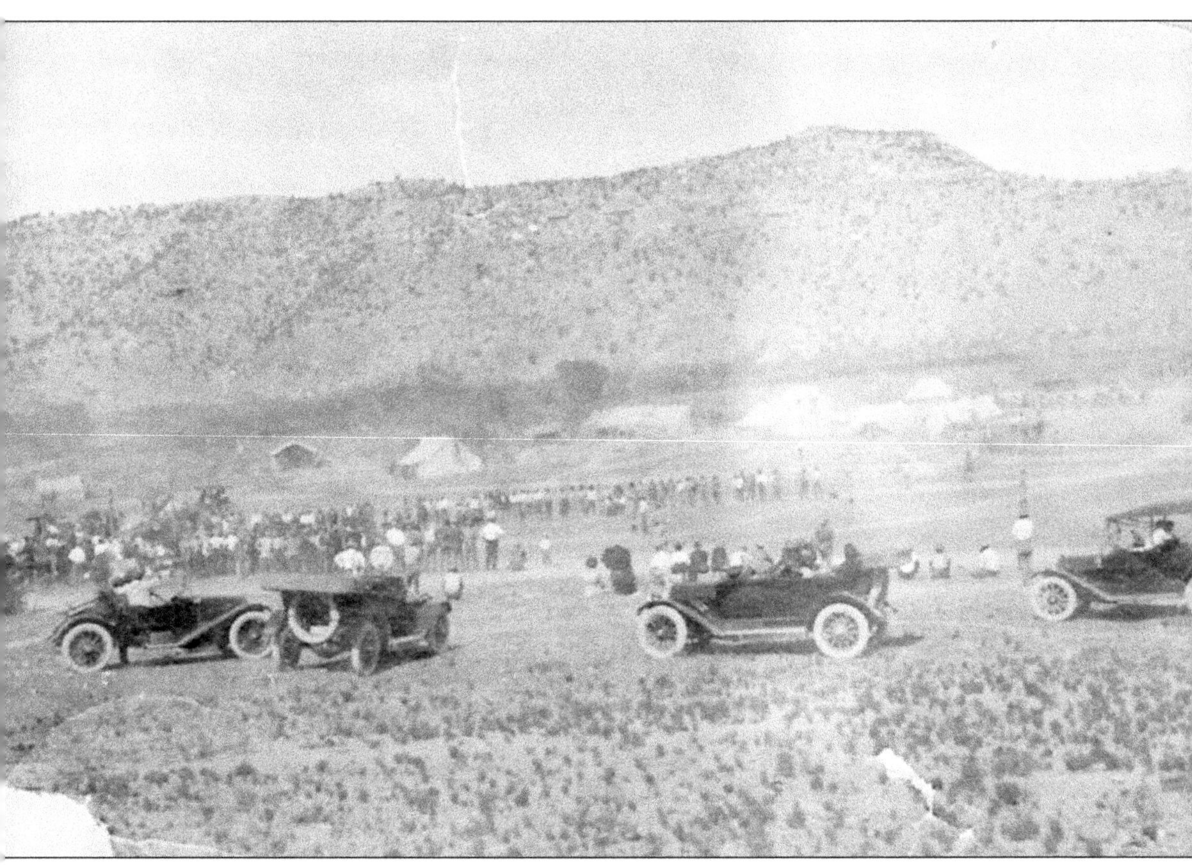

In 1913, with construction of the town just beginning, Clarkdale played a baseball game with Jerome beside the smelter site next to the river. This began a half century of Clarkdale's smelter teams and Jerome's mine teams competing in many sports and events. To win, both communities soon began hiring professional and college athletes for their teams. This was the time when baseball was played in about every town in America. (Courtesy Robert Love.)

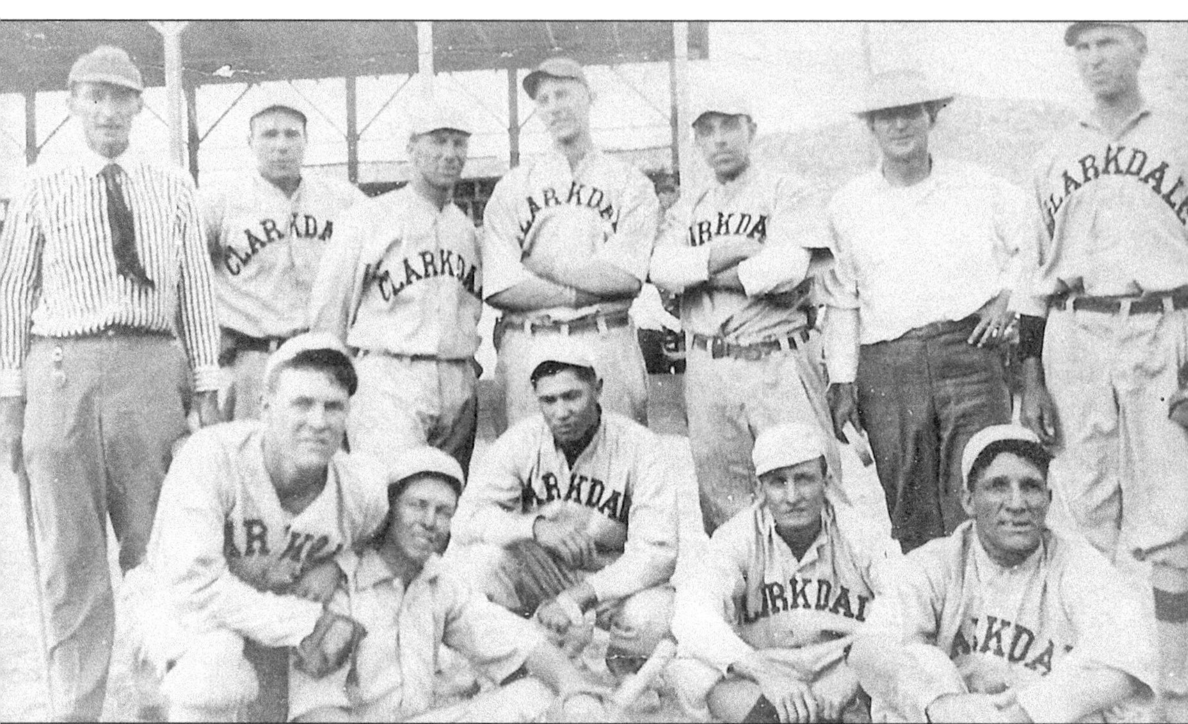

Pictured here is the Clarkdale semi-pro baseball team subsidized by the smelter in the 1920s. Other Clarkdale sporting facilities during the smelter days included a football field, an outdoor basketball court, a boxing ring, tennis courts, horseshoe pits, a bowling alley, pool and billiard facilities, a shooting range, a golf course, and swimming pools. Peck's Lake provided swimming, shaded picnic facilities, boating, fishing, children's swings, seesaws, and a merry-go-round. The lake provided a spectacular setting for Fourth of July fireworks. (Courtesy L. Best)

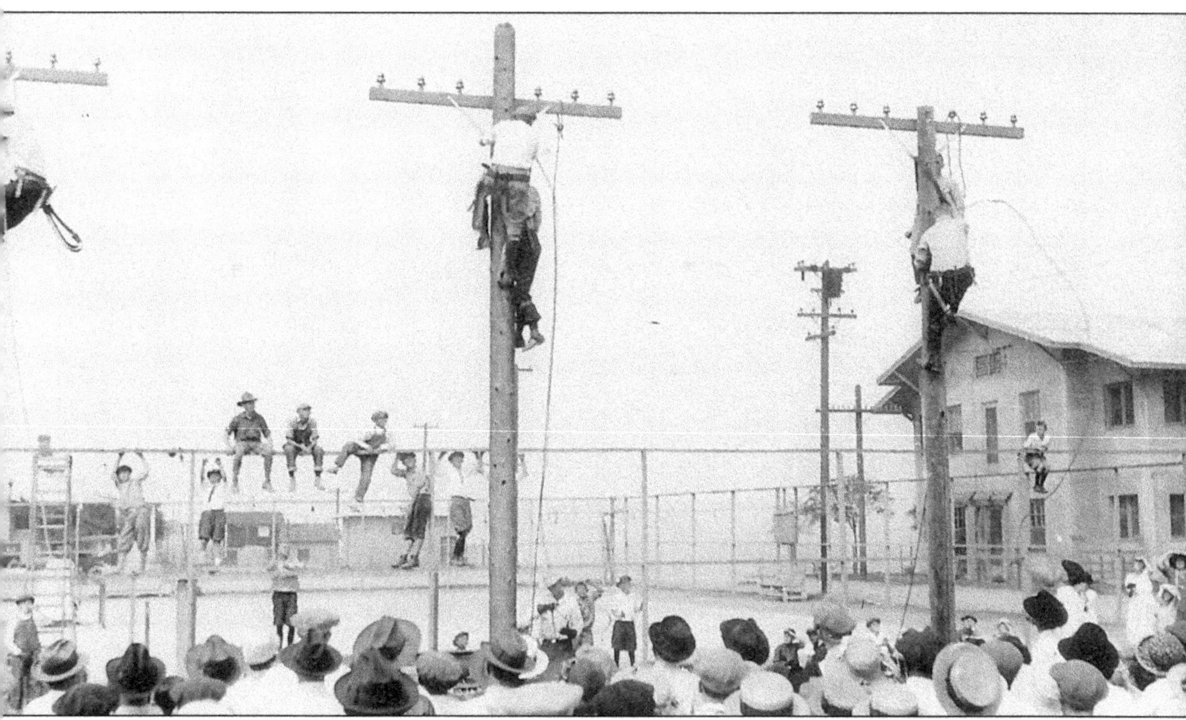

The rivalry between Jerome and Clarkdale expanded beyond the conventional sports arena into workplace contests, including emergency rescues, firefighting skills, hand drilling, and ore shoveling (mucking) competitions. This photograph shows a contest on the Clarkdale tennis courts between the mine electricians and the smelter electricians rescuing a simulated electrocuted lineman. (Courtesy K. Cannon.)

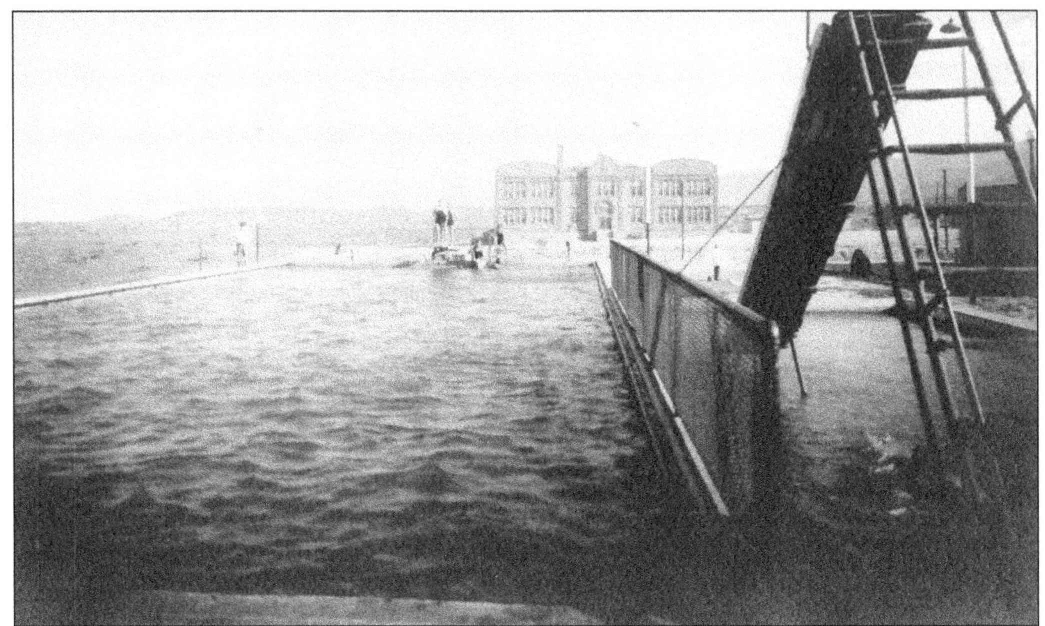

Residents of all ages enjoyed swimming in the swimming pool, reportedly Arizona's first in-ground pool, located behind the Clark Memorial Clubhouse. There was a second swimming pool in lower town for the Hispanic population. Red Cross swimming lessons were an annual summer event at both pools. Tennis on the four courts in Upper Town was enjoyed by residents of all ages. (Courtesy Clarkdale Historical Society and Museum.)

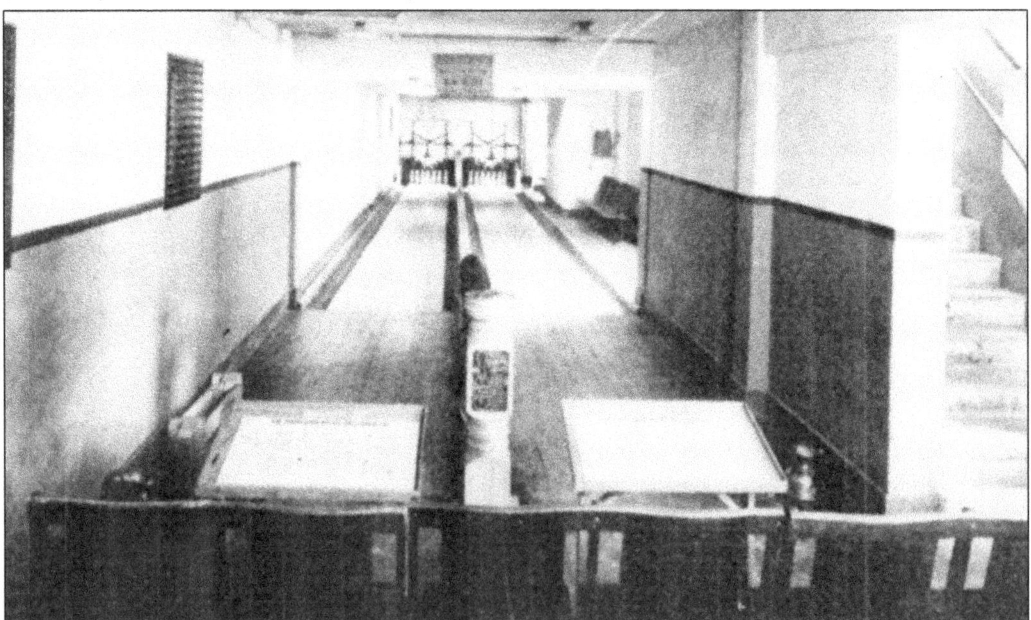

A major activity was bowling in the four-lane alley in the basement of the Clarkdale Memorial Clubhouse. There were men's and women's leagues, with some bowling activity scheduled every day. Sundays were reserved for tournaments against other towns' teams. Many teenage boys earned money as alley pinsetters. Poker and bridge card games were popular among the local citizens as well. (Courtesy Clarkdale Historical Society and Museum.)

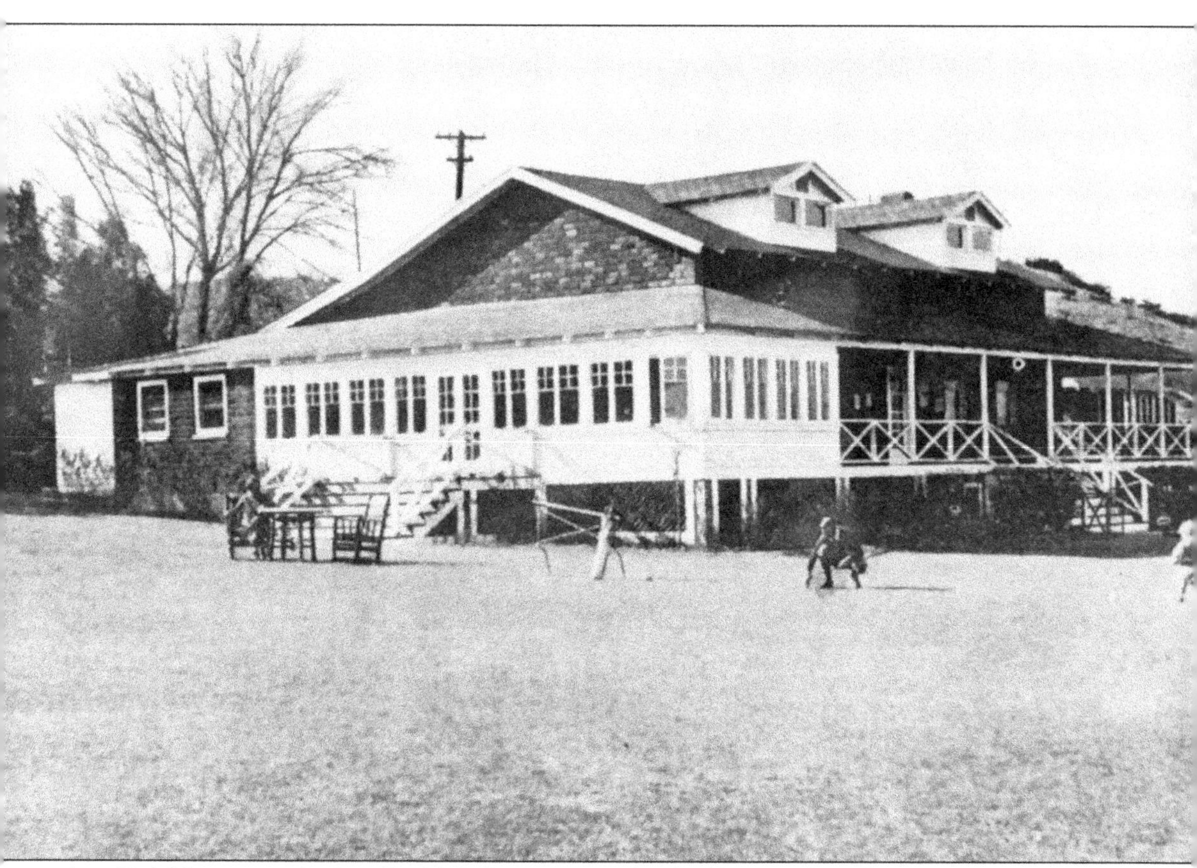

A golf clubhouse was built at Peck's Lake in 1922. This building, with its lounge, dining room, kitchen, and locker rooms for men and women, became the social center for many families for decades. In 1924, the picturesque 3,193-yard Verde Valley nine-hole course, Arizona's second golf course, was developed around Peck's Lake. This challenging course was where the Arizona State Golf Association championships were held in 1925 and 1929. (Courtesy John Bell Collection.)

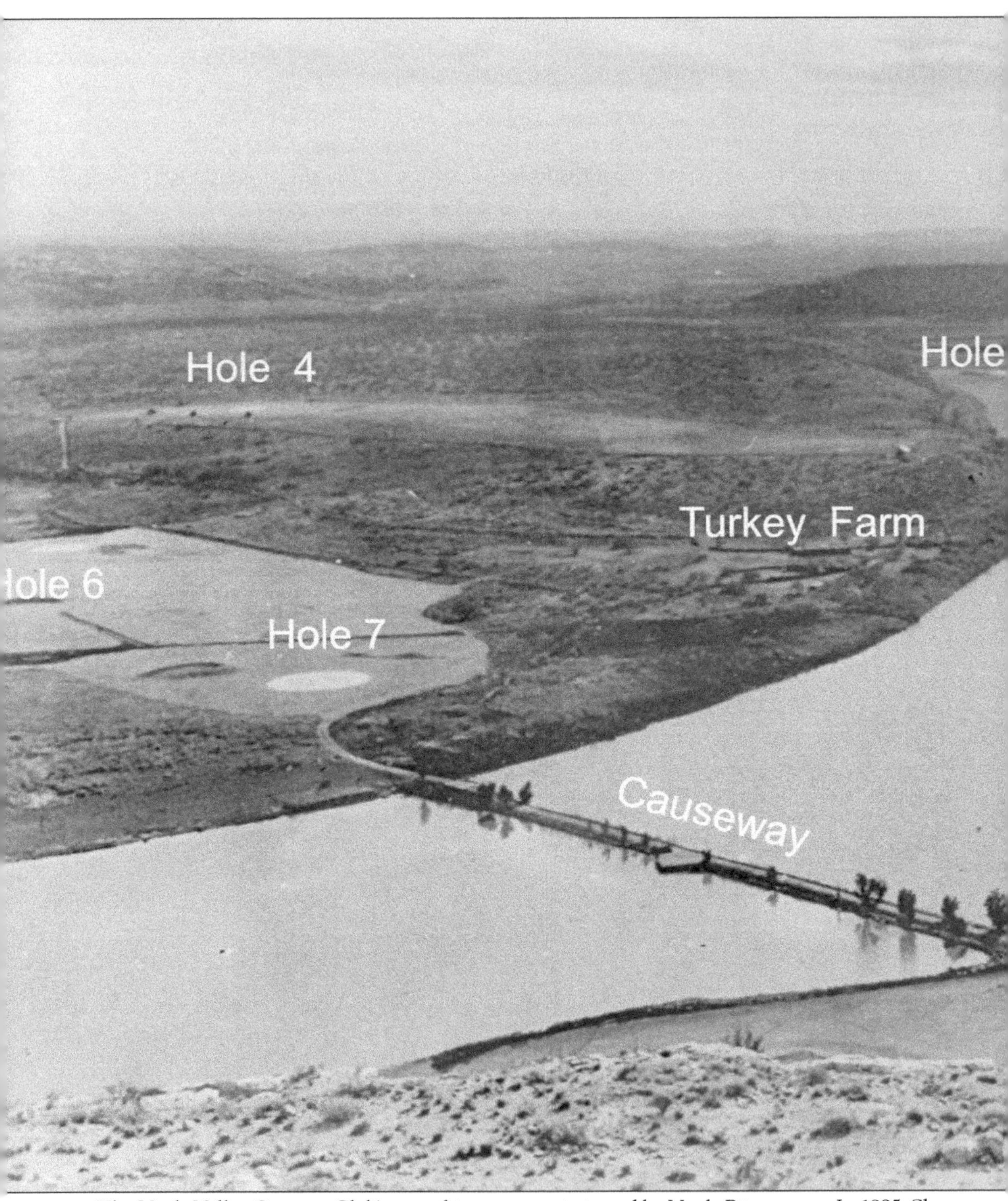

The Verde Valley Country Club's grass fairways were irrigated by Verde River water. In 1895, Shea, Rich, Brewer, and O'Keefe constructed a 475-foot-long, four-by-six-foot tunnel to deliver Verde River water to the Peck's Lake agricultural properties by pipelines, flumes, and ditches. Three decades later, the golf course became the beneficiary of some of this water. The surplus overflow resupplied Peck's Lake and continues to do so today. Peck's Lake provided this golf course with

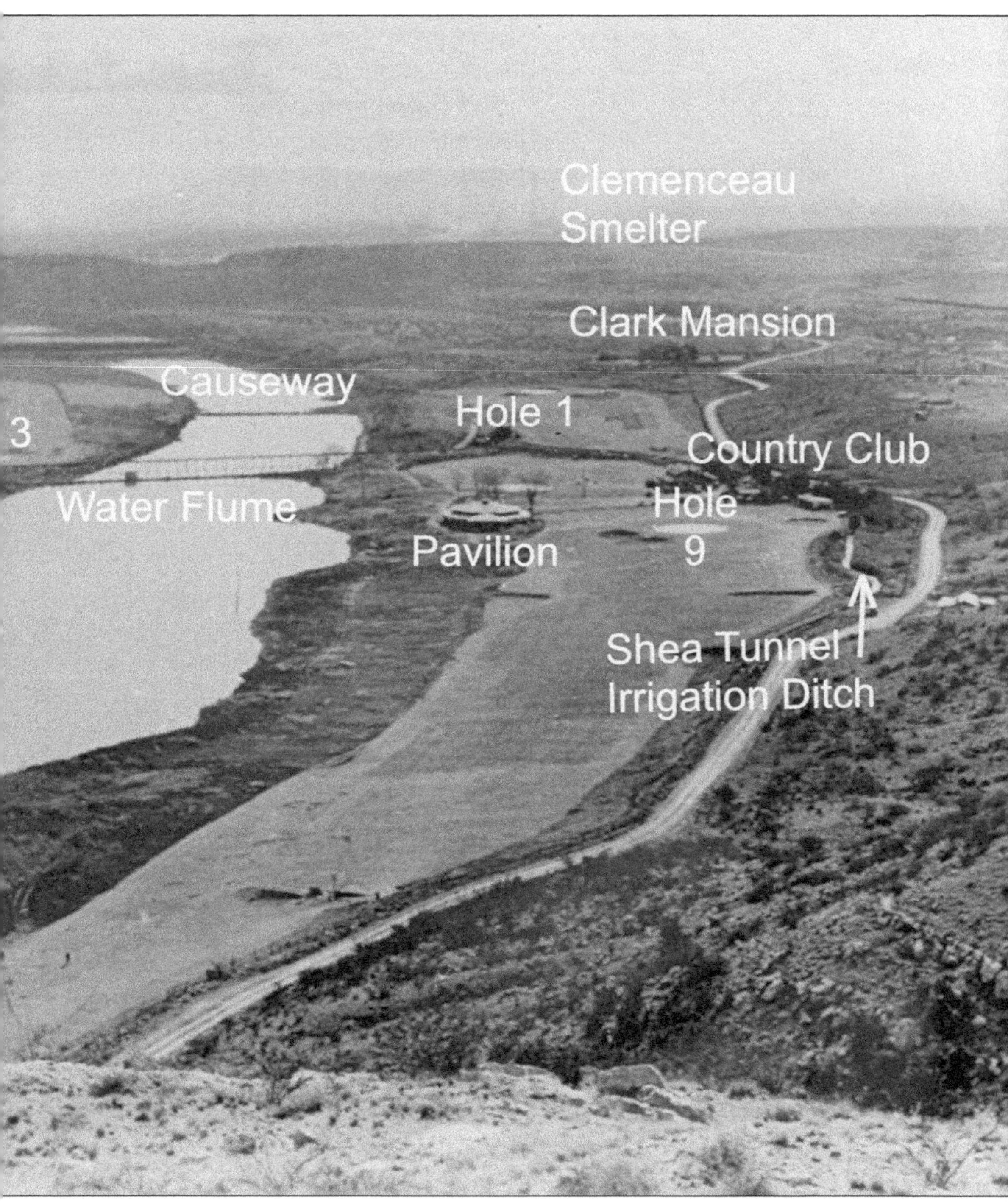

Arizona's only natural water hazards on two holes. The hilly course was scenic in its setting of mountains, cliffs, and the lake. In 1921, a secret Peck's Lake "recreation" activity was discovered deep within the Shea tunnel—a liquor still in a chamber excavated above the roof timbers over the four feet of running water. This was just one of many moonshine stills shut down around Clarkdale during Prohibition. (Courtesy John Bell Collection.)

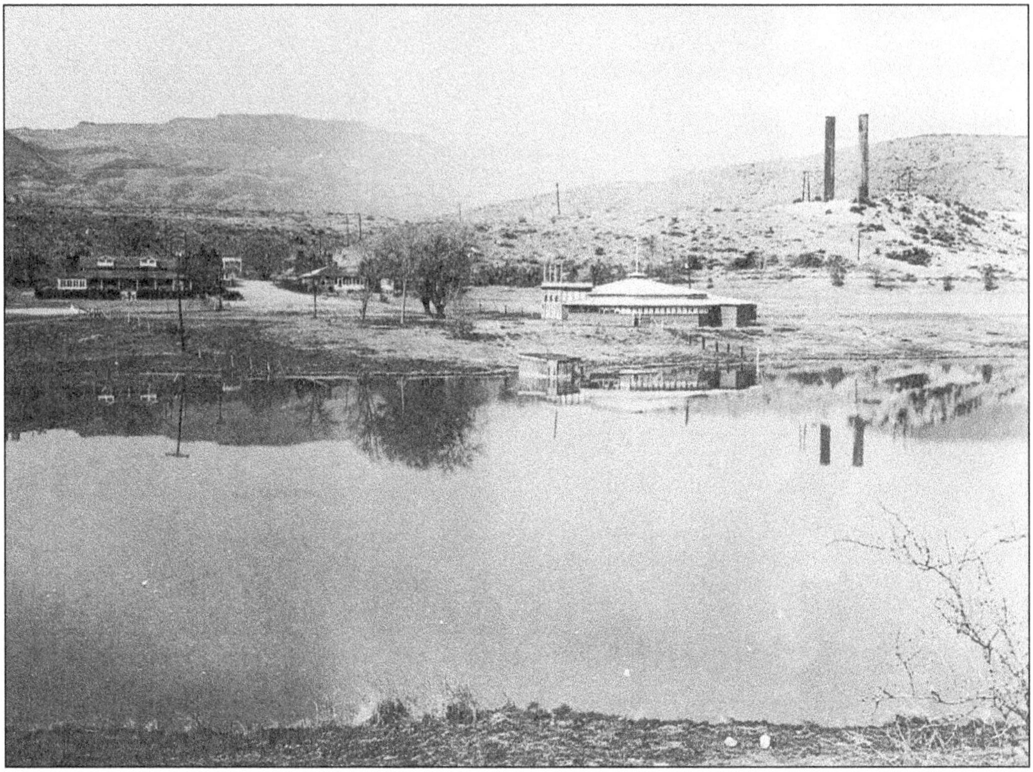

A pavilion was constructed near the clubhouse as part of the William A. Clark Memorial bequest. This pavilion was the site of many festivities, including monthly Hispanic dances and big band dances. A proposed real estate development around Peck's Lake's shores culminated in the closure of the golf course by the mining company owners in 1991. (Courtesy Bob Beltz.)

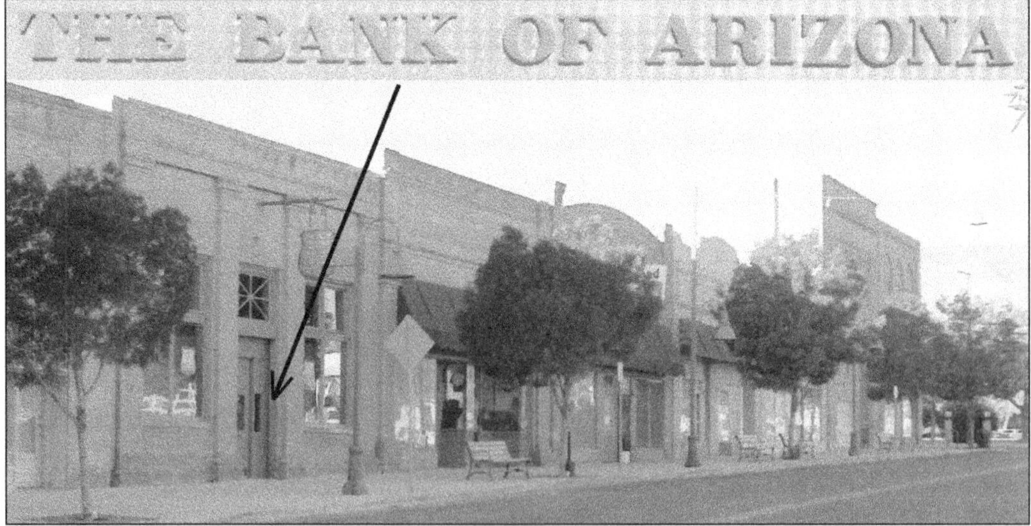

The Bank of Arizona on Main Street was the scene of an armed robbery in 1928. Two robbers held manager David Saunders, clerks, and customers hostage while grabbing more than $40,000. After putting the hostages behind the vault's gate, the thieves fled. Saunders immediately opened the gate, grabbed a revolver, and ran outside firing shots toward the bandits' car. (Author's collection.)

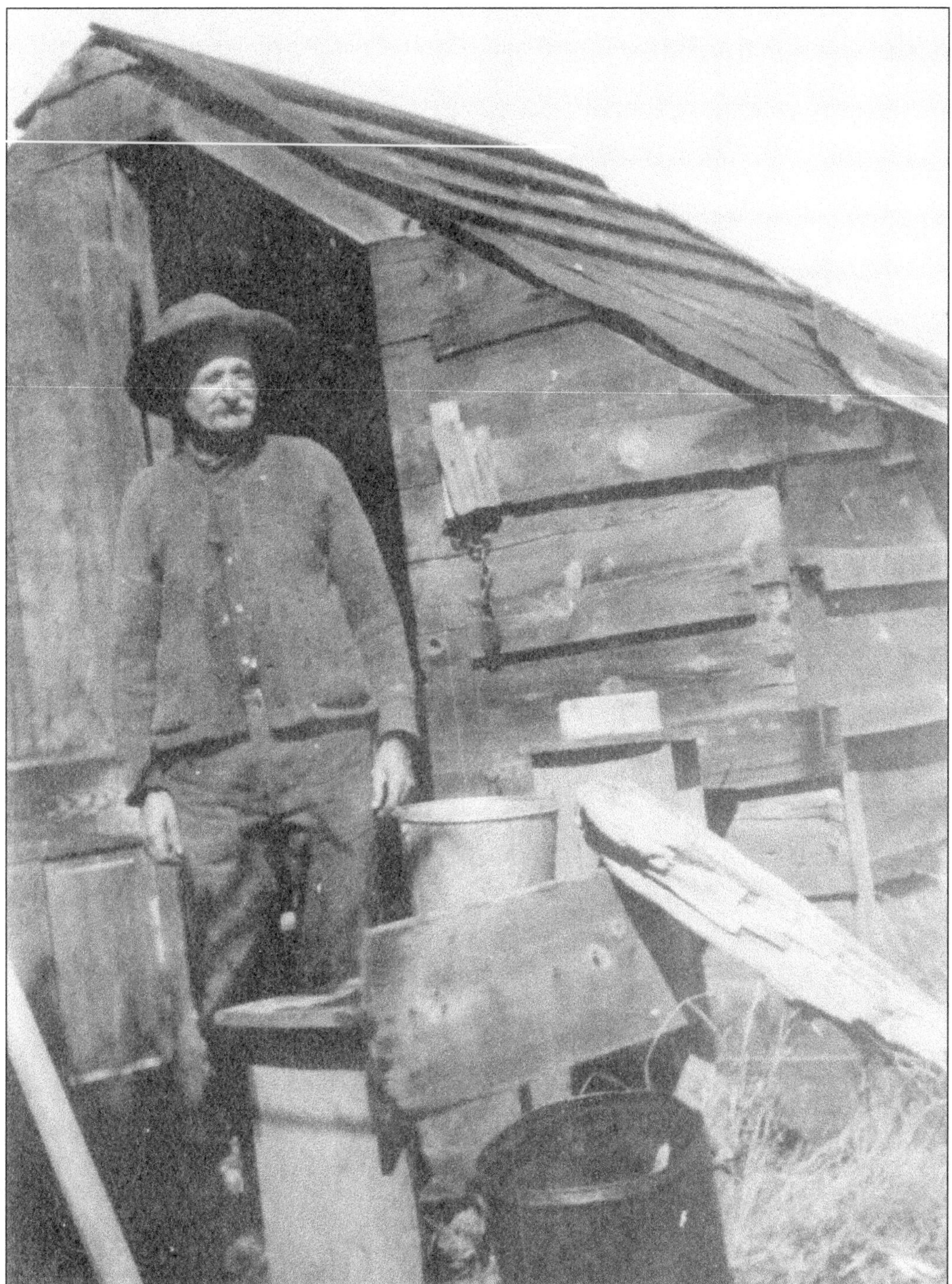

At the same time, Town Marshall Jim Roberts, a 40-year lawman with experience in many shootouts against criminals, was on a nearby sidewalk. He drew his .45 and fired. The car swerved and crashed into a pole. The driver was dead. The second thief jumped out of the car, only to be wrestled down by citizens in the schoolyard. Thus ended Clarkdale's only bank robbery. (Courtesy Sedona Heritage Museum.)

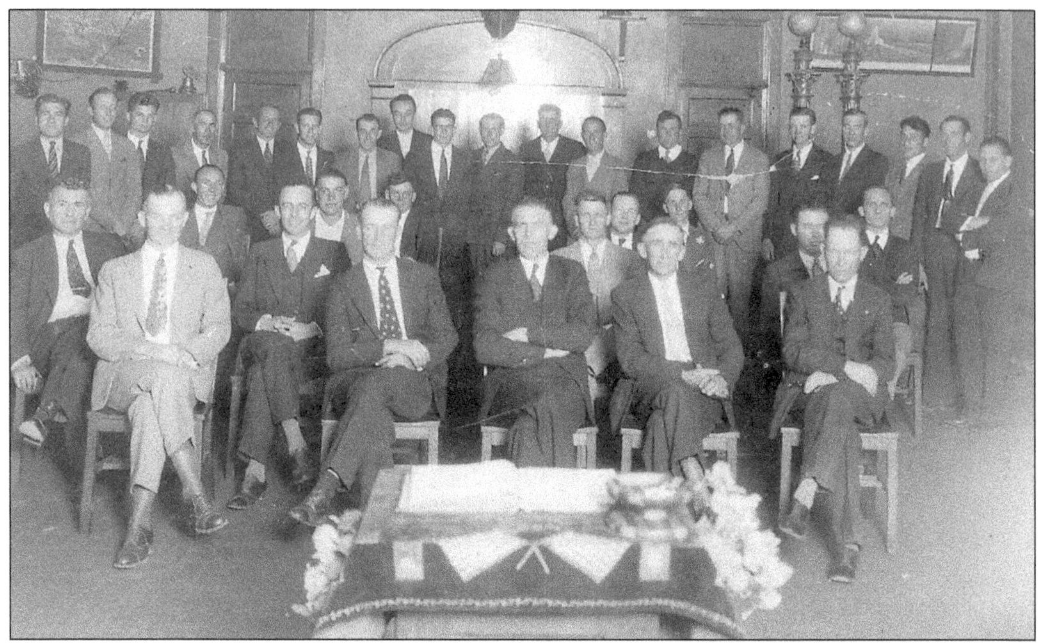

Clarkdale has had many social and volunteer organizations. Through the decades, these have included Moose, Elks, Rotary, Kiwanis, Masons, Knights of Columbus, Odd Fellows, Knights of Pythias, American Yeoman, Order of the Eastern Star, Rebeccas, Women's Club, Boy Scouts, Girl Scouts, and the Volunteer Fire Department. Theater, music, art, literature, and sports groups were formed during Clarkdale's first century. Many of these organizations met in the second-floor hall in the uptown business block. (Courtesy Jerry Wombacher.)

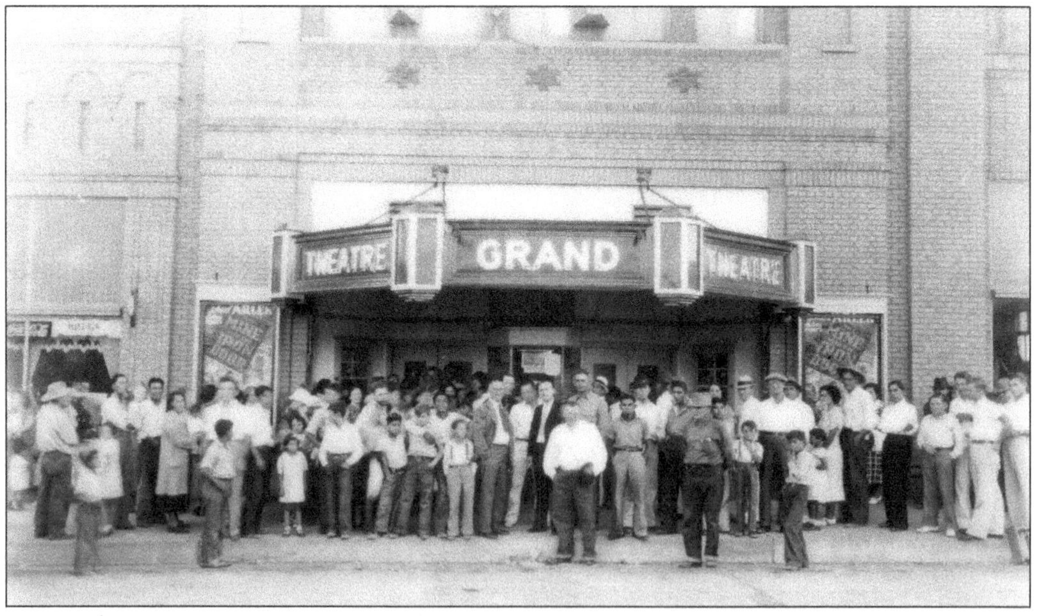

During the Depression, movies were a favorite form of entertainment and escapism in Clarkdale as in the nation. This crowd in front of the downtown Grand Theatre is waiting to see the 1936 movie *The Mine with the Iron Door* about an Arizona gold mine. On Thursdays, the movies were in Spanish for the Mexican population. (Courtesy William Cowan.)

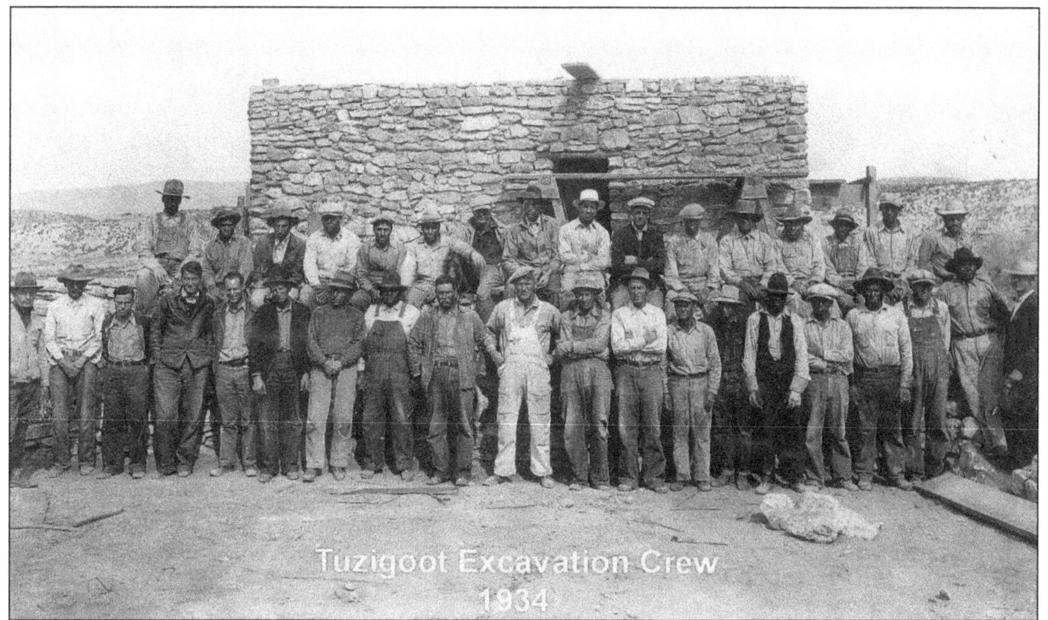

Tuzigoot National Monument is located on former UVCC and Phelps Dodge land donated to the federal government. The last donation was adjoining marshland in 2006. Benefiting from federal New Deal relief funds that provided jobs during the Depression, local unemployed workers excavated Tuzigoot in the mid-1930s. Franklin Roosevelt designated Tuzigoot a national monument in 1939. (Courtesy Tuzigoot National Monument.)

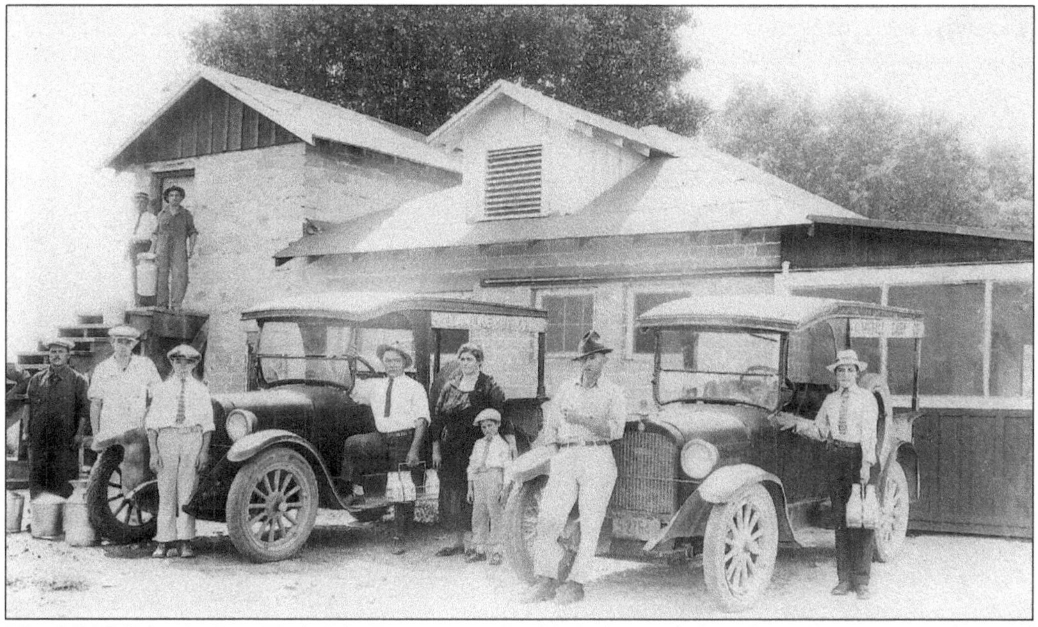

The UVCC built the Clarkdale Dairy near Peck's Lake and then leased it as an authorized monopoly to supply milk products within Clarkdale. Paul Tavasci, Guido Marianni, and Nat Rezzonico were the initial lessees. The dairy also sold milk to the surrounding communities in competition with other dairies. After the mine closed, the Clarkdale Dairy continued shipping milk as far as Prescott, Flagstaff, and Phoenix. (Courtesy John Tavasci.)

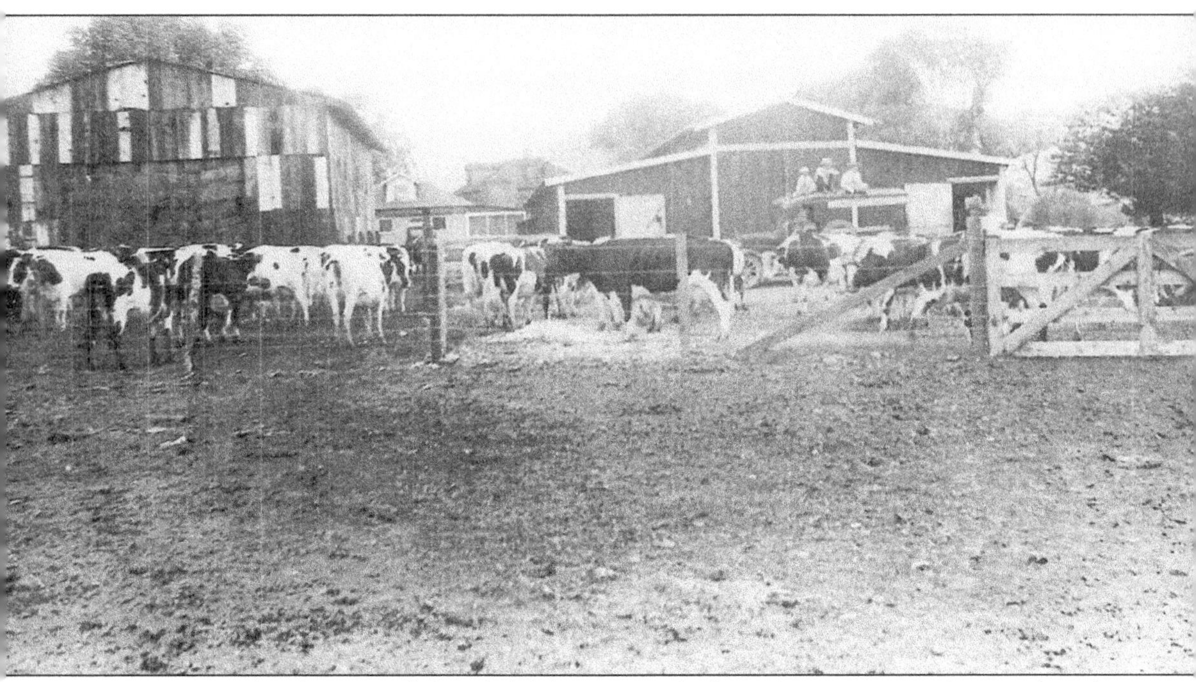

The Tavasci family operated the Clarkdale Dairy under lease from 1928 to 1965, providing dairy products to the Clarkdale region. The family children remember William Clark III, the UVCC heir designate, riding out on horseback to examine the dairy and its books for the mining company. After the visit, Clark tipped the Tavasci boys a prized silver dollar for holding the horse's reins. (Courtesy John Tavasci.)

Nine

1953–2013
Clarkdale into the 21st Century

In 1953, the UVCC mine ran out of ore and PD closed the smelter, ending Clarkdale's life as a smelter company town. The population quickly dropped from 3,500 to 900 as families abandoned their homes to find work elsewhere. Clarkdale was dying.

In 1954, the remaining residents who could make a local livelihood began buying their company homes. These citizens incorporated Clarkdale in 1957. Clarkdale's rebirth really began in 1959 with the opening of another resource industry. The Phoenix Cement Company's mine, plant, and cement trucking provided major employment opportunities.

In 1969, the Yavapai-Apache reservation was established with the development of a modern community within Clarkdale. Before the end of the 1970s, individuals and developers had bought most of the UVCC lands and buildings and the population increased as the town grew. The Town of Clarkdale acquired the former UVCC public buildings over the years. In 1975, Clarkdale annexed land that included the developing Yavapai College campus. Later annexations increased the community's area to 10.1 square miles.

Without copper company support, most recreational facilities were abandoned. A loss to all Verde Valley citizens occurred in 1991 when the land owners closed the golf course, followed 12 years later when access to Peck's Lake was prohibited.

Over the years, Clarkdale residents upgraded their homes and public-use buildings, saved and refurbished the Clark Memorial Clubhouse, built a K–8 school, built and equipped fire stations, created parks and trails, and redeveloped the downtown area. Senator Clark's community was listed in the National Register of Historic Places in 1989. Home construction mushroomed as people moved to Clarkdale's pleasant climate, comfortable lifestyle, and beautiful setting. In 2006, the town purchased Haskell Spring, the water source that had been Senator Clark's first Clarkdale land acquisition in 1906.

By 2014, the population grew to over 4,000. Today, people enjoy visiting Tuzigoot National Monument, riding the Verde Canyon Railroad, picnicking, boating, hiking, and birding along the Verde River, attending Yavapai College, and visiting the Clarkdale Historical Society Museum and the Copper Art Museum. Clarkdale celebrated its centennial in 2012, and looks forward to its next century both as "A Place of History" and as "A Place with a Future."

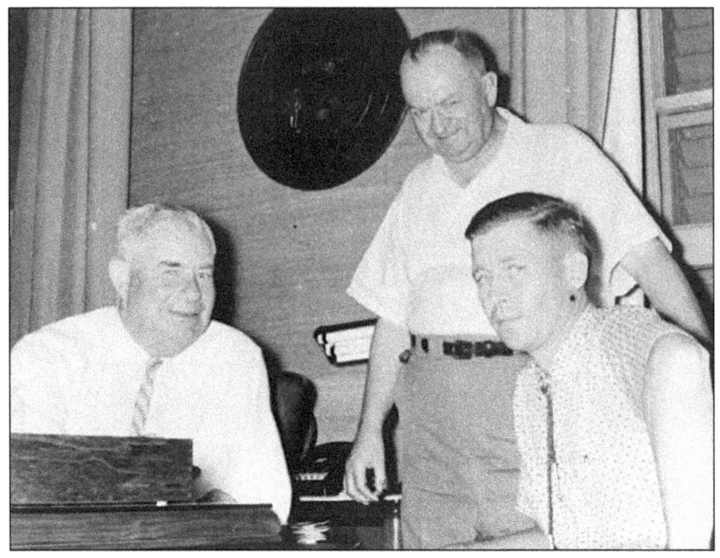

Clarkdale's residents, not happy with company rule, incorporated the town on July 1, 1957. The first mayor was M.O. "Bud" Lindner Jr,. shown in this 1957 photograph with his father, Arizona state representative M.O. Lindner (standing), and Arizona governor Ernest McFarland (left). Dr. Daniel Bright, Dr. Raymond Pecharich, Ed Starkey, and Joe Wombacher completed Clarkdale's first town council. (Courtesy Curtis Lindner.)

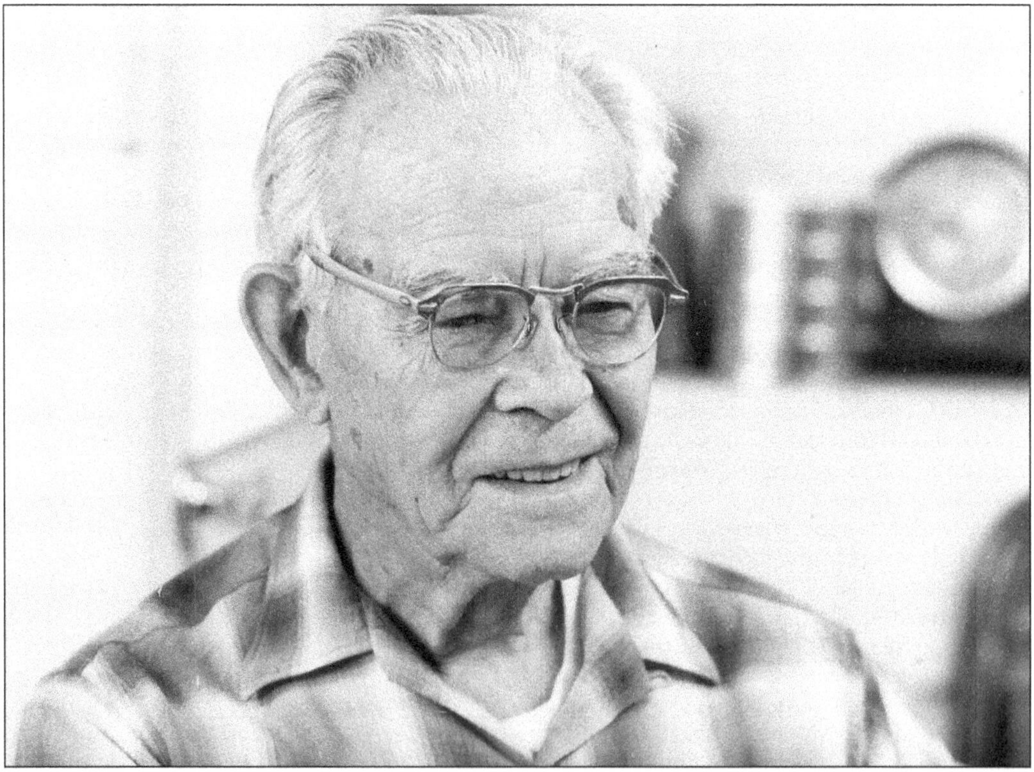

Herb Young (1887–1988) became a UVCC office secretary in 1912, and in 1915 he moved to Clarkdale, becoming secretary to upper management including Senator Clark. Young worked for the UVCC and then Phelps Dodge until the 1953 mine closure. He helped incorporate Clarkdale and became the town's first clerk, treasurer, and magistrate. A fiction writer in his youth, he returned to writing in his 70s, completing two highly regarded local history books. (Courtesy of JSHP.)

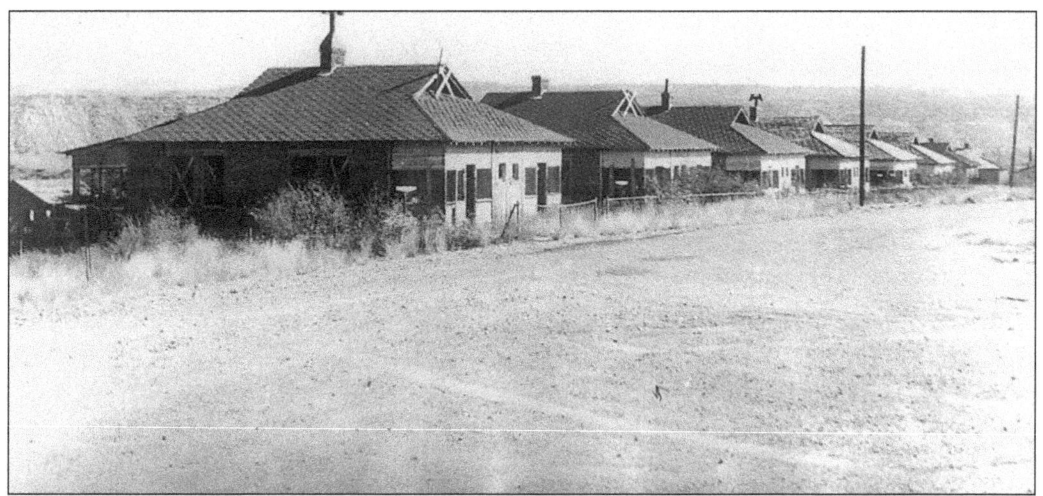

Following the UVCC mine and smelter shutdown, the company-owned buildings rapidly emptied as families vacated their homes and moved elsewhere for work. Soon, a majority of the company housing units had been abandoned. Clarkdale's population rapidly dropped from 3,500 to 900. The $1 million town built by Senator Clark seemed destined to become just another Western mining ghost town. (Courtesy B. Cimarolli.)

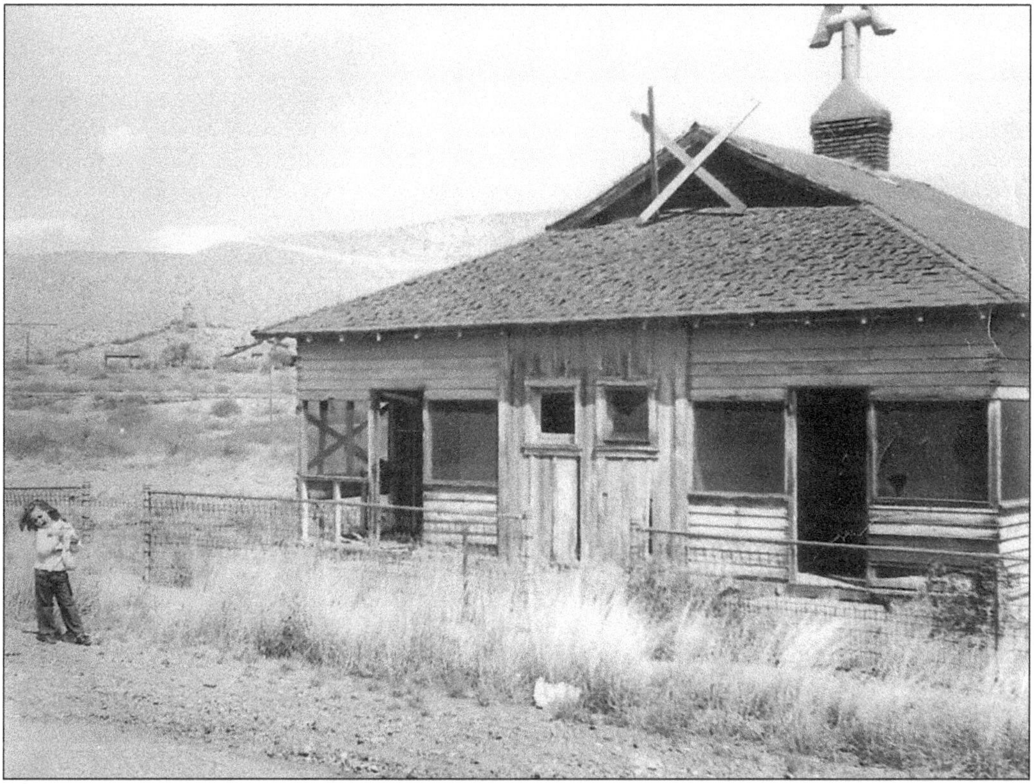

In the 1950s, Lower Town and Patio Town were nearly abandoned by the departing workers. Many of the original homes were neglected for more than a decade; since then, most have been repaired and remodeled. A resurrection of Clarkdale began in 1958 with the construction of a cement plant on the edge of town, giving the town a new chance of life. (Courtesy B. Cimarolli.)

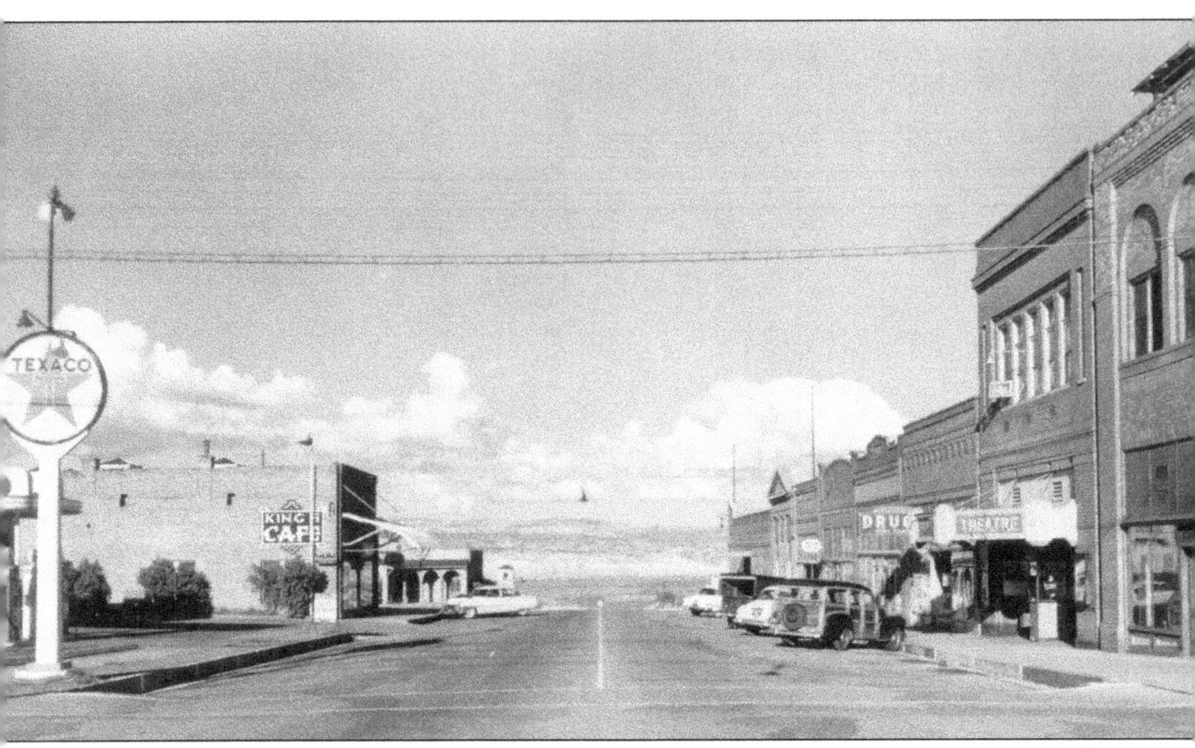

Phelps Dodge sold Clarkdale's houses, the smelter, and 2,475 acres of land in 1953 to Allison Steel for $250,000, followed in 1954 by a resale to Halliburton interests. Westfield Corporation purchased all the properties in 1959 for $1 million. Clarkdale Realty, a subsidiary of Westfield and Gulf States Land and Development, was organized to sell all the remaining company-owned buildings and land. (Courtesy S. Hill.)

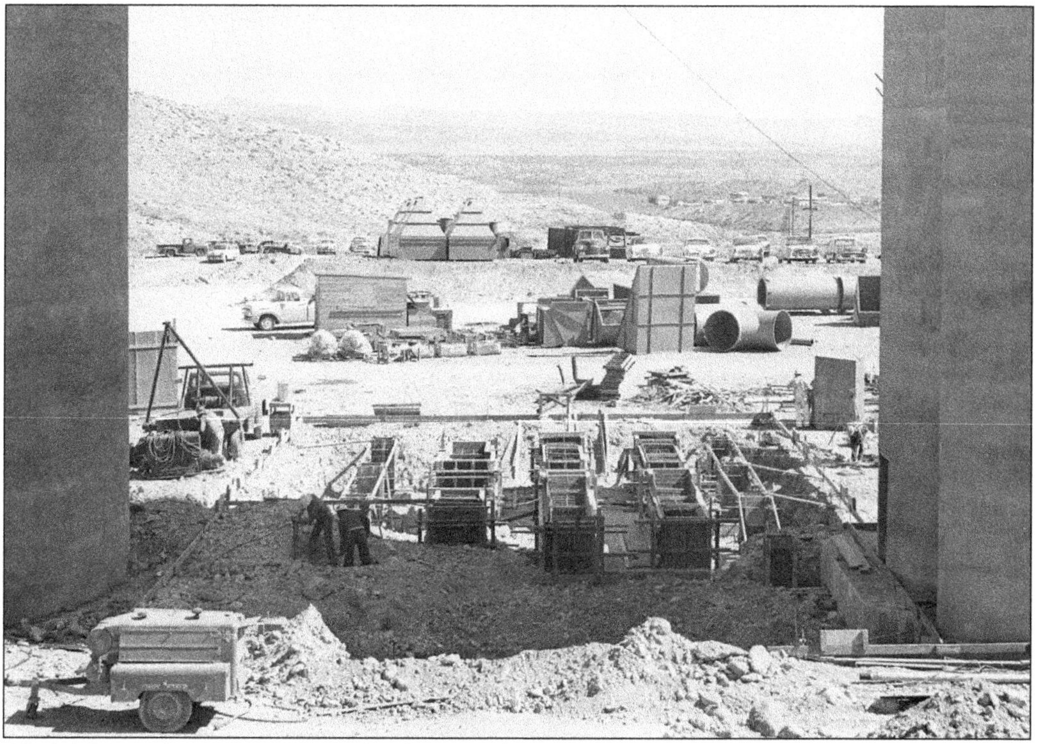

Clarkdale's geologic environment has high-quality limestone necessary to make Portland cement. Congress authorized the construction of Arizona's Glen Canyon Dam in 1956, which would require 10 million cubic yards of cement. In 1958, the Phoenix Cement Company began construction of a $16 million plant and mine on Clarkdale's west border (Clarkdale is in the background). The plant initially hired 400 employees, many of whom acquired Clarkdale's empty homes. (Courtesy M. Lindner.)

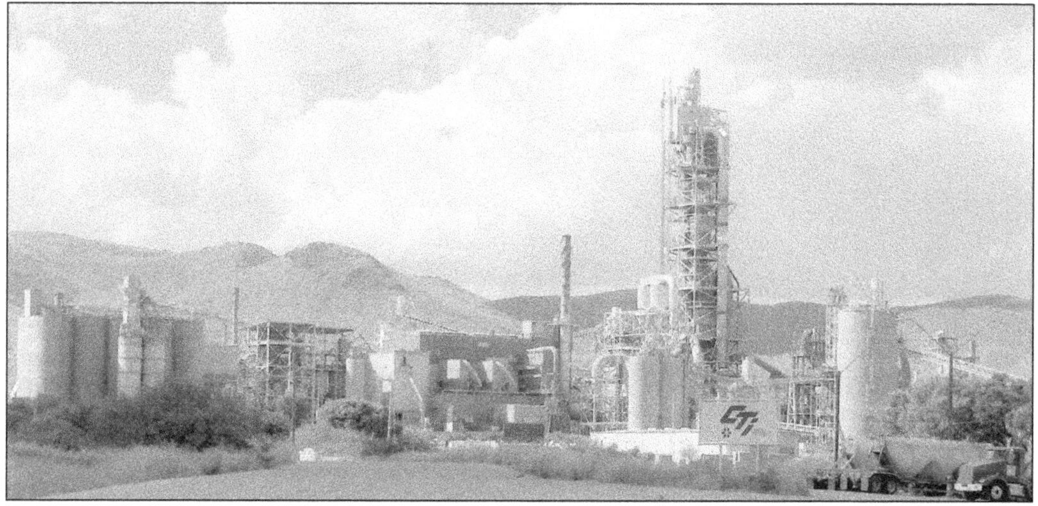

The operation started producing Portland cement in October 1959. Beginning in 1960, cement-laden CTI trucks drove from Clarkdale to the Glen Canyon project every 15 minutes, 24 hours a day, seven days a week—a 10-hour, 260-mile-round-trip. That continued until July 1964, when the 710-foot-high dam project on the Colorado River was completed. (Author's collection.)

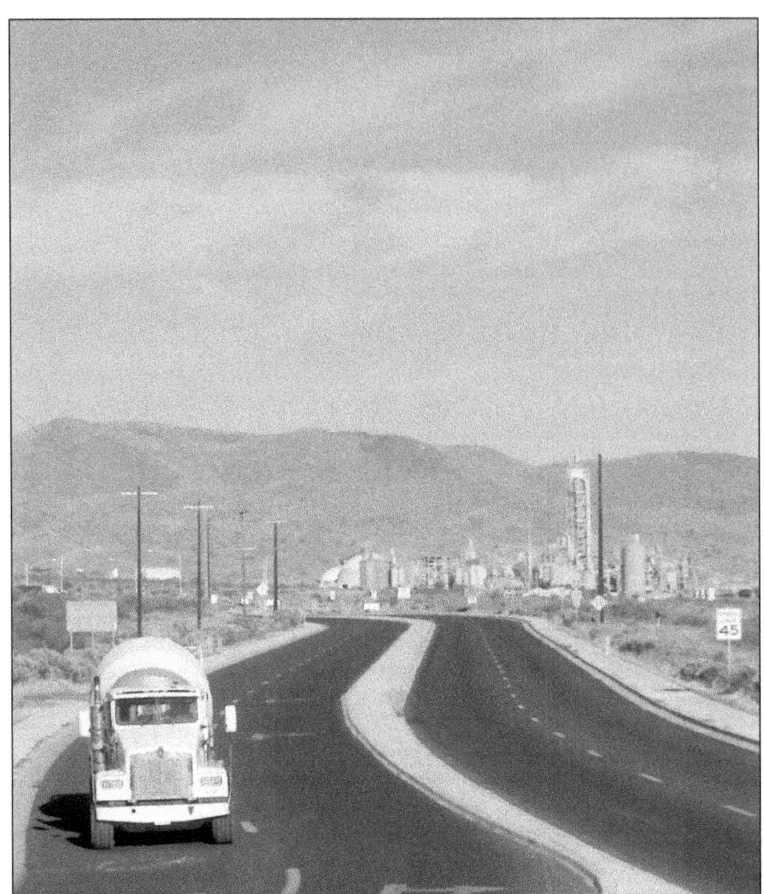

Recent modernization and upgrades amount to $160 million, 10 times the original investment. Since 1987, the cement plant has been operated by the Salt River Materials Group, owned by Pima and Maricopa Native American nations. The Clarkdale plant and mine have a long future, with more than two centuries of limestone resources remaining. (Author's collection.)

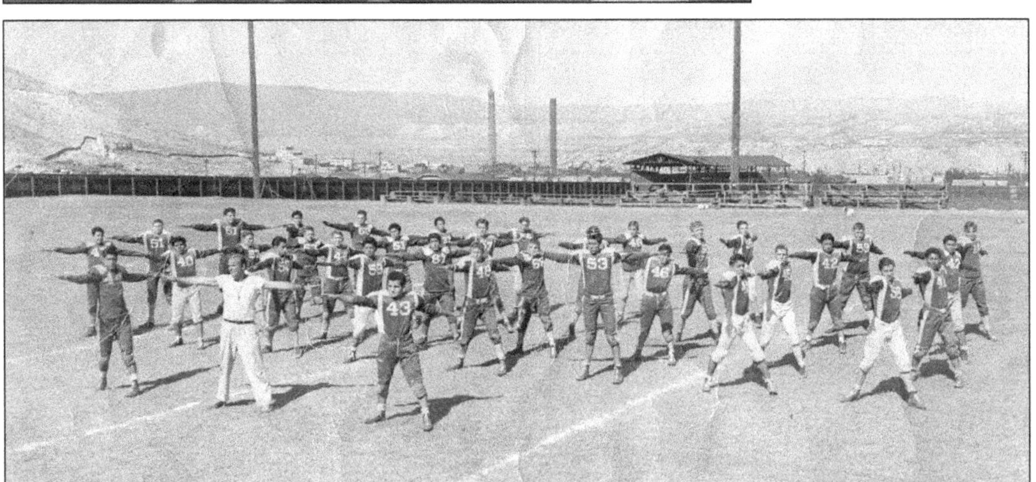

Due to the population losses after 1953, Clarkdale High School consolidated with Mingus High School in Jerome in 1960 forming Mingus Union High School (MUHS). With the combining of Jerome's school buildings and Clarkdale's athletic colors and playing fields (as seen in this 1946 photograph), decades of sports rivalry between the towns ended. After 1960, the Clarkdale school building was used as a charter school, a community college, an electronics plant, and now the Copper Art Museum. In 1972, MUHS moved to Cottonwood. (Courtesy M. Lindner.)

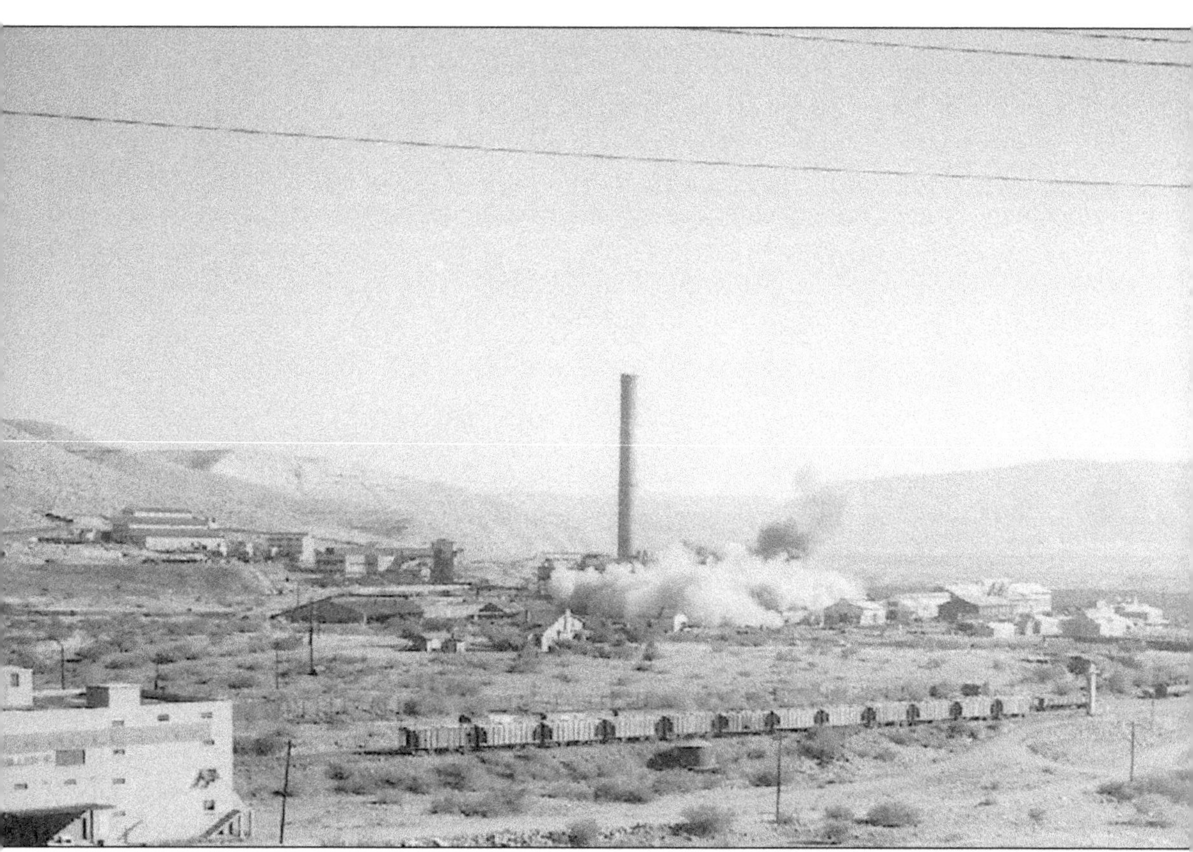

On October 2, 1966, the remaining brick smelter smokestack, built in 1922, was blown down in an event watched by the townspeople. The former mine company employees who still lived in town regretfully accepted that the smelter was never returning; Clarkdale's bonanza employment times were finished. The steel stack, built in 1914, had been demolished four years earlier on July 31, 1962—a half-century after Clarkdale's construction began. (Courtesy John Bell Collection.)

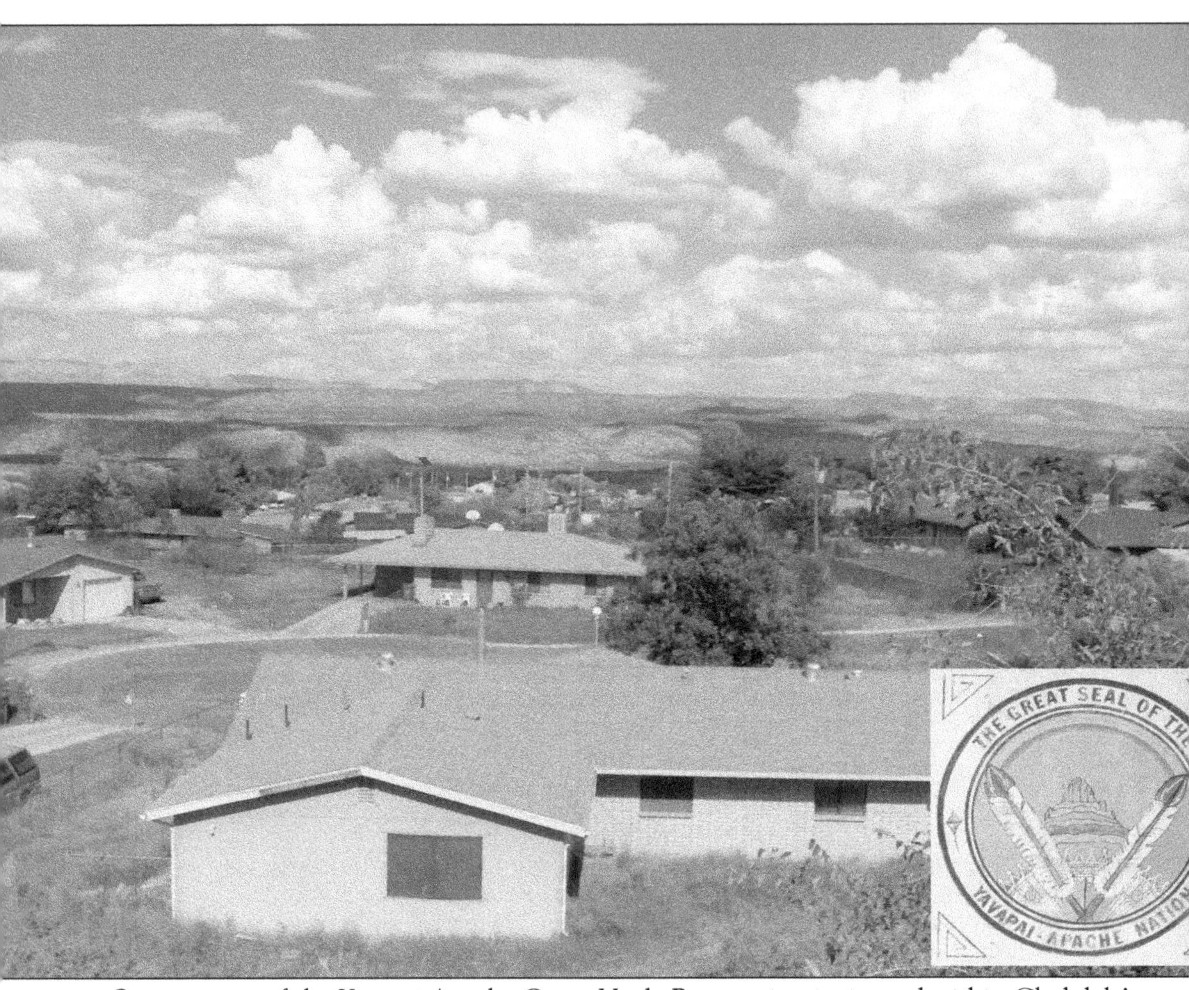

One segment of the Yavapai-Apache Camp Verde Reservation is situated within Clarkdale's borders. Indians had been living there without deeds since the early 20th century in old structures with limited utilities and substandard roads. In 1969, a total of 60 acres of land were granted to the nation. The Operation Turnkey federal program enabled construction of new roads, utilities, and buildings, including houses and community structures. (Author's collection.)

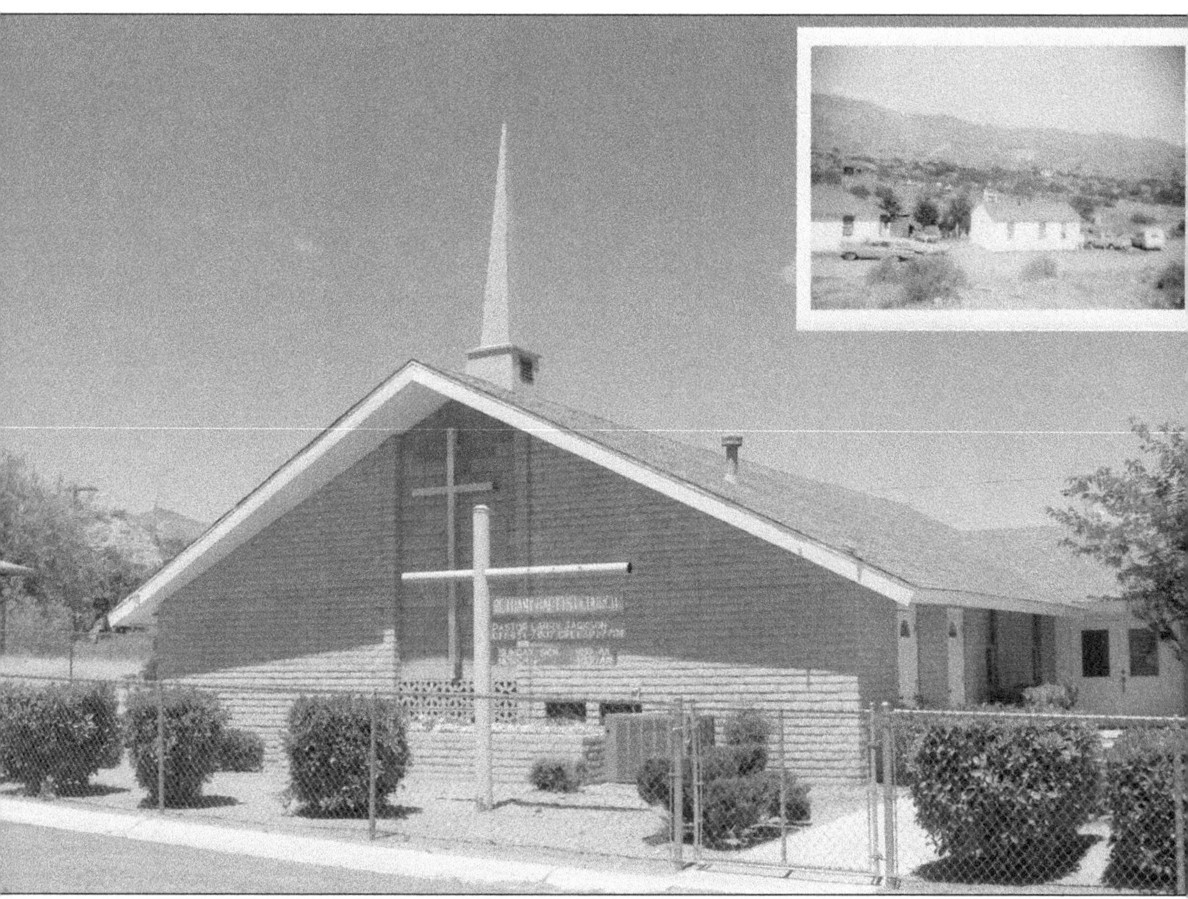

The Bethany Baptist Church is located in the Yavapai-Apache reservation in Clarkdale. The attractive building replaces the former old church (seen in the insert) built in the earlier pre-reservation years. Of the 2,300 Yavapai-Apache Nation's members, about 300 live in Clarkdale. Economic opportunities for the Native Americans arrived with the opening of the Cliff Castle Casino in Camp Verde in 1995. The casino and several other businesses have led the tribe out of their early-to-mid-20th-century poverty. (Author's collection.)

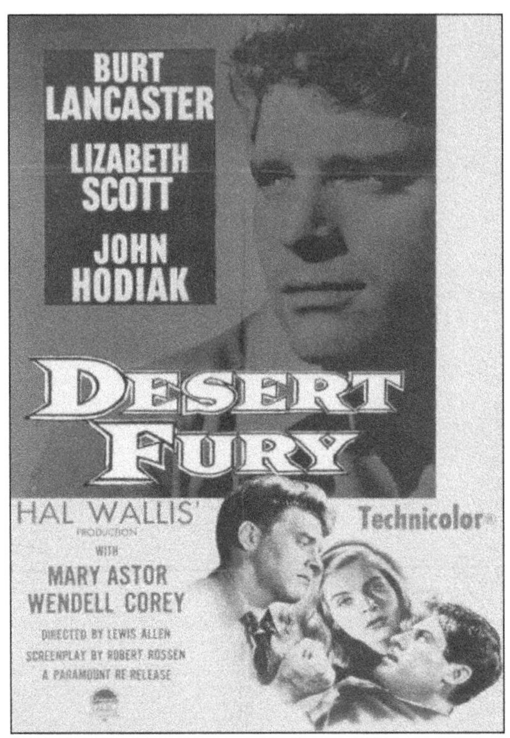

Clarkdale has provided settings for movies beginning with the 1947 film *Desert Fury*, starring John Hodiak, Lizabeth Scott, and Burt Lancaster. This movie includes scenes of the Clarkdale single-lane bridge and the smelter. Other movies filmed within Clarkdale include *Midnight Run* with Robert De Niro in 1988, *Universal Soldier* with Jean-Claude Van Damme in 1992, and *Benefit of the Doubt* with Donald Sutherland in 1993. Several other short films have utilized Clarkdale locations. (Author's collection.)

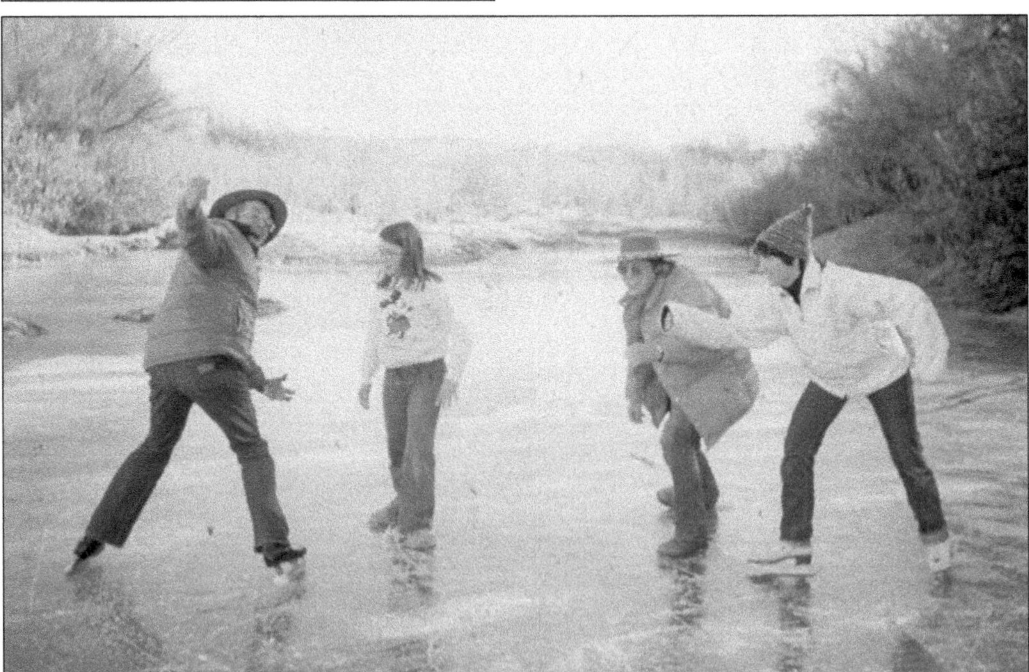

A wide pool in the Verde River below Tapco was Clarkdale's earliest swimming pool. In the late 1970s, an exceptional freeze turned this pool into a skating rink for the author and his children. Peck's Lake once froze hard enough to support vehicles. A record-breaking, one-week snowstorm occurred in Clarkdale in December 1967. The town received more than three feet, with double that snowfall in the surrounding mountains, isolating the entire Verde Valley. (Author's collection.)

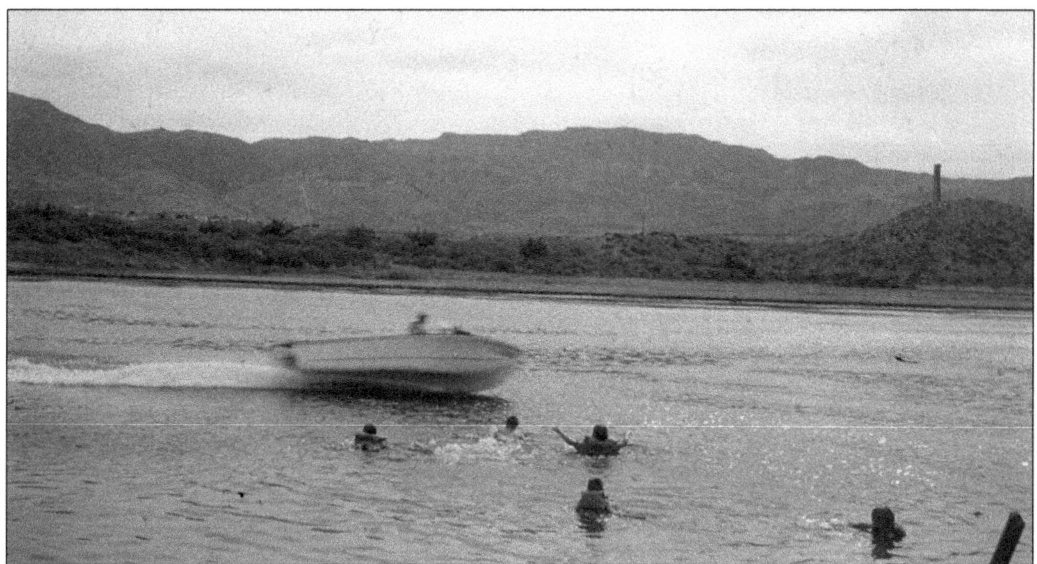

After Phelps Dodge obtained ownership of the UVCC in 1935, many of Clarkdale's original recreational facilities were abandoned over the following decades. Since the 1860s, soldiers, farmers, workers, and their families had lived, camped, played, boated, hunted, and fished at Peck's Lake. More than a century of recreational use of the lake by all Verde Valley citizens ended in 2003 when access to Peck's Lake was prohibited. (Author's collection.)

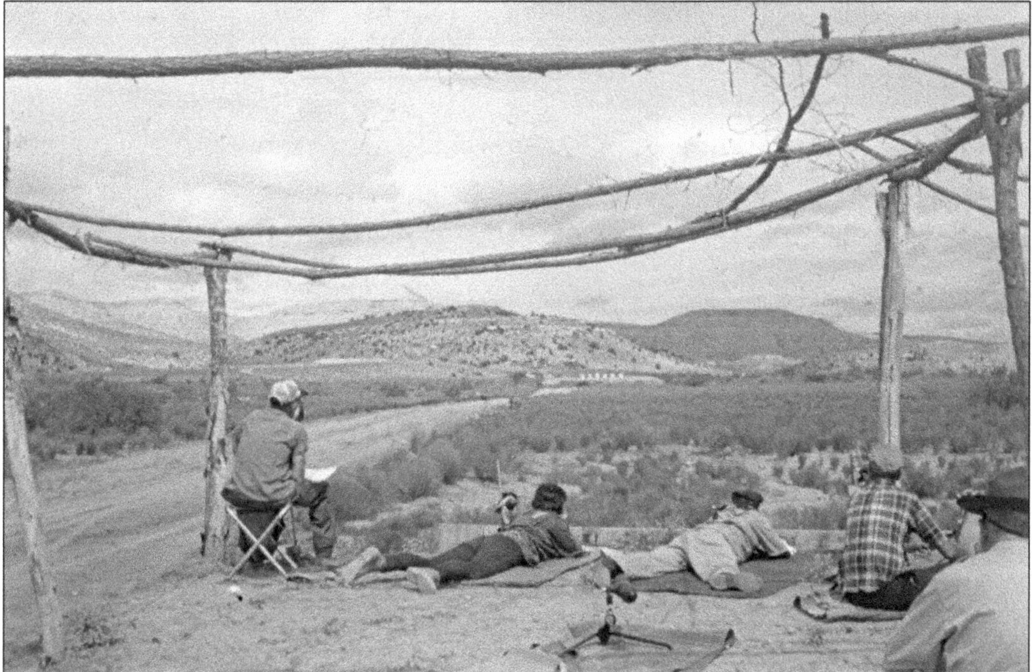

Before 1920, a 125-member shooting club built a clubhouse and rifle and shotgun ranges near Centerville and then later moved to a site near Tapco. In 1962, the local Verde Marksmen Club constructed a 600-yard rifle range and an archery course near Tapco. This range was active through the 1960s, hosting high-powered rifle competitors from throughout Arizona. It served as a training facility for the military until it closed in the early 1970s. (Author's collection.)

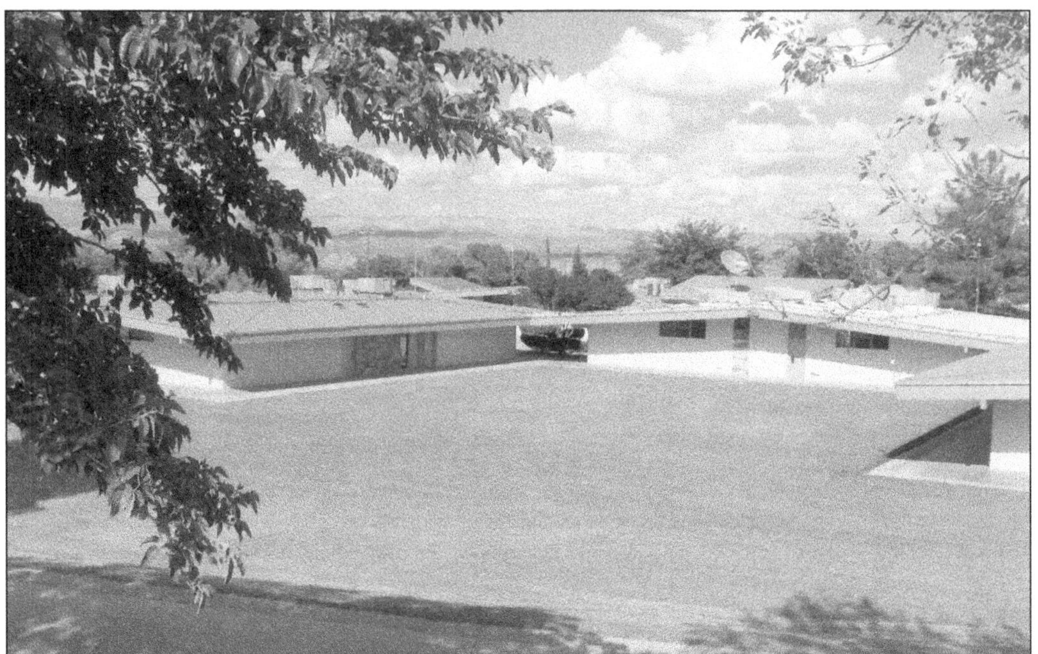

Clarkdale's current K–8 school complex opened in Upper Town in 1985. It consists of five pods with four classrooms in each plus an administration building. In 2013, it served about 450 students. This school adjoins the former high school athletic field, which—during the smelter days—was the site of a ball field with grandstand. (Author's collection.)

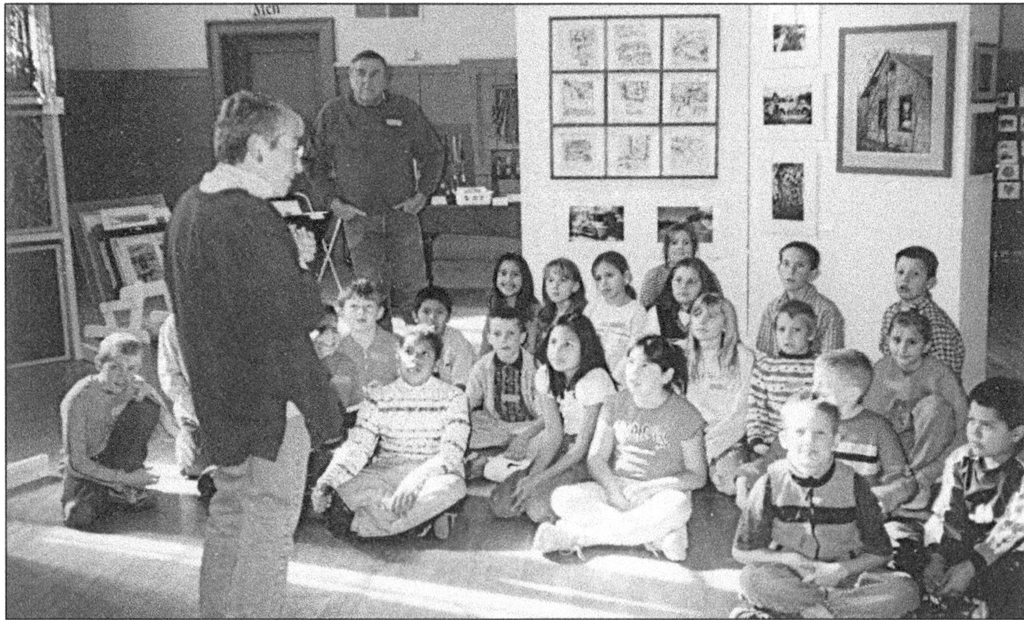

Clarkdale's resident artists host the Made in Clarkdale annual invitational art fair every December. In 1986, seventeen artists started this multimedia exhibition, held in the Clark Memorial Clubhouse. It has grown to exhibit works of more than 50 local artists. Clarkdale's Yavapai College offers an associate of fine arts program that complements the art scene with instruction in a variety of creative disciplines. (Courtesy Ellie Bauer.)

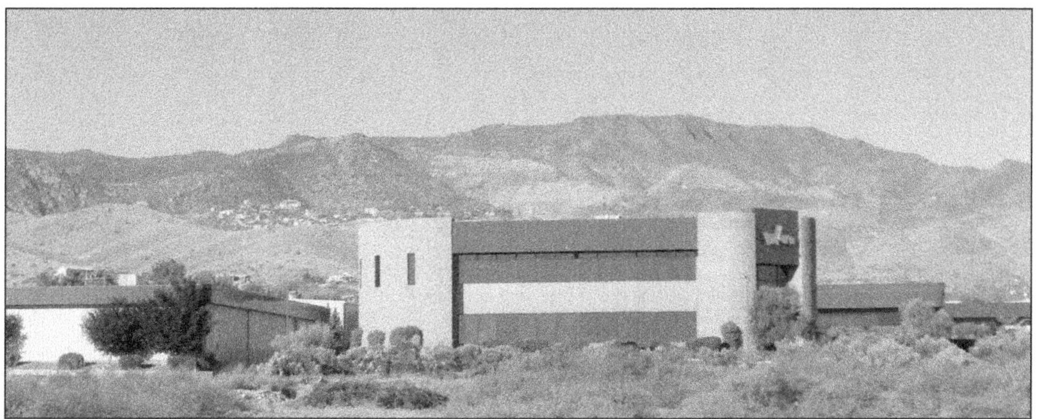

Clarkdale's larger employers are currently the Salt River Materials Group cement plant, Mold in Graphics (an international business making labels and decorations on plastics), CTI Trucking (cement hauling), Verde Canyon Railroad (excursions and hauling), and Bent River Machine (automation machine design and manufacturing). The biggest government employers are Yavapai College, the Clarkdale-Jerome School System, and the Town of Clarkdale. (Author's collection.)

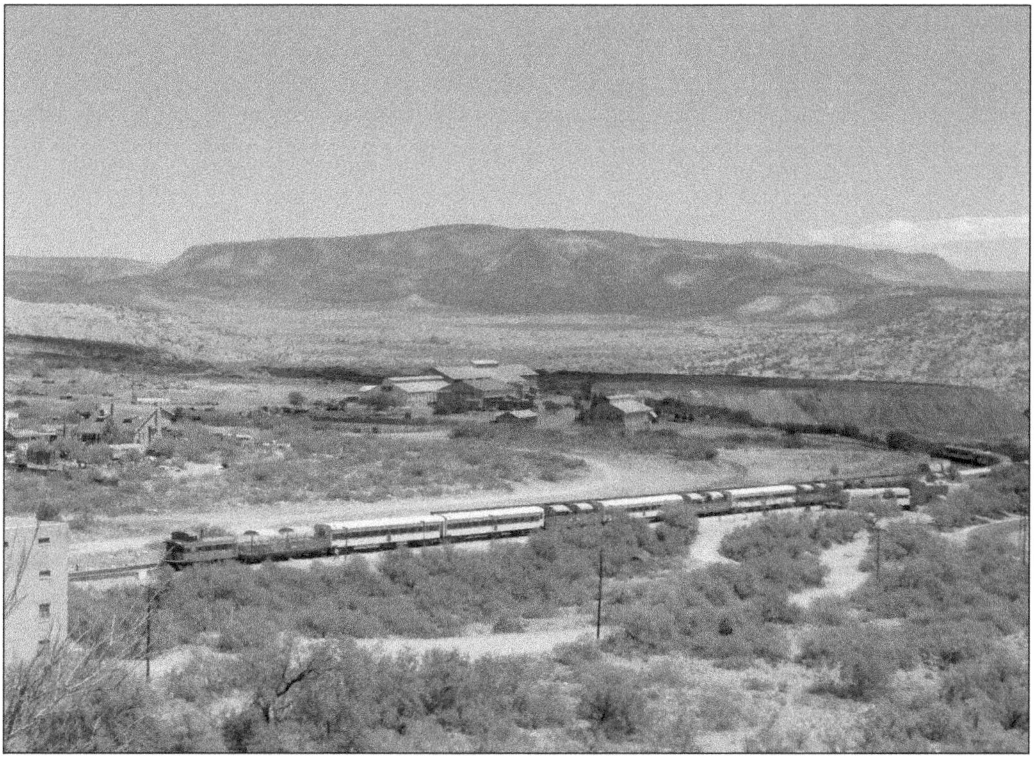

Opening in 1990, the Verde Canyon Railroad carries more than 100,000 tourists annually on roundtrip excursions along the Verde River Canyon, starting at the Clarkdale smelter site. The four-hour ride travels through 1.7 billion years of geologic time and a few hundred years of historical time. Wildlife sightings are frequent as the train passes by the Verde River riparian habitat and adjoining wilderness area. (Author's collection.)

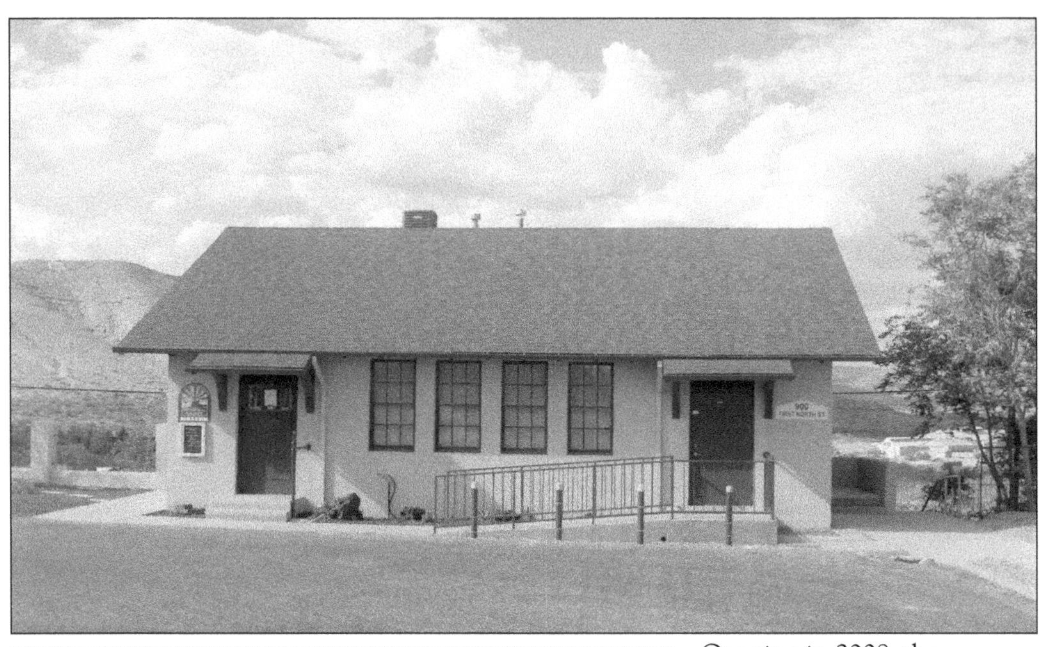

Opening in 2008, the Clarkdale Historical Society and Museum is housed in the former UVCC clinic-dispensary built in 1920. The museum contains rotating displays and archives of the history of Clarkdale. The building itself has a diversified history as a clinic, town office, emergency management office, police station, jail, state driver's license office, and library. (Author's collection.)

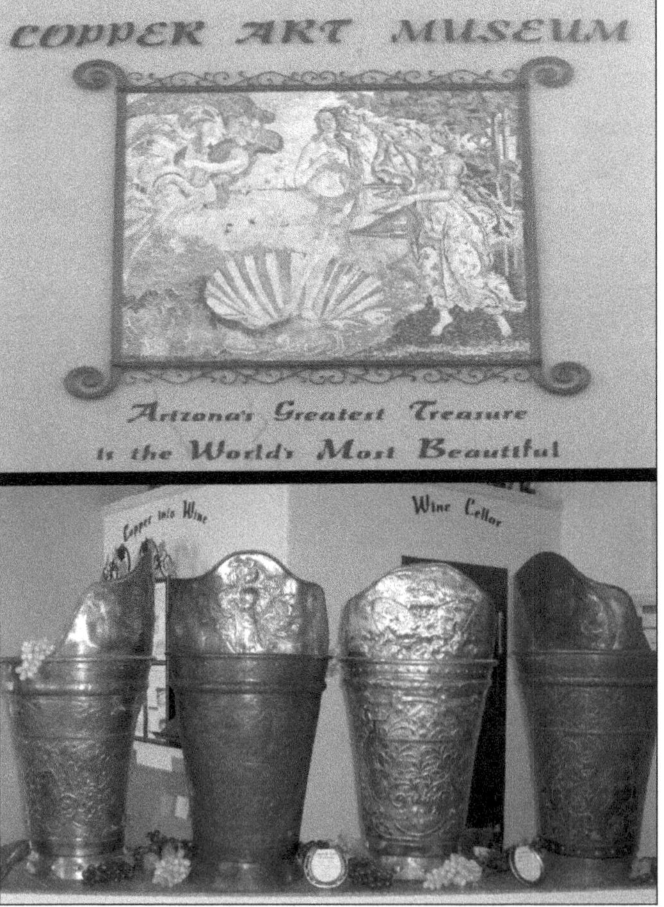

The Copper Art Museum, in the former Clarkdale High School, is Arizona's newest museum. Copper has been extremely important in the history of both Clarkdale and Arizona. Inside its copper doors, the museum provides displays and information on the origin of copper and its artistic uses through time in architecture, cooking, distilling, winemaking, and military art. (Author's collection.)

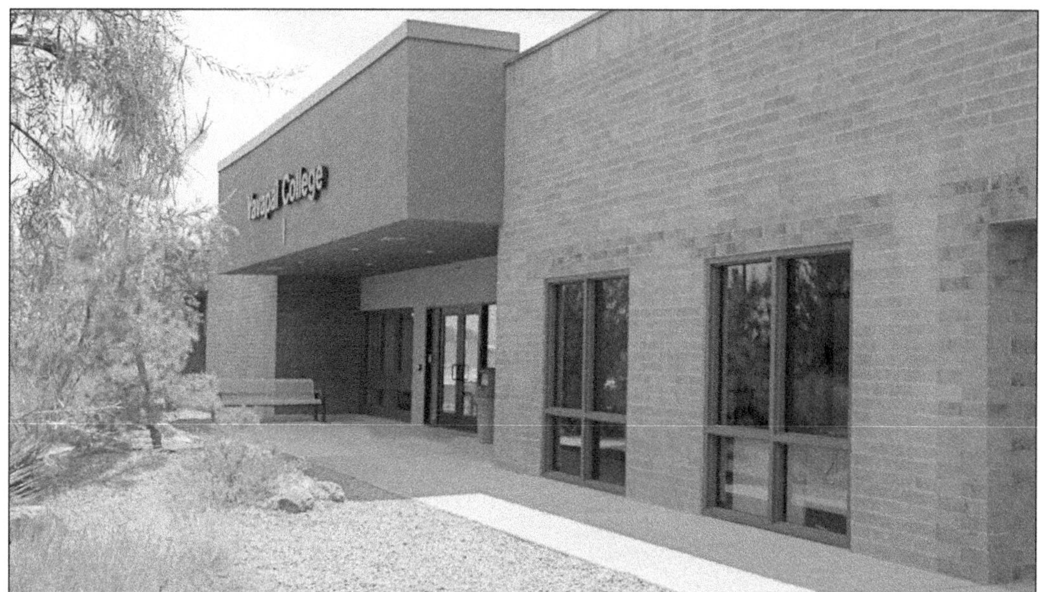

Yavapai College, located in Clarkdale, is the area's center for higher education. Since its ground breaking in March 1975, the 125-acre campus has experienced continual growth. Clarkdale's future will grow along with Yavapai College. The Clarkdale campus currently enrolls more than 1,700 full- and part-time students in more than 70 fields of study. Several associate degree programs provide vocational skills for 21st-century employment. Many retirees enjoy the adult education classes. (Author's collection.)

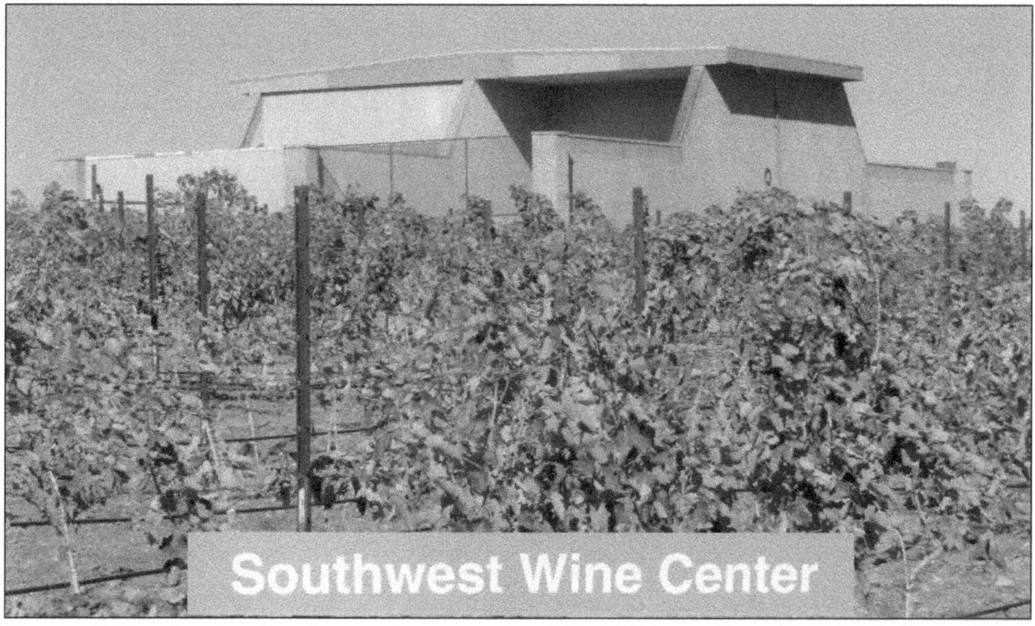

Yavapai College has developed an academic program in viticulture and oenology that will train future vintners in growing grapes, producing wines, and marketing the final product. The campus vineyards are located on the same land that a century earlier belonged to the Haskell-Kirwagen farm, whose orchards earned national recognition for their gold medal–winning fruits. Yavapai College looks forward to this land achieving recognition as a producer of fine wines. (Author's collection.)

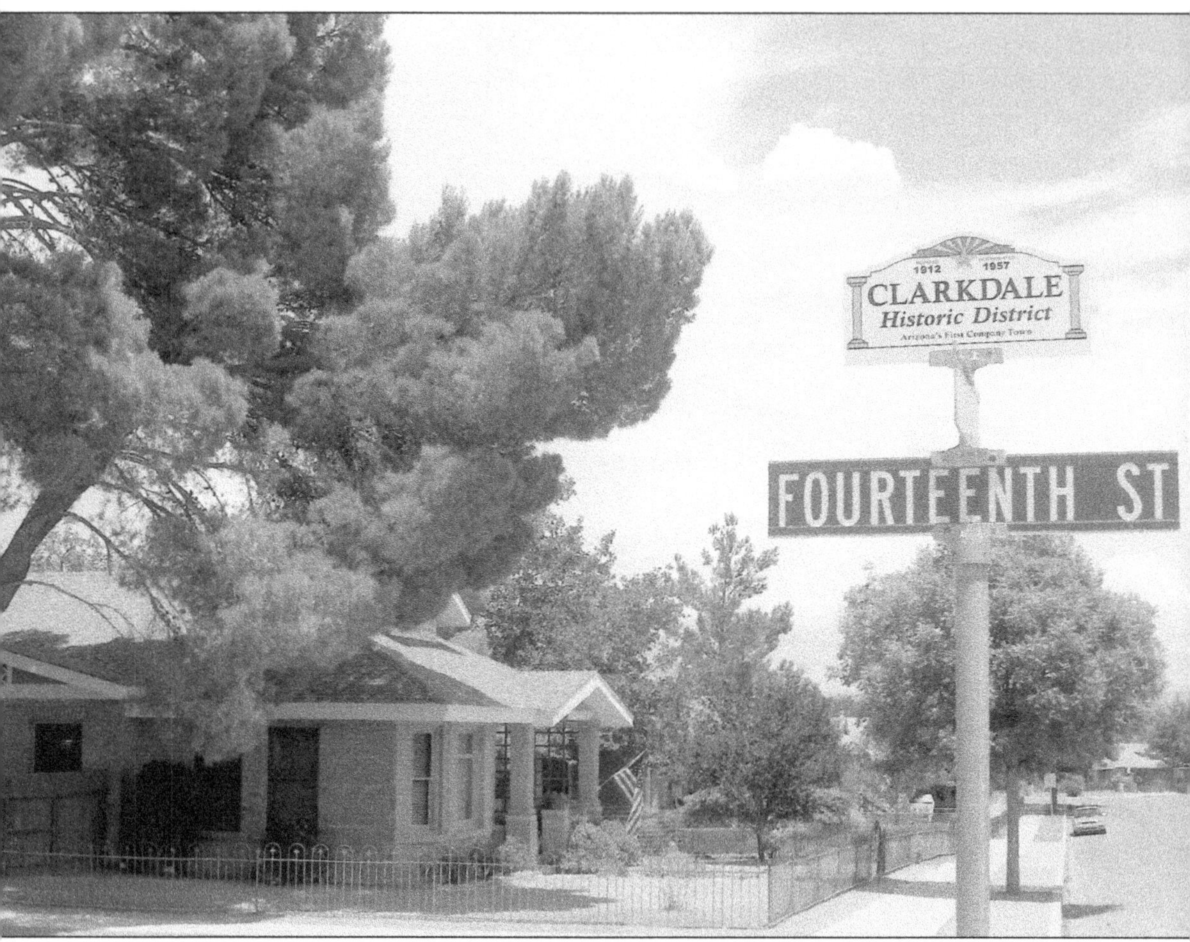

In 1998, Sen. William A. Clark's industrial town of Clarkdale was designated a National Historic District. This nomination was based upon Clark's pre-planning concept and the town's advanced engineering, attractive architecture, and nationally significant commercial history. The 4,600-acre, boot-shaped historic district (see page 68) includes 361 buildings and 20 structures. (Author's collection.)

Bibliography

Bartlett, Katharine. "Notes upon Routes of Espejo and Farfan to the Mines in the Sixteenth Century." *New Mexico Historical Review*, Vol. XVII. University of New Mexico, 1942.

Cottonwood Chapter 2021, American Association of Retired Persons. *Cottonwood, Clarkdale, and Cornville History*. Cottonwood, AZ: Fran's Print Shop, 1984.

Cowan, William L. *Verde Valley*. Charleston, SC: Arcadia Publishing, 2011.

Dedman, Bill, and Paul Clark Newell Jr. *Empty Mansions*. New York: Ballantine Books, 2013.

Glasscock, C.B. *The War of the Copper Kings*. New York: Grosset & Dunlap, 1966.

Handverger, Paul A. *The Story of the Rio Indian Reservation in Clarkdale, Arizona, 1874–1875*. Monograph No. 1. Clarkdale Historical Society, 2009.

————. *Ancient Metate Site near Clarkdale, Arizona*. Monograph No. 2. Clarkdale Historical Society, 2012.

Jordan, F. Ruth and B.T. Boudway. *Following Their Western Star*. Surprise, AZ: Moore Graphics, 2005.

Lanning, John, et al. *Mining Congress Journal Reprint*. The U.V. Copper Company, 1930.

Peplow, Bonnie and Ed. *Pioneer Stories of Arizona's Verde Valley*. Verde Valley Pioneers Association, 1954.

Wahmann, Russell. *Verde Valley Railroads*. Third Edition. Jerome Historical Society, 1999.

Young, Herbert V. *Ghosts of Cleopatra Hill*. Jerome Historical Society, 1974.

————. *They Came to Jerome*. Jerome Historical Society, 1972.

University of Texas Libraries. www.lib.utexas.edu

www.ingramcontent.com/pod-product-compliance
Lightning Source LLC
LaVergne TN
LVHW060933110826
845155LV00042B/722

9781467131391